THE ROT IN MALAYSIAN EDUCATION

And Other Essays

Also by M. Bakri Musa

Race, Religion, And Royalty: The Barnacles On Malay Society (2020)

The Plundering Of Malaysia: Najib Razak And IMDB (2020)

The Son Has Not Returned. A Surgeon In His Native Malaysia (2018)

Cast From The Herd: Memories Of Matriarchal Malaysia (2016)

Malaysia's Wasted Decade 2004-2014: The Toxic Triad Of
Abdullah, Najib, And UMNO Leadership (2016)

Liberating The Malay Mind (2013)

Moving Malaysia Forward (2008)

Towards A Competitive Malaysia: Development Challenges of
the 21st Century (2006)

From Malaysia, With Love (2004)
(With Karen E Musa)

Seeing Malaysia My Way (2003)

An Education System Worthy Of Malaysia (2003)

Malaysia In The Era Of Globalization (2002)

The Malay Dilemma Revisited: Race Dynamics In Modern Malaysia (1999;
Updated 2017)

THE ROT IN MALAYSIAN EDUCATION

And Other Essays

M. Bakri Musa

Library of Congress Control Number: 2020903823
Nine States Press, Morgan Hill, CA

Cover Design by Su and Jason Pittam

Author's website: www.bakrimusa.blogspot.com

"... [B]ahwa hiduplah untuk memberi sebanyak-banyaknya,
bukan untuk menerima sebanyak-banyaknya."

(Live to give as much as possible, not to receive as much as possible.)

The principle imparted by schoolteachers Pak Harfan and Bu Mus upon their precious handful of young minds entrusted to their care, in Andrea Hirata's bestselling novel *Laskar Pelangi* (The Rainbow Troops).

The best and most succinct encapsulation of the purpose of education.

Contents

8   Contents

Endless, Meaningless Reforms

Quality, Quantity, And Equity In Malaysian Education

The Role Of Private Sector In Education (In Six Parts)

Affirmative Action – Malaysian Variety

Potpourri of Malaysiana

Book Reviews

An American Voice

Index

About The Author

Preface

This is my third set of essays and commentaries on Malaysian affairs written since 2008; the first, *Race, Religion, And Royalty: The Barnacles On Malay Society*, and the second, *Plundering Malaysia: Najib Razak and 1MDB*.

The bulk of this volume covers education. Malaysia's failure to achieve her ambitious Vision 2020 goal of becoming a developed nation by 2020 is attributed in large part to her rotten system of education–her failing schools. The ancient Chinese wisdom that a nation's schools are its future in miniature is never more true than with today's Malaysia.

The rest of the essays are a potpourri of Malaysian topics including the local variety of affirmative action and reviews of books on Malaysia or by Malaysian authors.

As these essays have appeared as independent pieces before, it is inevitable that some ideas or even phrases may appear repetitious when put in one volume. Where possible and when they would not impact on the overall flow, I have excised them.

These commentaries have appeared in a variety of social and mainstream media. As with my preface to the other two volumes, I again thank those owners who have generously granted space to me, including blogs of Mr. Lim Kit Siang, Datuk Din Merican, *Malaysia Today*, *Malaysiakini*, The *Malaysian Insight* and *The Malaysian Insider*.

The cover design is by husband-and-wife team of Jason and Su Pittam. I thank them for this as well the designs in the other two companion volumes.

My wife Karen has been a constant help and collaborator in this as well as in all my previous writings. I thank her for her never-ending patience and endurance in my endless quest to express it right and clear.

May 2020
Morgan Hill, California
www.bakrimusa.com
bakrimusa@gmail.com

Introduction

Way back in 1989 and until not too long ago, the year 2020 was much anticipated. It promised to be a glamorous one, a coming out event of sorts for Malaysia to mark her achieving Vision 2020 aspirations. It was to be the year when Malaysia would be joining the exclusive club of developed nations.

It is 2020 now and not a word is being uttered on that once-lofty goal. No celebrations, no hoopla. All silent. It is as if there is a massive national conspiracy not to bring up the topic. Too embarrassing!

Malaysia is way far short of achieving her Vision 2020 goals set in 1990, a generation earlier. All those grandiose visions were but, as we Malays would put it, *angan angan Mat Jenin* (the wild fantasies of a Mat Jenin–the lovable clown in Malay folklore).

The man who articulated that grand plan was one Mahathir Mohamad. Today he is still Prime Minister, his second time around after a hiatus of over a decade and a half, and at 93 years old.

He first put forth his vision for the future of Malaysia in an address to the Malaysian Business Council. This was followed by a series of essays under the title "The Way Forward." The country then was still the darling of the West, recognized as an emerging or potential Asian Tiger, though not quite yet on par with Taiwan, Singapore, or South Korea. A British publisher later put those essays in a slim volume with the same title.

Mahathir's vision caught on and it became the basis of his Sixth Malaysia Plan introduced in 1991. It was to be the nation's blueprint for development for the next thirty years, the span of a generation, to end on–auspiciously–2020. As "The Way Forward" did not quite have a zing to it, the plan was later dubbed Vision 2020.

Ever the iconoclast, Mahathir eschewed the traditional criteria of a developed society, dismissing them as the parochial invention of the West. He fancied that he could better such traditional markers as the per capita income, level of industrialization, or the Human Development Index. Instead, he envisioned "a united Malaysian nation with a sense of common and shared destiny." His other goals were equally nebulous if not corny, as with a society that would be "robust," "economically just," and "psychologically liberated."

His paean to quantitative or measurable goals (and modern economics) was the doubling of the Malaysian GDP every decade, or a four-fold increase from its 1990 base. That would assume a consistent 7 percent annual growth. Quite a challenge, although South Korea and later China plus a few other nations had done it.

Mahathir's Vision 2020 fantasy was rudely disabused by the 1997 Asian contagion. He blamed the West for its rapacious capitalism that gave rise to such celebrated greedy currency speculators as George Soros.

Then as if not challenged enough by that economic crisis, Mahathir created a much unneeded and nearly crippling accompanying political crisis by picking a fight with his hitherto deputy and presumed heir apparent, Anwar Ibrahim.

Having steered Malaysia through that treacherous stretch of political and economic turmoil, he retired in 2003 and handed power to his handpicked successor, Abdullah Badawi. Ever the poor judge of talent, Mahathir's dud and soporific Abdullah nearly destroyed Malaysia, not willfully but through indifferent neglect. Mahathir then engineered to have Najib Razak take over. It was a walkover. Sleepyhead Abdullah was not awake enough to know what had happened.

If Mahathir had erred with Abdullah, then Najib was a disaster several quanta beyond.

Then at 93 year of age and having through a treacherous "redo" heart bypass in 2007, Mahathir together with a now invigorated opposition coalition crafted by his erstwhile nemesis Anwar Ibrahim, dislodged Najib's Barisan coalition in the 2018 election.

With that, Mahathir had the rare second chance to redeem himself, at an age where most are people are either dead or just existing. Malays decades younger than he is are content with spending time on the golf courses or suraus. Not Mahathir. He again fancied himself Malaysia's last redeemer, Allah's gift to Malaysia.

The result? Before he could savor the second anniversary of his second coming, he was out maneuvered. He resigned in shameful failure. By March 2020 when Malaysia should have been basking in the glory of his Vision 2020, the country was hit by the Covid-19 pandemic, with a government totally inept to meet this grave new challenge. Worse, its government is led by an inept, cancer stricken Muhyiddin Yassin, though much younger than Mahathir but biologically much older. The leadership of Muhyiddin and the government he leads has yet to be ratified by parliament as of May 2020. What a legacy for Mahathir!

Mahathir now has a convenient excuse for his failed Vision 2020. During its first decade he could convince himself and Malaysians if not the world that it was the West that did in the country. In the second, he blamed the soporific and detached Abdullah, and the third, Najib with his insatiable greed. That crook Najib nearly wrecked Malaysia with his 1MDB heist.

Mahathir may have convinced himself in blaming others for his failure, but he does not convince me.

The more plausible reason, and this applies not only to Malaysia but also all those other countries still struggling in their undeveloped or developing mode, is much simpler and more fundamental.

Blindfold me and then place me in a school compound on any school day in any country. By removing my blindfold, I could tell right away whether that country is developed or still an undeveloped one.

The essence of my observation is captured by the ancient Chinese wisdom: The schools of a nation are its future in miniature.

The contrast between a Japanese or South Korean school versus that in Egypt or Mexico could not be more startling. You would have to be blind or an idiot not to notice the stark differences.

Visit a Sekolah Kebangsaan and compare that to any school in Singapore, and you would know that Malaysia is behind that island republic, and why. A generation or two ago the schools in both countries were comparable.

In First World America, there are scattered isolated enclaves of Third World. Visit the schools in the Blue Mountains of Appalachia, the deep rural south of Mississippi, America's inner cities, or the Native Indian Reservations, and the reason would be apparent—their rotten schools. Obvious too would be the solution—improve them!

American inner-city schools are but massive ugly warehouses for her young, with ubiquitous metal detectors at the entrances and highly visible armed guards. Learning or nurturing centers for the young they are not.

Malaysia may still be in the Third World, but tease the economic and demographic statistics, and you would discern definite clumps of First

World, just like America and her Third World pockets. The per capita income of the Chinese and the condos or bungalows they live in rival those of the First World. The rural kampungs and those blights of urban high-rise edifices (*Rumah Pangsa*) inhabited by Malays, well, their inhabitants' per capita income matches their Third World existence.

Then visit their respective schools. Ever wonder why Malays now are increasingly enrolling their children in those Chinese schools? That is reminiscent of the Irish Catholics of the 1950s sending their children to the much superior "Godless" Protestant schools of the English despite threats of being excommunicated.

With his Vision 2020 now all but forgotten, Mahathir coined another grand but much less heralded scheme, his "Shared Prosperity 2030." This time he wisely chose a much shorter time span, a decade instead of a generation. At 95 it would be unlikely for him to be alive at the end to see whether it would be successful. I was certain that back in 1990 when he chose Vision 2020 with its time span of thirty years, he too did not expect to live to see its conclusion.

Mahathir may or may not be around come 2030 but Malaysia would. If present trend continues, with continued deterioration of the schools, then Shared Prosperity 2030 would meet the same ignoble fate.

If Mahathir were to live long enough to see the failure of his Shared Prosperity 2030, I wonder who or what he would blame it on then. I am uncertain if his surviving till 2030 would then be a blessing or a cruel divine punishment.

No nation could progress unless it has an enlightened system of education and pays attention to its schools, colleges, and universities. Ireland, Taiwan, Singapore, and South Korea would not be where they are today had they not done that.

The world today rightly lauds China for uplifting hundreds of millions of her citizens out of poverty and making her economy rival that of America. China is poised to take over soon.

The world attributes China's success to her joining the global mainstream, as with her entry into the World Trade Organization as well as her embracing capitalism and free enterprise. Those may be contributing factors, but the pivot point was Deng Xiaoping's early decision to rehabilitate China's schools and universities devastated by Mao's madness.

As revealed in Ezra Vogel's biography of the man, soon after taking over from Mao and early during America's initial tentative rapprochement with China, Deng asked the head of a junior American delegation visiting Beijing to ask President Carter to accept a few hundred young bright Chinese students into top American universities. A very modest request that Carter readily acceded to.

A generation later—the same time span as Vision 2020—America hosts hundreds of thousands of Chinese students. Those American-trained students are leapfrogging China into becoming a leader in IT, biotechnology, and solar technology, among others. They are the ones transforming China.

The traffic was not only all one-way. I was visiting Beijing in early 2000. The plane was full of American teachers, lecturers, and professors bound for China. International schools, especially British and American, blossomed in China. Hundreds and thousands of Chinese students flock to attend cram courses for TOEFL (English test for non-English speaking foreign students wishing to attend American colleges), SAT (America's matriculating examination), GRE (for entry into American graduate schools), and GMAT (for graduate business schools).

Those Chinese students and leaders were not at all worried that by embracing English and the West generally they would be guilty of not *mentarbatkan* (dignifying) their own language or culture, the current obsession with Malay leaders.

There is a lesson there for Mahathir (as well as other Third World leaders) and Malays. Focus on education if you want your society to join the ranks of the developed. Improve your schools and colleges. Set the bar high for students and make them sit for the same tests as those from advanced countries, not the local SPM and *matrikulasi*. Modernize the curriculum. Import foreign teachers if that is what it would take.

That is not a secret recipe. It has been time-tested both in the East (Taiwan and Singapore) as well as in the West (Ireland).

For Malaysia, failure to correct these deficiencies in her education system would doom her citizens to perpetual mediocrity and the nation a permanent member of the Third World.

These essays are my views towards Malaysia achieving that end. In essence they are updates of my earlier book, *An Education System Worthy Of Malaysia* (2003).

A Systemic Rot

Education Minister Maszlee Should Be More An Executive, Less A Professor

August 6, 2018

New Education Minister Maszlee Malik should be more an executive and less a professor that he was. He now leads an organization with an annual budget well over RM280B and a staff of over half a million. That ministry, like all others, is not known for its crispness.

Forget about grand plans and overarching policies. All would be for naught if your staff and organization could not execute them, or if they were consumed with such trivia as campus newspaper subscriptions and pupils' shoe colors.

Maszlee should focus on shaping up that flabby organization. Enlist someone with a solid MBA or credible business experience to help him be an effective and efficient executive. There is a universe of difference in being a professor and an executive. Business meetings are unlike academic seminars. You want results and decisions, not endless intellectual musing and more research.

Maszlee should assess the capabilities and weaknesses of his staff. Forget about *wacanas* (talk shows), town hall meetings, or press conferences. To his credit, he has already made many personal visits for first-hand assessments.

The challenges facing Malaysian education are as overwhelming as they are obvious, the consequence of long neglect, incompetent leadership, and political meddling. The difficulty is not in identifying the issues but to pick three or four of the more pressing ones and tackle those first. Maszlee has articulated some of those–greater university autonomy, making students at least bilingual, enhancing STEM teaching, as well as fixing dilapidated schools. Those four would occupy and challenge him for some time. There is little need and would serve little purpose to go beyond, as with recognizing UEC (the Chinese schools' terminal certificate), sending a team to Finland, or issuing edicts on the color of students' shoes.

Maszlee's first and continuing public task, as with all the other ministers, is to "walk the talk." He cannot profess to champion university autonomy and then order the dismantling of campus gates and make the universities have speakers' corners! The universities should do those on their own initiative. By issuing that directive, Maszlee missed out on a splendid opportunity to assess his Vice-Chancellors' responsiveness to citizens' rising expectation for greater openness.

Maszlee should elicit from the universities' leaders their three or four most immediate challenges and ask how he as minister could help. They, not him, know best (or should) as they are closest to the problems. If they could not articulate them or were more concerned with a welcoming ceremony for him, fire them.

Firing university leaders should be done only if they are found wanting or fail to gain the confidence of the greater campus community, and not because they were appointed by the previous administration. Doing so would only perpetuate the blight of political interference that is the bane of local institutions.

Likewise, the stressing of the importance of English. Maszlee would best demonstrate that not through endless speeches but with an executive decision to make MUET (Malaysian Universities English Test) mandatory for universities and teachers' colleges. Likewise, give extra allowances and preferential choice for quarters to teachers of English (as well as STEM). He could also direct schools to increase their hours of instruction in English or have another subject be taught in that language.

If he were to encourage his staff to communicate in English and make its proficiency a requirement for promotions and entry into the permanent establishment, that would demonstrate the importance of English. Emulate what Rafidah Aziz did at MITI (Ministry of Trade and Industry) decades ago.

Make 12 years of schooling the norm. Bring back the old Form VI and reduce it to one year. Start it in January together with the rest of the school. Make the transition from Form V to VI as seamless as going from Form IV to V. That would bring order to the current chaos for school-leavers post-Form V.

The current seven-month hiatus following Form V and before the start of Form VI or *matrikulasi* is a colossal waste of time and presents a precious loss of learning opportunity, more so for the academically inclined. The rich enroll their children in private colleges. Most Malay students idle their time away. Much attrition of good study habits would occur during that long break. Idle time is also the devil's workshop.

Get rid of *matrikulasi* and the universities' foundation courses. Those waste scarce expensive resources. Universities should focus on undergraduate, graduate, and professional education, not high school.

As for fixing schools, Maszlee has demonstrated the dire need for that by his many photo-ops showing him sitting at pupils' broken desks. At the macro level the best solution would be to prevail upon Treasury to have MOE's tenders be open to competitive bidding. That would achieve more with less.

At the micro level, the Minister would achieve even more and much faster while at the same time streamline the process if he were to give the money directly to the headmasters. Let them prioritize the repairs and choose the local contractors. If you entrust them with the nation's most precious assets—the brains of our young—then you should also trust them with a few million *ringgit*.

Back to the teachers, Maszlee should not get bogged down with administrative trivia as with requests for transfers and maternity leave. Let your human resources people deal with those. Stay out of that.

Execute these basic matters well and Maszlee would earn the gratitude of millions of Malaysians, quite apart from making a significant contribution to the betterment of the nation.

Make Malay College Exclusively International Baccalaureate

May 14, 2017

Malay College Kuala Kangsar (MCKK) is being yanked left and right as well as up and down by the Ministry of Education (MOE) and other agencies. The college is *directed* to be Sekolah Kluster Kecemerlangan (Cluster of Excellence School), Sekolah Berprestasi Tinggi (High Prestige School), and School of Global Excellence. Even the government-linked conglomerate Khazanah is in the act, the college being its "Trust School," whatever that means.

Neither excellence nor anything of great value could come from those who are being told what to do. The college should chart its own course and then convince those in authority the merits of its ideas, not the other way around.

MCKK's governing board glitters with luminaries. Its chairman, the Sultan of Perak, is an Oxford graduate and a Harvard PhD. However, unless the board can demonstrate leadership with great ideas and their effective execution, then those glittering qualifications of its Board members would be nothing more than distracting window dressing.

I suggest two possible futures for MCKK. One, become an exclusive International Baccalaureate (IB) school; two, collaborate with a degree-granting institution for an accelerated program where its students would complete their high school simultaneously with the first two years of university, and earn an Associate Degree.

Since I left in 1962, Malay College has been through only three major academic changes. One was its initiation of a science stream while I was there; two, elimination of Sixth Form in tandem with switching of the language of instruction into Malay in the late 1970s; and three, introducing IB's Diploma Program (DP) in 2011. That last one took over a decade in the planning.

The introduction of the pure science stream in the 1970s was the only unqualified success. That initiative also brought the Sixth Form science block. The consequences of that move were the many current and past STEM professors at local universities, as well as many of the nation's leading scientists and medical specialists.

That move grabbed national headlines then, and rightly so. However, not to gloat but to put things in perspective, my Tuanku Muhammad School in rural Kuala Pilah started its pure science stream years earlier, *sans* any fanfare.

That one positive change was soon undone a decade later with the switch in the language of instruction to Malay and the discontinuation of Sixth Form. Without Sixth Form, MCKK was emasculated to a glorified and expensive middle school. Concomitant with that was the de-emphasis on science. Today the college could not even meet the ministry's minimal 60:40 goal of science to non-science students.

As for the college's IB program, it is too soon to tell. This much we do know. The program does not attract its own students; it has to advertise to attract applicants. The results of the first few years lag the region's average. More telling, the program is *not* the first choice with the college's own students. Very unusual! Nonetheless, last year the college expanded the IB to the Middle School Years (MSY).

Time to reassess the college. That should begin with considering who its peers are or should be. They should *not* be the other local residential schools or the likes of SMK Ulu Kelantan, rather Britain's Eton, Singapore's Raffles Institution, America's Groton, and South Korea's Daewon. Daewon is a recent institution but already has a reputation as a leading feeder school for elite universities. As for local peers, I suggest KL's International School and Penang's Chung Ling.

Making the college all IB should be next, sparing its students from having to sit for local examinations. That would be liberating, for them and their teachers. IB would become the college's crown jewel academic offering, and not as at present, only an expensive ornamental add-on. Were MCKK to do that, it would become the biggest of such schools in the world. MCKK could start a trend in being truthful by posting its IB results. Currently many schools with hybrid IB have artificially excellent results because they screened their students, allowing only their very top students to sit for the test.

IB's Diploma Program is two years; the full Middle School Years (MSY), five. You do not have to subscribe to the full MSY. I suggest only the last two. Students would enter a preliminary "prep" year of full English immersion, reminiscent of the old Special Malay and Remove Classes. They would then continue with years 4 and 5 of MSY before proceeding to DP, making their stay at Kuala Kangsar a total of five years, just as at present. The only difference is that these students would enter in midyear of their local Form II instead of at the beginning of Form I as at present.

That prep year would be critical; IB is English-medium and emphasizes critical thinking, the polar opposite of the Malaysian curriculum which is in Malay and heavy on rote learning. Making MCKK exclusively IB would also eliminate the students' current wasteful half-a-year hiatus following their SPM (Year 11) examination.

Changing the school year from January to July could pose problems with regards to inter-school sports and other competitions, as well as with families coping with different school holidays. However, with more schools now offering IB, they could form their own leagues. The second problem would entail major adjustments for families.

The major cost for residential schools is for food and lodging. MCKK could double or even triple its current output without much additional costs by dispensing with its hostel. It could also begin charging fees on a sliding scale based on parental income.

With the increasing popularity of IB, and with Western universities becoming exorbitant, I envisage a need soon for a local university to cater for these graduates. It would be great if MCKK were to be instrumental in initiating a new trend in tertiary education in the country and region.

As for the second option of an accelerated high school-college program, Bard College has a successful one with New York City's schools. A high school in my area has one with a nearby college, focusing on STEM subjects and underrepresented minority students.

It would be difficult for Malay College to start a comparable program in Kuala Kangsar seeing that there are no degree-granting institutions nearby. The plan would be feasible for residential schools in Klang Valley because of the numerous universities in the area. Penang's Tri-Chung Ling High Schools' leaders once contemplated having their own tertiary institution integrated with their school system based on similar rationale.

MCKK started as a colonial institution to train children of the feudal elite for junior administrative positions. Only later did it become a school, and its admissions liberalized. It is time for another transformation.

I look forward to someday reading headlines of the school's Speech Day not on the many royal guests in attendance rather the headmaster announcing with unconcealed pride the list of elite universities his graduating students would be attending. *That* would mean more to and reflect better the college's students, teachers, parents, and leaders than any award the sultan or ministry could bestow.

Swap STAM For STEM To Enhance Malay Competitiveness

March 5, 2017

In 2016 nearly nine thousand students [the total for 2018 was 10,000], all Malays, sat for the Sijil Tinggi Agama Malaysia (STAM-Religious High School Certificate). A related event, and with even greater significance and accompanying fanfare, was the glittering mega event at Putrajaya, "Reviving The Islamic Spirit" (RIS) conference. That was the first time it was held outside the Muslim-minority West and in a Muslim-majority country. The organizers made a big point on that.

Careful observation would reveal that, the government excepted, in the modern sectors of Malaysian life and economy, Malays (and thus Muslims) remain very much in the minority and at the margins. Only the overwhelming presence of the Malay-dominated government in the marketplace masks this stark reality. Malaysia's ostentatious minarets and other very visible artifacts of Islam give visitors and natives alike a false sense of achievement.

In the greater scheme of things, having RIS in Malaysia did not alter the conference's traditional and overall Muslim-minority ambience.

Judging from the luminaries in attendance and the trappings, the conference must have cost a bundle. However expensive, it pales to the opportunity costs of the squandering of precious Malay brains through STAM. Malays and Muslims would advance more if Malaysia were to get rid of STAM and revamp her religious schools.

Religious schools in Malaysia and elsewhere in the Muslim world should be more like those in the West. Meaning, they should produce their share of the nation's scientists, entrepreneurs, and engineers. These schools should not be monasteries or a refuge for Malays wanting to escape from this world.

The world is heavy into STEM (Science, Technology, Engineering, and Mathematics) but Malays are rushing into STAM. Ever wonder why the community is still left far behind? The only sliver of hope was the slight drop in the number of candidates last year.

The Islamic cachet sells with Malays, with more Malay parents enrolling their children in Islamic schools. This is further greased by the deterioration of the national stream.

STAM's curriculum is narrow, restricted to Islam and Arabic. Even Malay is not offered, while English is only an elective, not as a formal subject but a prep course for the Malaysian Universities English Test (MUET). Malays forget that the language of RIS is English. How could they understand the message of the conference without knowing English?

The only universities STAM students could enroll in, apart from local ones, would be Arab ones, hardly the leading centers of learning. The courses those students could pursue would be even more constricted.

Outside the religious establishment, the only jobs STAM graduates could get would be as tour guides for visiting Arabs. These students could not even be their camel herders. Even if they were lucky enough to be one, the only thing they could do for their sick herd would be to pray.

Islamic education in Malaysia and the Muslim world is outmoded and irrelevant. The Arabs are scratching their heads on how to modernize their archaic system. However, do not expect any utterance at the RIS conference on this critical daunting issue facing Muslims.

The central fallacy if not arrogance of contemporary Muslim scholars is their obsession with the "Islamization" of knowledge, the view that there is a uniquely Islamic version or perspective. That conceit flies in the face of reality as evidenced by the wide spectrum of views within Islam throughout history as well as now. Muslim ulama and leaders would prefer that the flock be like sheep, subscribing to the only one true version of Islam, as *they* (leaders) see it.

Ancient Muslim scholars saw no such distinction between the secular and religious; the leading ones were both scientists and ulama. Those ancient Muslims did not hesitate learning from the atheistic and polytheistic Greeks. Early Muslims would go to China if they had to in the pursuit of knowledge. The Chinese did not believe in Allah.

I do not know whether there was any irony intended when Syed Naquib Al Attas, the champion of this Islamization fad, was honored with the Al Ghazzali Achievement Award at this RIS!

A saying attributed to Martin Luther has it that a Christian cobbler would best demonstrate his devotion to God not by carving intricate crucifixes on the shoes he makes but to make them sturdy and cheap and thus durable and affordable. You serve God by serving your fellow man, not by endlessly reciting His Glory. God does not need that.

The Muslim comparable would be a hadith where a man was admitted into Heaven because he once removed a thorn from a path, thus saving others from hurting themselves; likewise, a prostitute who brought water to a dog dying of thirst. If those were the rewards in Islam, imagine what it would be for the engineer who built the road or bridge so villagers could bring their produce to market or their sick child to the hospital! Referring to the thirsty dog, imagine the reward for a veterinarian!

STAM does not prepare students to be an engineer or a veterinarian. The current Islamic education reduces Islam to a set of rituals, and our Holy Koran to a talisman, no different from the dried grass strands our animist ancestors hung at the entrance of kampung houses to ward off evil spirits. Want to pass your examination, recite the Koran; want to heal your illness, likewise.

This vast chasm separating Islamic leaders, religious and otherwise, from reality and the masses is the most formidable challenge facing the ummah.

Consider corruption, the blight of all Muslim societies. Not a word was uttered at that RIS conference. I met one of the American speakers before he left for Malaysia. Knowing that I was from there, his first words after the customary salutation was, "Return the billions to the people!" he jested, referring to the 1MDB scandal. I hope he did mention that at the conference.

Another speaker at RIS was Afifi al-Akiti, a local celebrity being the first Malay to be appointed an Oxford don. He was once asked while on a government-sponsored trip back home about the scandalous corruptions now blighting Malaysia. He grinned and pleaded ignorance, his being away from the country for so long! What a cop out! Either that or he was so cloistered in his cramped Oxford office and equally restricted discipline to be aware of the outside world.

Throughout history, ulama and scholars were formidable bulkheads against the excesses of leaders. Today these scholars have been co-opted by the state and given impressive titles and equally generous stipends. I am reminded of the wisdom encapsulated in the hadith that Heaven is full of rulers who were close to scholars, but Hell is full of scholars who befriended rulers.

If Muslims were to be serious on reviving the spirit of our great faith, begin with the simple Koranic injunction: Command good, and forbid evil. The rest of the Holy Book is but commentary. Condemn the corruption, injustices, and the flagrant human rights abuses of your host country–that would be an excellent start. As for serving God by serving mankind, young Malays would achieve this better through pursuing STEM than STAM.

If Malaysia were to do those things, when RIS would again be held in this country, it would be truly in a Muslim-majority country in all respects and meaning.

The Impact Of Growth Of International Schools

June 5, 2012

The government had gone beyond removing quotas, as with granting tax and other incentives, to encourage the growth of international schools. However, growth would depend more on market forces, principally the demand, which in turn would be related to costs. Lower the cost and you expand the market, elementary economics. Reducing red tape, as with making it easy to get permits and secure visas, would lower costs far more effectively than any other move.

If there were to be a market and profits to be made, entrepreneurs would come in. That is the beauty and genius of capitalism. I have no problem with education being "for profit". That would be no different than the health and other sectors. Profit is just another measure or reflection of discipline, effectiveness, and productivity.

Some educator-entrepreneurs would focus only on quality education and dispense with fancy gyms, Olympic swimming pools, and ornate entrance arches, thus making their services affordable. Some parents would accept slightly crowded classrooms in return for affordability. After all they chose international schools and paid those huge expenses; they and their children would thus be motivated and could handle the larger classes. They would not need much pampering–just quality Western education. They would not be interested whether their children would be playing soccer with the children of Mat Salleh diplomats and expatriates.

These local children would be diligent no matter how big the class is; their parents would ensure that. Besides, there is little correlation between class size and students' achievements. The most important factor to a child's success in school is parental involvement; and motivated parents (meaning, those who have fork out tons of money) are involved parents.

Those newer and less expensive schools would not be competing against Tunku Jaafar College or KL International Schools, rather Malaysian national schools. Their major selling point would not be that these schools are "international" rather that they use English and have a Western curriculum. You could be assured that even with the removal of quotas there would still be no lineups at the comparable Chinese or Indonesian International School.

With the increased demand, I envisage Malaysian government-linked companies would be tempted to set up international schools. After all they are already involved in owning and running private hospitals. MARA could also set up such schools or even convert their existing junior colleges. Imagine those colleges being sources of revenue instead of draining it!

Removal of quotas for international schools was an important first step, but only that. The government's next major role should be to protect the public by keeping out hustlers and fly-by-night operators more adept at ripping off customers than serving them. One provision would be to require performance bonds so that if the school were to close, parents would be reimbursed, plus an appropriate penalty. That should be the minimum "soft" requirement; there of course would be other "hard" requirements aimed at ensuring pupil safety.

At the next level, the government should ensure quality, again to protect consumers. However, I do not think that the teachers at Tuanku Jaafar or Bukit Kiara would look kindly to overbearing Ministry officials setting the standards. Instead the ministry should encourage self-regulation and accreditation. The process aims at the enhancement of quality and not be subverted to become hidden barriers to new entrants, or worse, another source of corruption. That would only increase costs.

Increased competition would result in the trickling down of affordability. This is true for education as well as aviation. The success of Air Asia ("Now Everyone Can Fly!") is testimony to that. The government's projection of 75,000 students and 87 schools by 2020 could easily be exceeded. Thailand already has over 200 such schools. Based on the economy and tradition of English education, aided by the deplorable quality of Malaysian public schools, the potential local market is even much larger and ready for massive expansion.

Impact of More Malaysians at International Schools
Those who enroll in international schools are no ordinary Malaysians; they are the children of the rich, powerful, and highly motivated. As such these children would be destined to play major roles in the nation's affairs. They would have a clear path to the top because of their superior education and parental influence, though more likely in the reverse order, this being Malaysia. At present their impact of international schools is minimal because of their small numbers. With the anticipated growth, their influence would grow.

Even if they were to become only teachers (not to slight the profession) of national schools, they would bring new styles and perspectives to their classrooms. They would be noticed though initially only by their students but later, fellow teachers and the general community. That could only be positive, for the pupils, fellow teachers, the school, and the entire system. Were they to end up as headmasters, professors, senior civil servants, and executives helming major GLCs, their impact would increase that much more, to the benefit of Malaysia.

Prime Minister Najib bragged of his Administration's "transformation program". However, it would be too much to expect present ministers and civil servants to effect that. Brought up under the current system and having reached the top under it, they would not likely find fault with it. To them, the ingrained ethos of the civil service, *kami menurut perentah* (We follow orders!) would be hard to break. Their schools and universities have not taught them how to think critically and independently, only to regurgitate what had been fed into them, and to perform according to what had been programmed in them. Their career successes have been predicated on complying diligently with the commands of their superiors. When they reach the top, they would perpetuate that culture.

The only hope for change would be to have a critical mass of Malaysians brought up through Western-type international schools to become policymakers and head the various departments. That would be the more significant long-term benefits.

Meanwhile in the short term expect some difficulties. The initial accompanying educational inequities would be aggravated and potentially be explosive especially when tied to race. With the rise of the Malay upper class (either legitimately or otherwise), and with international schools becoming less expensive, there could soon be a critical mass of these Malays with Western liberal education.

The flip side is that with affluent and influential Malay parents abandoning national schools, the impact on those remaining would be severe. With the top creamed off, the average in national schools would go down. Whereas before those parents would demand higher expectations from these schools, now that they are gone, there would be little impetus for improvement. That would grease the slide of national schools.

It would not be long before a culture of mediocrity and low expectation would become entrenched. Malaysian national schools would then be like America's inner-city public schools, dangerous and dysfunctional warehouses for the young, the breeding grounds for Mat Rempits and Minah Karans.

Such a dismal future is not destined. Creatively handled, the removal of quotas for international schools could be the impetus for improving national schools. For one, for every local child enrolled in an international school means that there would be one fewer pupil in national school and one less associated expense. The saved resource could then be showered on those remaining. Even if there were to be an exodus out of national schools, consider the bright side. Those schools would be less crowded, and the teachers could afford to spend more time with their pupils.

With quality international schools being the new model, there will be the associated general uplifting of educational expectations among Malaysians. Malay parents would now aspire an education for their children the caliber of that offered at Tuanku Jaafar, not Malay College or MARA Junior College. Consider the example of the retail sector. Now with clean, air-conditioned supermarkets found even in small towns, Malaysians demand fresh products, efficient services, and pleasant environment. Those sundry store operators with their bare armpits contemptuously "serving" their customers would have to change or risk being out of business.

That would be the positive impact on national schools with the removal of quotas on international schools. Malaysians would have to strive to achieve that end; it would not happen by default.

The alternative would be to suffer the consequences of local national schools being reduced to the status of America's inner-city schools, dysfunctional human warehouses thus condemning future generations of Malays.

Removing Quotas In International Schools A Positive Development

May 26, 2012

In striking contrast to the horrendously expensive and unbelievably stupid idea of sending Malaysian teacher-trainees to Kirby, the Ministry of Education's other decision to remove quotas on local enrollment in international schools is positive and much welcomed. The Minister assured everyone that because of the small number of students involved, the move would not impact national schools. I disagree. His confidence was misplaced, and analysis flawed. On the contrary, this measure would have a tremendous impact on national schools and ultimately the nation, for good or bad depending on how it would be managed.

Consider the liberalization of higher education instituted in 1996. The rationale was to increase access and save foreign exchange by keeping at home those who would have gone abroad. It achieved both, the most successful of government initiatives. And it did not cost the government a *sen* (penny) except for the pay of government lawyers who drafted the enabling legislation.

The policy's impact went far beyond. It forever altered in very profound ways the academic landscape of local public universities. Their current emphasis on the use of English for example, is the consequence of the impact of these private universities. Local employers (other than governmental agencies of course) made it clear that they prefer these graduates over those from public universities because of their demonstrably superior English skills.

There were initial attempts at imputing ugly racial motives to this preferential treatment of private university graduates as most of them were non-Malays. That worked, but only temporarily. Ultimately the horrible truth was exposed. That realization was the impetus to the current greater use of English in public universities, with their erstwhile nationalistic Vice-Chancellors now fully embracing the move. They had to; the pathetic sight of their unemployed graduates was a constant and painful reminder.

Liberalizing higher education aggravated the inequities between Malays and non-Malays, specifically with respect to their employability in the private sector. It did however, force public universities to change their ways, as with emphasizing English. That ultimately benefited their mostly Malay students.

Removing limits on local enrolment in international schools would have the same profound and irreversible impact on national schools and on Malays. Initially expect that aggravate gaps in educational achievements, again especially between Malays and non-Malays, but in the long run it would jolt Malay leaders to make the necessary adjustments to national schools. Either that or face the prospect of future generations of young Malays doomed to perpetual mediocrity and unemployability.

At present the locals in these international schools are children of the super-rich, and thus overwhelmingly non-Malay. Even the upper middle class (with slightly greater Malay representation) could not afford these schools. The concerns expressed that this liberalization would exacerbate educational inequities between rich and poor are therefore valid and reasonable. However, the rich are already different in many other ways; educational advantages for their children would just be another.

It bears reminding that the impact of any policy is dynamic. Yes, there would be the expected increased inequity in the beginning, but with time people would adjust and you get radically different reactions and consequences, as was seen with the earlier liberalization of higher education.

Those harping on inequities ignore economic realities. There is demand for these international schools because they offer quality albeit expensive education. The imposition of quotas only aggravates the situation. Its removal would expand the market, enticing new players. Greater competition puts downward pressure on price, an economic truism that cannot be ignored. This is already happening in Thailand where international schools are found even in small towns and within the financial reach of the middle class, at least those families prudent enough to think of their children's future and not on current conspicuous consumption. The lower costs in small towns would make these schools even more affordable.

There are three ready markets for international schools. One would be the super-affluent Malaysians who already have children in schools abroad. That is a miniscule market; besides, those parents are not likely to change course. The cachet of an overseas education still sells. A much bigger market would be the next tier of the wealthy. Those parents value education and recognize only too readily the inadequacies of local schools. At present they would require special dispensation from the minister and face other hurdles to enroll their children in international schools; money alone would not do it.

It is not a surprise that local students (especially Malays) in these schools are the children of Malaysia's "Politburo" members. If you wonder how they could afford the costs based on their parent's official pay, then you have not appreciated the culture of negotiated contracts, "Approved Permits," and other quirks of the New Economic Policy, as well as the "Malaysian way" of doing business.

The third, and sizeable market would be those parents in Johore who now send their children to schools in Singapore. To be sure, Malaysian international schools are still considerably more expensive than the republic's public schools, nonetheless after factoring in transportation and other costs, quite apart from wasted time and energy in commuting, these parents might well fork out the added expense and opt for the much superior local international schools. After all their reasons for choosing Singapore are to get an education in English and avoid local public schools; Malaysian international schools offer both.

To repeat because of the potential political significance, these three markets are dominated by non-Malays. Expect a racial angle to the argument for reinstating the quota. If not handled skillfully, political pressure would build up to jettison the policy. Already the Parent Action

Group for Education (PAGE), otherwise made up of liberal professional Malays, is already against the idea though for reasons other than race.

Ironically, PAGE advocates the greater use of English in national schools especially in the teaching of science and mathematics. Perhaps PAGE could be persuaded that international schools are but a backdoor path towards this objective (and beyond), albeit available only to those who could afford it. This path also conveniently sidesteps possible constitutional conundrum of having English-medium public schools. Fortunately, Malay language nationalists are not sophisticated enough to see through this.

In truth, the constitutional hurdle, like all man-made ones, is surmountable. Consider that the International Islamic University uses English. It overcomes this legal barrier by being registered under the Ministry of Trade and Industry, not Education, hence exempted from the language rule.

Expanding international schools would be a far superior move than the bringing back the old English schools or increasing the number of hours devoted to the subject in national schools, as many including PAGE are advocating. The deficiency with local national schools goes beyond its medium of instruction. International schools (especially those following the American pattern) have a much different curriculum and pedagogical philosophy, far from the stultifying ones that plague national schools.

On a related issue, if there were to be a blossoming of Arabic or Indonesian International Schools with this liberalization, with Malays flocking to enroll their children there, then the community would not be further ahead. Malays would still regress. The two systems of education are not worthy of emulation.

Western international schools enjoy two complementary advantages. One is of course their superior curriculum, facilities, and teaching, quite apart from the international ambience. The other and perhaps more important is that the quality of local schools is atrocious. The recent rescinding of the policy of teaching science and mathematics in English only made matters worse. Consider that today's Malay elite would rather send their children to Garden International School over supposedly exclusive Malay College Kuala Kangsar.

Where the public schools are excellent, few locals would opt for private schools, as in Alberta, or international ones as in Finland. The clamor for Malaysians wanting to send their children to international schools reflects a much greater and more basic problem—the lousy local national schools. Seen from this angle, for PEMANDU and the government's transformation program to view the growth of international schools as positive could only be construed as misplaced and misguided. Only if you are convinced that our national schools are beyond redemption would you consider this a positive development. And I do.

Resurrecting Kirby Is Fiscally Irresponsible

May 20, 2012

It is incomprehensible that with the Ministry of Education still reviewing its schools, the Minister and his Deputy saw fit to announce two decisions that could potentially have a profound impact on the system. The first would resurrect the old Kirby/Brinsford Lodge teacher-training program of the 1950s, and the second, would remove the current quotas on local enrollment in international schools.

Before analyzing the two decisions, it is worth pondering as to why they were made *before* the completion of this "exhaustive review." A cynical interpretation would be that the current "review" is but a charade rather than a serious deliberative process. If that were so, then it would be a terrible insult to those distinguished Malaysians who have been co-opted or have volunteered to serve on the panel. On a moral level, it would also be an unconscionable fraud perpetrated upon citizens, especially parents who have been banking on the review to improve their children's schools.

Another view, equally less charitable, is that the Minister and his Deputy are not fully aware of the many ramifications and enormous consequences of their decisions. A more practical explanation would be that both announcements reflect the typical seat-of-the-pants style of policymaking typical at the upper levels of the government. It would have been more reassuring had both proposals been first vetted by this review committee.

In the absence of the panel's analysis, I will examine the merits and demerits of the two initiatives.

Resurrecting Kirby

The old Kirby and Brinsford Lodge program was undeniably superb and successful. Thousands of young Malaysians had benefited from the tutelage and influence of those dedicated professional teachers who were trained at both institutions. Many of those teachers went on for their baccalaureate and graduate degrees to become distinguished Professors of Education at home and abroad, reflecting the high caliber of their talent.

If Malaysia were to resurrect the program, it is important first to elucidate the many contributing factors to its earlier success, and to remember that conditions today are vastly different from those of the 1950s. That may be obvious but is often overlooked. For example, to say that the current Form Five graduates—the potential trainees—are different from those of the 1950s would be a vast understatement. If Malaysia were to send those with Form Five qualifications to Kirby today, the results would also be vastly different if not disastrous.

The success of Kirby and Brinsford Lodge had less to do with their being operated by the British or located in England, rather with the candidates selected to undergo the training. As mentioned earlier, they were simply superior to begin with. It is well to remember that in the 1950s only the top five percent (or less) of Fifth Formers could go on to Sixth Form and from there, to universities. The next level would be the potential Kirby candidates; they may not have been at the very top nonetheless they were still high up there above the 90th percentile. I knew a few who were qualified for the local university but instead opted for Kirby simply because of the opportunity to go to England, thus deliberately settling for a teacher's diploma instead of a degree from the University of Malaya.

Today the top 25 percent of Malaysian students are headed for universities. Those left for teacher training would be the next tier, those at the 75th percentile at best. Unless Malaysia gets the top students (those above the 90th percentile) to go into teacher training, she would never get good, much less great, teachers regardless where or how they would be trained, and by whom.

This is the crucial lesson from countries like Finland that have excellent schools. They get the best students to go into teaching; the best students make the best teachers. If the lure of spending a few years at Kirby would attract the best and brightest to apply, then resurrect the program. After all, many bright students change their career choices simply because of the opportunity to go abroad. I have met many who dreamed of becoming doctors but instead pursued accounting or engineering simply because of the chance to go abroad.

Economic Aspect of the Proposal

Kirby and Brinsford Lodge had a total of about 600 students at any one time. Assume that the cost today would be about RM100K per student per year (a reasonable estimate), for a total of about RM60 million annually. A hefty sum! That is the total outflow of foreign exchange from Malaysia. The money would be spent in Britain with zero multiplier effect on the local Malaysian economy.

Imagine if that sum were to be spent locally but for the same purpose and by the same personnel. Meaning, bring those British lecturers to Malaysia. Using a faculty/student ratio of 1 to 15 as a guide (comparable to top universities), we would need about 40 professors. With a generous pay package of RM300K per year we would have no difficulty recruiting them. The total cost would come to about RM12 million annually. With another RM3 million for non-academic support staff, the total payroll would be about RM15 million. We would still have RM45 million remaining!

If we were to pay the trainees RM600 each per month, that would certainly interest top students, and the cost would be just over RM4 million. To entice them even more, incorporate elements of the major matriculation examinations into the curriculum so that those students could sit for their STM, GCE A Level, or SAT tests while in training. Then reward those successful students with scholarships to pursue their degrees in return for their committing to teaching.

Having done all that, we would still have RM41 million left. Out of that I would spend RM6 million for soft costs (food, computers, library books), and still RM35 million left over. Assume that to be the annual mortgage payments. Spread that over 30 years (the typical amortization period for real estate loans) at 4 percent interest rates, you could build a campus costing about RM600 million. Even after accounting for the inevitable leakages through "negotiated tenders" and "facilitation fees" to local politicians, we could still build quite a fancy facility, almost luxurious and definitely far superior to the old barn-like and warehouse structures of old Kirby and Brinsford Lodge.

Then think of the economic impact of RM60 million being spent locally, with the multiplier effect from the construction workers to the gardeners as well as the local *teh tarik* and *nasi lemak* peddlers to the hair saloon owners. About the only foreign exchange loss would be the remittance by those British professors. After paying for their housing and other living expenses, (which would be high for expatriates), as well as their hefty Malaysian income tax, they would be lucky to have RM40K at the end of the year to send home.

The total outflow of foreign exchange would be under RM2 million in a year. Contrast that to the outflow of RM60 million in cold cash if Malaysia were to send 600 trainees to Britain, thirty times more expensive! And I have not included the multiplier economic benefits of the RM60 million being spent locally.

There are other non-economic benefits, the most important being academic and scholarly. Those professors would be interested in doing local research and be consultants to local schools and institutions, as well as conduct workshops for the continuing professional education of local teachers. Leading education journals would carry articles with the footnote, "From Kuantan Teachers' College, Malaysia."

The Minister's objective would still be achieved, that is to have Kirby-trained quality teachers. The signal difference between my plan and Muhyiddin's is that I would import Kirby-quality professors to train local would-be teachers while he would export those trainees (and precious foreign exchange) to Britain.

Kirby would like Malaysia to send her trainees there and would lobby hard to secure that contract. Consider that such august institutions as the London School of Economics would engage in shady deals with Third World dictators like Muammar Ghaddafi to secure lucrative contracts and endowments. Expect those Kirby folks to engage in similar intense lobbying to influence the Minister of Education.

Muhyyiddin felt that the only effective way for local would-be teachers to learn English would be to send them to an English-speaking country. I would suggest that he visit Tuanku Jaafar College in rural Malay-speaking Mantin, Negri Sembilan. Not only do those students speak impeccable English, they also have acquired some of the finer

Anglo-Saxon habits. It would not surprise me that they prefer tea and crumpets instead of *goreng pisang* and *tea tarik* for their snacks!

Those students sent to Kirby in the 1950s were already well versed with matters English, at least in theory from their textbooks. They may be ignorant of the practical aspects as with using knives and forks, chewing with their mouths closed, and not burping at the table, nonetheless their English fluency enabled them to learn and adapt quickly. It did not take them long to appreciate Beethoven as well as tea and crumpets. Sending today's trainees to Kirby would only aggravate their culture shock. Far from enjoying and benefiting from the English ambience, they would recoil and retreat to their little kampung on campus.

It was unbelievably stupid and fiscally irresponsible for Muhyyiddin to put forth that proposal. I began by suggesting that he may be unaware of the potential consequences, monetary and otherwise, and that his announcement merely reflected the seat-of-the-pants *modus operandus* at upper levels of our government.

Or there could be a more mundane explanation. Sending trainees to Britain would be the perfect excuse for Ministry officials to make frequent "official" tours there. If that be the reason, it could easily be remedied; give those senior officers paid annual trips to Britain. That would be considerably cheaper.

The Wisdom Of The Students

July 6, 2011

In a remarkable display of professorial prowess, University of Malaya Vice-Chancellor Ghauth Jasmon recently engaged his students in a two-hour dialogue on what it would take to make their university great. With humility, pedagogical skills, and great stage presence he enthralled his audience while imparting an important message. They in turn were not at all shy in telling him the challenges they faced. It was truly a dialogue, not the usual one-way pedantic pronouncements.

Those students had a clear message for their Vice-Chancellor as well as the country's leaders and policy makers: Listen to us!

The session was even more remarkable as it was held after lunch, typically siesta time in the tropics. Anyone who has faced a classroom of students at that time of day knows how difficult it is to get their attention. Yet there they were, a professor and his students intellectually engaging each other, interspersed with frequent cheers and laughter.

The Vice-Chancellor listed the five criteria of an elite university, as judged by the rating bodies—academic reputation of its faculty (40 percent of the weightage); faculty citations (20); student-faculty ratio (20); employers' assessment of its graduates (10); and the institution's internationalism as reflected by the number of foreign students (5) and faculty members(5).

For parents and students, the fourth factor—the employers' assessment—is for practical reasons supreme. Ghauth focused on that. To employers, local graduates are deficient in such important areas as English proficiency, critical thinking, and problem solving. He emphasized the lack of English fluency.

The first three major criteria, comprising 80 percent of the total, are beyond the students' control. Those are the responsibility of the university, specifically Dr. Ghauth. Students' contribution would be limited, as the Vice-Chancellor humorously suggested, to existing foreign students encouraging their friends and family members to enroll at UM.

In a Kennedyesque twist, Ghauth asked his students what they could do for their university to make it great. Specifically, he asked them for ways on improving their English proficiency if for no other reason than to make them acceptable to local employers.

The students' responses were illuminating. To be sure, most were the usual and predictable, "Use English more frequently," or "Befriend more foreign students." One student stood out for the frankness of his opinion and sharpness of his observation. He also had a deft sense of humor, outclassing the Vice-Chancellor's. He introduced himself as "Azlé from Kelaté" (Azlan from Kelantan) in that distinctively Malaysian east coast accent. That brought the house down.

Azlan freely admitted to his mediocre English and bravely committed to improving it to "C-grade" over the semester. Amidst the ensuing laughter, many missed his sharp observation, made difficult by his frequent resorting to Malay. In Malay, he articulated his problems and challenges eloquently.

He related how his teachers back in Kelantan had to resort to using Malay when teaching English! The atmosphere was no better on campus. His friends and classmates would for example, mock and berate him whenever he tried to speak in English. It was obvious that opportunities for him and others like him to learn and practice his English were as limited on campus as they were back in his Kelantan village. That was his crucial message.

As indicated, Azlan could not escape the irritating and jarring Malaysian habit of mixing Malay and English at will. I can readily excuse him because of his admitted lack of English fluency; inexcusable however, were Dr. Ghauth and the other supposedly English-proficient students.

"Soft" and "Hard" Obstacles To Achieving English Fluency

I would have stated Dr. Ghauth's central question differently: How could the university enhance the English proficiency of its students? A good start would be to follow up on Azlan's insights.

What Azlan related as the "soft" obstacles were the subtle cultural and peer pressures. The mindset that dictates learning English is tantamount to hating your own language is part of this "soft" problem. It is a formidable obstacle precisely because it is so amorphous; you cannot easily put your hands around it.

Then there were the "hard" obstacles he alluded to, like the lack of competent teachers or students not taking the subject seriously. Ironically, because these are concrete barriers, we could readily get a handle on them and thus come up with workable solutions.

Take the obvious, the poor teaching of English in schools and lack of competent teachers especially in rural areas. To train these teachers the university must have a strong Department of English. Yet UM's department has only 11 faculty members and three tutors to serve a campus of 25,000 students. To its credit, nine of its faculty members have doctorates, a higher percentage than the rest of the university.

The department's size is not consonant with the great needs of the university and country. Considering that it was one of the first if not founding departments, the lack of growth of its English Department must have been deliberate. That was short sighted and must be rectified so students like Azlan could have a place to learn and practice their English.

Emulate many American campuses including elite ones like Harvard that have facilities to improve the math and writing skills of their students.

Dr. Gauth should go further and persuade his fellow Vice-Chancellors to impress upon Malaysian policymakers on the importance of teaching English in schools and universities. They should not remain silent in the face of such regressive steps as the discontinuing of teaching of science and mathematics in English.

As academic leaders, these Vice-Chancellors could also mandate a pass in the Malaysian University English Test (MUET) for admission. That single move would make students take English seriously. There would be severe opposition from some students and Malay language nationalists, part of the soft obstacle I alluded to earlier. To soften the impact, I would add this proviso: If a student is otherwise qualified except for his MUET score, then he would be given a year to remedy the deficit before being admitted.

If academic leaders like Ghauth believe on the importance of English for their students, as they profess often, then they should go further and make English mandatory for all freshmen. Have a placement test so students could be assigned to the appropriate class. That is common practice on American campuses.

Dr. Ghauth could also require all students write no fewer than 30 extended essays (term papers) during their undergraduate years. Again, this is the norm at good American universities. I would also have a similar requirement for essays in Malay. It would be a great shame and make a mockery of their attending a Malaysian university if they were unable to read and write in Malay.

Overcome the "hard" obstacles and the soft barriers would disintegrate like a mud wall in a downpour.

This emphasis on English, though well placed, should not distract the authorities from the other problems. English proficiency is no panacea; otherwise those Indian and Filipino graduates would be competitive.

Deficiencies in critical thinking and problem solving are not English language dependent. As Azlan attested by his performance, you could still think through things and be logical even if you were to be English illiterate. The inability of Malaysian students to think critically is not because of their limited English-proficiency but the consequence of the nation's pedagogical philosophy as well as in the approach to teaching and testing. Far too often what goes on in Malaysian schools and universities is not education but indoctrination. Education in Malaysia is, to borrow Noam Chomsky's phrase, "a system of imposed ignorance … a system of indoctrination."

Consider how Malaysia tests her students; it is nothing more than an exercise in regurgitation. If we design the questions so students could have "open book" examinations, then we would be truly evaluating their critical thinking and problem-solving abilities instead of their talent for regurgitation. Professor Ghauth had demonstrated a teaching style that engages his students and make the intellectual traffic flow both ways.

I applaud the university personnel for doing a professional job in videotaping the session and then posting it on the social media. I hope Dr. Ghauth will have other similar sessions with his faculty, the public, and policymakers.

Anticipating that, I offer some suggestions on improving local universities. One, strive to have all faculty members with terminal qualifications. Later elevate that by requiring new recruits to have substantive post-doctoral experience. Two, fund faculty members so they could present papers at international meetings. That would encourage them to submit their papers to international bodies. Three, grant all faculty members automatic research funding equal to their annual salaries, and spread over three years. Four, I would supply each faculty member with free laptops and unlimited Wi-Fi access so they could download lectures by leading scholars elsewhere for presentation to the students, as well as access professional journals. Many of those publications offer free access to academics from the Third World. That alone would pay for the computers, by sparing the library from having to subscribe to those expensive journals. Five, I would treat academics with great respect, beginning with getting rid of that idiotic *Akujanji* (I promise) pledge.

If Malaysian policymakers think that my suggestions are expensive, think how much more it would be to have local universities remain in the academic cellar and continue producing mediocre products! That would be the greatest disservice to the students, as well as to the country.

Attracting The Best To Teaching

June 29, 2011

Early this year the US Department of Education, together with OECD and the Asia Society, convened a summit of education ministers, master teachers, and union leaders from 15 countries. The theme was on attracting, training, and retaining the best teachers. Those were no ordinary countries participating; their students had consistently excelled in the Program for International Student Assessment (PISA).

America has some of the finest private and public schools, while its colleges and universities regularly dominate anybody's list of the best. Yet there was US Education Secretary Duncan sponsoring this symposium and be its opening speaker. That reflected the seriousness with which American leaders and policymakers consider education. It also showed their humility and commitment to learn from the best. I long for such traits in Malaysian leaders and educators.

The core assumption of the summit was that you cannot have excellent schools without excellent teachers. "Great teachers are not just born that way," Secretary Duncan noted in his opening remarks. "It takes a high-quality system for recruiting, training, retaining, and supporting teachers over the course of their careers to develop an effective teaching force," he continued.

This emphasis on schools and education was well placed. As OECD Secretary-General Angel Gurria put it, "The prosperity of our nations depends on whether we succeed to attract the brightest minds into the teaching profession, and the most talented teachers into the most challenging classrooms."

Pivotal Role of Teachers

You cannot have good schools without good teachers. Good teachers in turn come from good students, and good students need good schools to shine. This is not another version of the old chicken-and-egg riddle. Rather what these countries with exemplary schools and outstanding teachers have demonstrated is the pivotal position of the teacher. Finland

and Singapore have shown that you can intervene and make teaching an attractive profession, to be the first-choice career for the talented.

In Finland, teaching is a much-sought occupation, with ten applicants for every position! The teaching profession there attracts the best applicants in part because teachers get competitive pay. Singapore aggressively recruits from among the top third of its students, and those interested in and committed to teaching are paid while still in school.

Keen competition by itself is no indicator of quality. In Malaysia, there is a glut of applicants for religious teachers, but no one would dare claim that the applicant pool is made up of top-tier students. There is similar stiff competition to be teachers in Egypt, but its schools and students rank at the bottom in international comparisons. The reason for Egypt's glut of would-be teachers is that its economy is in such a rut that teaching is the only job available. The same dynamics apply to Malaysian religious teachers.

Recruiting top talent is only the beginning. Rookies' enthusiasm would get you only so far. Teachers must also be given superior initial training; then there must be a mechanism for continuing professional education and training.

Finland has an exceptionally superior system; hence it is attracting the best talents. Teachers there get training to the master's degree, even for primary school teachers. They are rightly treated as professionals because they are rigorously trained and more importantly, they behave as such. They are also trained to be diagnosticians to recognize not only the different learning styles but also potential learning problems.

A unique feature of the Finnish system is that each teacher is also a researcher, participating in research in collaboration with the local university. The best way to keep abreast in your field is to be involved in research even if only tangentially.

Being true professionals, Finnish teachers have considerable autonomy, as are their schools. The Finnish Ministry of Education is more a resource center than a command-and-control one. Its bureaucrats are not control freaks, as in Malaysia and most Third World countries.

Finland and other advanced countries are actively widening the talent pool for recruitment to include those from underrepresented minorities as well as those seeking mid-career change. This has particular relevance for Malaysia; she too must aggressively recruit from among Orang Asli and other minority groups especially in East Malaysia. It is important for minority students to have role models that they could readily identify with from among their teachers.

No professional would be satisfied unless he or she is assured of career advancement, as well as appropriate reward and recognition for a job well done. In Singapore teachers are career tracked to be master teachers, school leaders, or specialists in curriculum or research. The government regularly tracks what competing sectors are paying their workers in order that teachers remain competitively paid.

Reforming Schools

The other significant lesson from the summit is that school reforms when effectively executed would bear positive results quickly. Poland is an example. It initiated reform only in the late 1990s but within a decade it has dramatically reduced the number of its poorly performing students and cut in half the variations in performance among its schools. Previously Polish students performed below average level of OECD countries; after their reform they were on par with Americans.

Reforming school is the rage everywhere, Malaysia included. The consensus at this conference is that teachers must both be the active agents for and effective implementers of reform.

This creates a dilemma for Malaysia. Where teachers are well trained, thoroughly professional, and highly effective as they are in the Scandinavian countries, they should be actively involved with the reform process. In Malaysia however, the teaching profession is far from that. It has been significantly degraded with respect to standards and professionalism, as reflected in the quality of their products—the students.

Having been brought up under the current system it would be unrealistic to expect these teachers to be agents of or advocates for change. Their position is essentially that the system was good enough for them; it should be good enough for the present and future generations. Stated differently, current teachers are part of the problem; they are not part of the solution. This does not mean that they cannot be trained or persuaded to be part of the solution, but we should not underestimate the difficulties and challenges.

The reform in Poland was, as expected of a former communist country, a top-down affair. Yet it was successful. A generation ago

Singapore faced similar problems where teaching was not the first choice of careers for her top students.

Thailand too has its "Malaysian problem;" the Thais solved it in their own unique patient way. Recognizing the futility of persuading existing teachers to agree for reform, the government just bypassed them by liberalizing the school sector to let the free entry of foreign players. Consequently, international schools blossomed in Thailand. Yes, they are an option only for the elite and rich. These schools are educating the children of the influential. As such these students are destined to hold key positions in their country, their superior education and social standing would assure them of that. They would then be the effective agents of change.

In reforming Malaysian schools, we could pursue either the top-down approach of Poland and Singapore, or the slower but surer Thai way. To date I do not see the necessary enlightened and intelligent leadership to effect meaningful top-down reform, nor do I see a farsighted leadership to initiate the slow Thai way.

Quality of Schools and Fertility Rates

On perusing the list of countries whose students excelled in PISA, one fact stands out: Those countries also have low fertility rates. The latest addition to the list of top performers is China, specifically Shanghai. China's almost inhuman "one-child" policy has many critics but there is no questioning its benefits. For the past few decades China was spared the burden of feeding and housing over 300 million potential new Chinese. Imagine the savings in not having another Bangladesh within your borders! Spared of those huge expenses, the Chinese could now divert their resources to improving their schools.

The reverse however is not necessarily true. That is, low fertility rates alone do not guarantee good schools. Sri Lanka is proof of that. Low fertility would only give the country a much-needed breathing space

In Malaysia, the fertility rate for Malays, while declining, is still nearly doubled that of non-Malays. The wide discrepancy in academic achievement and other social indices between Malays and non-Malays is directly and indirectly attributed in large part to this difference in fertility rates of the two communities.

If today there were to be an effective and acceptable family planning program for Malays, meaning, one that is enthusiastically endorsed by the religious authorities, the positive impact would be felt almost immediately. First, there would be the drop in the number of pregnancies, and the associated drop in expenses in dealing with the expected complications. Nine months later would come the decline in the number of births, and the related savings in medical care. Six years later when those potential babies would be ready for school, the savings would be even greater as there would be no need for new schools and teachers.

Those savings would be cumulative; they would continue. Spared those expenses, the nation could then divert resources to improving the quality of life of the people, as with providing good schools and superior teachers.

Those OECD countries could focus on making their schools superior because they have the resources to do so; they have been spared the expenses that would have been incurred had they had high fertility rates. This basic link was not discussed at the summit; it was taken for granted. For Malaysia however, it is a reality that is not yet even been acknowledged, much less addressed.

The wisdom of those eminent educators from OECD displayed at the summit is still valid, and Malaysia could usefully adopt them provided our leaders and policymakers bear in mind that we have a more basic problem outside the realm of education but related to it. We have to tame our fertility rates first; then with the savings we would have the resources to address the challenges in education.

Improving The Odds For Disadvantaged Students

June 22, 2011

Students from disadvantaged backgrounds face many challenges. It is not a surprise that they would be behind academically and in many other ways. This has always been true and accepted as normal. The consequence to this acceptance is that the students' disadvantaged background becomes too ready an excuse for teachers and policymakers not to address the issue of widening educational achievement gap, blaming instead such factors as poverty and lack of parental involvement.

While those are relevant, there is much that schools, teachers, and policymakers could do to turn disadvantaged students into "resilient" ones. A recent OECD study, "Against The Odds. Disadvantaged Students Who Succeed in School," confirms this. "Resilient" students, as defined by the study, are those from a disadvantaged socio-economic background relative to students in their country, and yet attain high scores by international standards.

Across OECD countries, about a third of disadvantaged students are "resilient;" in Finland and South Korea, nearly half. The bottom line, as the report asserts, is: "Disadvantaged students can and often do defy the odds against them when given the opportunity to do so."

At first glance the report may be stating the obvious. We all can recall examples of those from disadvantaged backgrounds who have overcome their many obstacles. Some would attribute their success to their innate ability, sheer grit, and unwavering determination. Those of humbler persuasion would credit other factors—talented teachers, superior schools, and opportune openings.

This OECD Report marshals impressive data to support its contention that when the disadvantaged are given equal opportunities to learn, foster their self-confidence, and effectively motivate them, they can exploit their potential. The Report collates and summarizes the experiences of those member countries that have been successful in executing their strategies and achieved those desirable objectives.

Learning From OECD's Experiences

Malaysia could adopt with some enhancements the findings of the Report. Granted, the disadvantaged in an OECD country are a universe away physically, economically and in many other ways from their counterparts in Malaysia. Consider that in America students from poor families get free textbooks, transportations, and school meals. They are also spared the expenses of uniforms and examination fees. Malaysian parents, rich and poor, are burdened by these ancillary expenses which make a mockery of the Malaysian brand of "free" schooling. A good beginning would be to get rid of all such burdens.

Malaysia could go further and reward parents who pay attention to their children's schooling. Brazil's *Bolsa Escola* and Mexico's *Progressa* programs *pay* parents if they were to keep their children in school. Such "Conditional Cash Transfer" initiatives are powerful incentives. If Malaysian poor fishermen and rice farmers are paid to keep their children at school, that would reduce the dropout rates. Add a bonus in the form of extra payments if their children were to excel, then watch those parents become diligent in ensuring that their children attend school and do their homework.

A universality of the human trait is that we respond to incentives. The secret is to find the right one. For many, it is still cold cash.

The key finding of the OECD study is that resilient disadvantaged students attend more regular lessons at school than those who are not. Transferring this to the Malaysian context, that would mean extending the hours of kampung schools to a full day and increasing the number of school days from the current 180 to 220 per year, as in Japan.

That would mean single-session schools. If these disadvantaged children are in school for much of the day, well fed, well taught, and well supervised, then we could not care less if their parents were unable to help them with the homework or read to them at bedtime. With an extended school day, the afternoon could be devoted to enriching extracurricular activities like athletics and fine arts. Instead of loitering in the afternoon or otherwise getting into mischief, they would be in school practicing their music or participating in sports. Those extracurricular activities help nurture a more wholesome development; they are also true and tried confidence builders.

Nurturing Self-Confidence

As for self-confidence, the Report emphasized the importance of instilling this, especially in disadvantaged children. This cannot be achieved merely by participating in cheerleading rallies and endlessly proclaiming our supposed glorious past.

Instead, and this is another key finding of the Report, resilient students spend more time studying science. Excelling in science boosts their self-confidence; this in turn spills over in other areas. This benefit is most pronounced with disadvantaged students; the more disadvantaged they are, the more they benefited. The same could be said by participating and excelling in extra-curricular activities, especially sports.

Resilient students spend more class hours on the subject. In France, Germany and the Netherlands these students spend an hour and 45 minutes more in science classes per week than disadvantaged low achievers. Malaysia must not only expand the school day of kampung schools, but also increase substantially the hours devoted to science. Their enhanced science proficiency, apart from boosting their self-confidence, would also improve their employability.

For disadvantaged Malay students, another effective way of boosting their self-confidence would be to improve their English proficiency. Malay leaders without end exhort these students to learn English, as if that could simply be wished upon or achieved by waving a magic wand. As the experience with science proficiency of resilient students in OECD countries demonstrates, devoting more hours to the subject would be a more effective strategy. If more subjects were to be taught in English, then those students could practice their language skills. In this regard, the burden of the recent decision to end the teaching of science and mathematics in English falls disproportionately on kampung (meaning, Malay) students, the very group Malay leaders profess to champion.

That fluency in English could boost a student's confidence is demonstrated in California. The state has large numbers of immigrant children with disadvantaged backgrounds and who cannot speak English. In the days of bilingual education, they would be taught in their mother tongue (most commonly Spanish) as well as English at the same time.

That policy ended with the passage of an "English Only" referendum in 1998. Today these students would have to spend their first year in an English immersion class, and only when they are sufficiently fluent would they join the regular stream.

The results of that experiment are now clear. Whereas in the past these pupils would perpetually be handicapped by their limited English ability and remain at the bottom of their class right up to their final years in school, with the mandatory immersion classes, their ability to speak and write English improved quickly. That boosted their self-confidence, which in turn spilled over onto other areas. Those students mixed well in the playground with the other children and were fully engaged socially and in many other ways at school. In the past they would segregate themselves as they felt inadequate; they had low self-esteem because of their language handicap.

Today California would not wish to return to those bad old days of bilingual education; nor would those children and their parents. California's success, widely acknowledged, contradicts the widely quoted UNESCO study that purported to show that mother tongue-based bilingual education has a positive impact on learning and learning outcomes.

The self-confidence of Malay students would be boosted if they were to be fluent in English. We could achieve this by replicating California's experience of English-immersion classes. Malaysia had something akin to that with the "Special Malay" and "Remove" classes of yore. Better yet, bring back the old English schools to the kampungs where the need for enhanced English fluency is the greatest.

Supplement that with an increase in school hours, enriched curriculum with more hours devoted to mathematics and science, and full extracurricular activities, then watch kampung kids blossom. If Malay leaders fail to provide those, then they have no right to blame those students for being lazy and not motivated.

Parental and social factors are important, but there is much that schools and teachers can and should do to improve the current abysmal academic performance of kampung kids.

Learn from the OECD countries. Adopt the measures discussed in its Report, then watch the miracles unfolding with kampung kids. The link between disadvantaged background and low academic achievement can and must be broken.

Improve Schools, Not Tinker With Examinations

September 5, 2010

In about two weeks nearly half a million Malaysian school children would be sitting for their UPSR, the national examination taken at the end of Year Six. Today there is raging debate on abolishing that as well as the PMR taken at Year Nine. A decision is expected within weeks. An issue less discussed is the timing of those examinations, administered as they are so early in the school year.

This year UPSR would be on September 20th, with PMR two weeks later. From then on till the year-end holidays in December, there would be no effective teaching or learning at these schools. With the examinations out of the way, the entire school—students and teachers alike—would be in holiday mode. The staff would effectively be *makan gaji buta* (paid but not working). At best they would be but babysitters. One would think that freed from examinations, those "free" weeks would be a splendid opportunity for the teachers to organize field trips or engage their students in such things as drama, debating contests, or science and environmental projects.

As it is come January when these students resume their classes, they would have already suffered considerable attrition in their learning skills because of the long break. The first few weeks if not months of the new year would be diverted to re-learning lessons of the preceding grade.

The problem gets worse when they sit for their SPM examination (at Year 11). Although that is held in mid-November, the results would not be out till late March. Visit Malaysia at the end and at the first half of the following year, and you would see thousands of these teenagers loitering in the malls and elsewhere. When queried, the typical answer would be, "We are waiting for our SPM results!"

Then after getting their results they would still have to wait as *matrikulasi* and Sixth Form would not start till June.

With UPSR and PMR, these students would waste away only a few months; with SPM they would be fritting away over half a year, a substantial period in a young student's life.

This terrible wastage of time escapes the attention of policymakers. They should be addressing this more pertinent and pressing issue instead of the non-productive controversy over abolishing UPSR and PMR.

Better Timing of Examinations

I fail to see why UPSR and PMR be set so early in the third term. Delaying it to mid or even late November would extend the students' instructional time by at least a couple of months. Substantial!

In the same vein I cannot comprehend why the Examination Syndicate would take such an inordinately long time to process the SPM examination. The Syndicate should ban its staff from taking holidays from October till the results are out so they could devote their time exclusively to processing the examination. Additionally, reduce the number of subjects tested to a few core ones like language, science, and mathematics. As for the rest, rely on the teachers' assessments or the schools' in-house evaluations.

Another option would be to have the final examination contribute only about 60-70 percent to the total score, with the rest made up of the student's year-round work. With modern statistical techniques we should be able to reduce inter-school variations in teachers' assessments.

I see no reason why students could not proceed directly to *matrikulasi* or Sixth Form come the following January after they finished their Fifth Form. In the 1960s there was a special entrance examination set in September whose only function was to select students into Sixth Form. Alternatively, use the SPM trial examination as the basis for selection. That would give the examination some clout! An even better proposal would be to make Form Six an integral part of secondary schooling.

Keeping those Fifth Formers with their raging hormones unoccupied for over six months would only invite trouble. Idleness is the root of mischief; we ignore that at our peril. That is quite apart from the learning attrition that occurs during the long hiatus.

Rich parents have wider options for their children, as with enrolling them in the many excellent private pre-university programs. Those are expensive, beyond the reach of the poor. In the context of race-conscious Malaysia, this means Malay and Indian children.

By June when Sixth Form and the other public pre-university programs begin, those children of the rich who are accepted there would have a head start since they had spent the past six months in private pre-university programs. That gives them a substantial advantage in what typically is a one-to-two-year program.

I recently met a group of students enrolled in such a program, this one meant to prepare them for American universities. There was an incentive put into the program whereby if the students were to excel in the first six months, they would be sent abroad earlier.

Of the students who excelled and were thus sent abroad earlier, a disproportionate number were non-Malays. In the poisonous sociopolitical landscape where race considerations are never far from the surface, those poor Malay students not unnaturally felt their acute sense of deficiency, feeding the already ugly stereotype they have of themselves.

Query those Malay students as to what they did in the interim between sitting for their SPM and enrolling in the program, to a person they replied that they did nothing! They idled the time away while waiting for their SPM results. In contrast, those non-Malay students who did well were already ahead of them at the time of enrolment as they had been in private pre-university classes during the six-month period while waiting for their SPM results.

Of interest, of the Malaysians who were privileged to attend elite American universities, few were from *matrikulasi* or Sixth Form. Instead they came from the many private pre-university programs in Malaysia. That is an indictment of the national education system, specifically its post-Form Five programs.

Malay College IB Program

Malay College (MC) would be embarking on its IB program next June, after about ten years in the planning. That program is long awaited and much needed. Up till now MC is nothing but a glorified middle school; its students would have to go elsewhere to prepare for university.

Back in the 1950s and 60s MC had difficulty filling its Sixth Form, and the program was frequently threatened with closure if not for the many Malay students from other schools to fill in the vacancies.

With MCs current IB, the students would sit for their SPM in November and then wait for the results. Come June the following year, and based on their SPM results, they would return to begin their IB.

IB is radically different to what these students have been used to. For one, it is English-medium while MC, like all national schools, is Malay-medium. Those students would encounter significant language and other adjustments.

As such I would have expected the policymakers to anticipate the problem and plan an appropriate "Pre-IB" program to prepare those students. What better time to do that than in the six months intervening. At the very least those students should have intensive English immersion classes.

Without such careful preparation, those first batch of IB students would risk not being successful. Were that to happen, then those otherwise bright and promising students would forever suffer the blight of being tagged a failure, and with that the ugly stigma of the presumed inadequacies of their race.

Public pressure would then be to terminate the program. That would be a monumental tragedy not only for those students but also for MC and Malays. Thus far there is little concern among college and ministry officials in avoiding this possible disaster. Based on past experiences, this lack of concern is unjustified.

The Minister of Education and his policymakers should not distract themselves with such non-productive issues as scrapping the UPSR and PMR. They should focus on making 12 or 13 years of schooling as the new norm, as they do in Germany. Make Form Six an integral part of secondary education. Unlike the Germans however, we should stream our students into the academic, general, and vocational streams (comparable to their *Gymnasium, Realschule and Hauptschule*) not at Year 5 but at the upper secondary (Year 10).

Such a move would better prepare our students for the increasingly competitive world and help advance our economy up the value scale. Tinkering with examinations does nothing; it is but a "make busy" project for policymakers.

Making Monsters Out Of Our Students
The "Lucifer Effect" On Campus

July 4, 2010

I commend Defense Minister Ahmad Zahid Hamidi for his swift action in reassigning the commandant of the Royal Military College (RMC) over the death of one of its students, Naim Mustaqim, during a ragging incident. Earlier, the college had expelled the alleged abusers. Likewise, I praise Higher Education Minister Khaled Nordin in issuing a stern warning of his "zero tolerance" for ragging in public universities.

Ragging is now an entrenched culture in local universities and residential schools, creating monsters out of their students, the "Lucifer Effect" being operative (more on that later). The ensuing scars and damages are consequential, both physical and psychological. A few like Naim get killed.

Ragging is one of those unsavory "traditions" of the colonial British that the Third World natives have picked up with a vengeance. Malaysians denigrate everything associated with the colonials but somehow when it comes to ragging, they have no qualms in quickly adopting it. Malaysians have bested the Indians and Sri Lankans in the savagery of their hazing.

The only effective way to end this scourge that has plagued local schools and colleges is to initiate a "shock and awe" intervention that would impress upon everyone the evilness of this hitherto foreign ritual.

Strong Individual and Collective Actions Needed

Malaysia needs aggressive actions at both the individual and system levels. At the personal level, help the family of Naim Mustaqim launch lawsuits against not only his alleged abusers but also RMC authorities and personnel, including the reassigned commandant. They have been negligent in failing to provide a safe environment for those placed under their trust and care. Initiate criminal proceedings; those in supervisory positions including the wardens and teachers should be prosecuted.

Naim's family would not get their young son back, but by instituting civil and criminal actions they would make those responsible pay for their culpabilities. Criminal behaviors lurking beneath 'tradition' should not be tolerated.

It is reprehensible that those who have been given the awesome responsibilities for nurturing our young have neglected their duties, resulting in one promising young man being killed. Naim's teachers and wardens had been with him for over six months, literally day and night, and yet they failed to notice the signs of his desperate need and cry for help. I wonder how they would feel if their loved ones had been similarly neglected.

The first order of business for RMC's new commandant must be to impress upon his staff their obligation to look after the safety of those under their charge. His second, to punish those who had let this ugly situation occur. Those are his two immediate priorities, and not, as he was quoted, "to safeguard the college's image and moral (*sic*) of students, staff, parents and the public alike."

At the systemic level, the responsible minister should issue directives to the vice-chancellors as well as principals of all universities and residential schools indicating that they would be held responsible for any ragging on their campuses. Were that to happen, they would suffer the same fate, or worse, as the former re-assigned commandant.

Impose specific rules and lists of "don'ts," and the penalties for infringements, upon the students and their parents before these students enroll. They (as well as their parents) would have to sign that document acknowledging their full understanding of its content.

Be strict for a few years and we would effectively get rid of this scourge of ragging. Our students could then look forward coming to a safe campus for a different experience, one more welcoming and nurturing.

I was privileged to be spared from attending a local university and as a result had a vastly different college experience. One of the sweetest and most comforting words that greeted me on my arrival on campus in Canada decades ago was an upperclassman extending his hand and saying, "You must be Bakri, from Malaysia! Hi! I am Ray, your resident advisor!"

Yes, during orientation week we still had to wear that silly beanie and were made to steal apples from the nearby orchards, but nothing beyond that. What I remember most was my seniors helping and guiding me. It was to them that I turned to in seeking advice on classes and what was appropriate to wear to campus functions.

That is what orientation week is supposed to be, to help incoming students adjust to their new campus environment.

Lucifer Effect: How Good People Turn Evil

While I advocate severe punishment for the abusers of Naim Mustaqim, I am mindful that these kids are not intrinsically evil. On the contrary, what we have learned from the Stanford psychologist Philip Zimbardo's famous prison experiment in 1971 is that those students who became torturers (and in Naim's case, murderers) were normal human beings. Given a different set of circumstances they could well become heroes.

Zimbardo's "Lucifer Effect" (after Lucifer, God's favorite angel who turned evil; the Koranic version is Iblis who, banished by Allah from Paradise to earth for disobeying Him, made it his mission to convert as many mortals to his Satanic ways) phenomenon is what made otherwise ordinary soldiers into sadists and murderers in Iraq's Abu Ghraib prison. Those who have read the accounts of Kassim Ahmad, Syed Husin Ali, Raja Petra and others incarcerated under the ISA would immediately recognize the local variation of this Lucifer Effect. The difference between Kamunting and Abu Ghraib is a matter of degree, not kind.

In his experiment, Zimbardo recruited ordinary college students looking to make a few dollars as subjects in a human psychology experiment simulating the prison experience. What he discovered about human nature from that innocent experiment shocked him and forced him to prematurely terminate the study.

What Zimbardo discovered was that students who were randomly assigned to be "guards" soon became vicious, senselessly brutalizing and inflicting gratuitous punishments on their "prisoners." Even though those students were aware that they were being monitored and that it was only an experimental situation, nonetheless they persisted in their brutish ways.

There are other experiments along the same vein where the social situation, in short, peer pressure, made the subjects do things they would not otherwise do.

The Lucifer Effect illuminates how otherwise good people can turn evil, given the "right" circumstances. Humans are like pet dogs. In the calm and nurturing environment of a quiet home with a caring master, it is the most docile, playful, and obedient pet, indeed almost angelic. It would not bark even if your toddler were to yank its tail. However, let it loose with his canine friends to maraud in the neighborhood as a pack at night, and they would become vicious predators.

We must make sure that the environment in local schools and universities would not turn our promising young students into evil fallen angels. Those in charge, from the ministers down to the teachers and custodians, have an awesome responsibility to make sure that this would not happen. If they fail, then they must be made to pay a stiff price.

Chaining The Children Of The Poor

July 12. 2009

The ancient Chinese bound the feet of their baby daughters so they would grow up with deformed tiny feet, thus limiting their mobility and participation in life outside the little world of their homes. Those women would then be totally dependent on their men.

In rescinding the policy of teaching science and mathematics in English, the government is likewise binding the intellectual development of Malaysian children. They and future generations would grow up with warped intellect. They would then be dependent on the government, just as ancient Chinese women with tiny feet were on their men.

Fellow commentator Azly Rahman has a more apt and colorful local metaphor. Malaysia is condemning her future generations to the *Pekan Rabu* (weekly farmers' market) economy, capable only of selling pirated versions of Michael Jackson albums. That would be the extent of their entrepreneurial prowess and creative flair. They are only subsistence entrepreneurs and 'copy-cat' creators.

The government's professed concerns for the poor and those from rural areas notwithstanding, reversing the current policy would adversely and disproportionately impact them. The rich and those in the cities have a ready escape, through private English classes. Urban children already high levels of English in their family and community.

The most disadvantaged would be poor kampung kids, meaning, Malay children. The supreme irony if not perversity of the champions of *Ketuanan Melayu* actively pursuing a policy that would ensure Malay children be perpetually trapped economically and intellectually! I thank Allah that I grew up at a time when the likes of Muhyiddin were not in charge of the education system. Otherwise I would have remained trapped in my village.

The idiocy of this new move is best illustrated by one startling example. In 2012 when the new plan will be implemented, students in Form IV will be taught science and mathematics in Malay, after learning the two subjects in English for the past nine years. Then two years later when they will be entering Sixth Form or the Matriculation stream, they would again have to revert to English.

Pupils in the vernacular schools would have it worse. They would learn the two subjects in their mother tongue during their primary school years, then switch to Malay for the next five while in secondary school, and then switch again, this time to English, in Sixth Form and university!

Had these policymakers done their homework and did some diligent downstream analysis, such idiocies would not have cropped up. Then again this is what Malaysians have come to expect of their civil servants. They have been brought up with their minds bound up; they cannot think. They depend on others to do the thinking for them.

Najib Razak's flip-flopping on this major national issue eerily reminds me of similar indecisiveness and lack of resolve of his immediate predecessor, Abdullah Badawi. No wonder he supports Najib in this policy shift. Najib should not take comfort in that, unless he expects a similar fate as Abdullah's. Abdullah was kicked out by his party; with Najib, it would be the voters who would be kicking him out. Public sentiments are very much against this policy switch.

Failure of Policy Versus Failure of Implementation

The cabinet reversed course because it deemed the policy did not produce the desired results. However, in arriving at this pivotal decision the cabinet failed to address the fundamental question on whether the original policy was flawed or its implementation ineffective.

It assumed the policy to be flawed. Muhyiddin and his senior officers relied heavily on the 2005 UNESCO Report which suggests that 'mother tongue first' bilingual education *may* (my emphasis) be the solution to the dilemma of members of minority linguistic groups in acquiring knowledge.

Muhyiddin and his advisers misread the Report. It was concerned primarily with the dilemma at the societal level of members of a linguistic minority having to learn the language of the majority ("national language") versus the need to maintain linguistic diversity generally and minority languages specifically. UNESCO was rightly concerned with the rapid disappearance of languages spoken by small minority groups. The Report was not addressing specifically the learning of science and mathematics.

Malay language is not at risk of disappearing, far from it. It is the native tongue of a quarter billion people. To extrapolate the UNESCO recommendations for Malay language would be inappropriate. That would be an oversimplification and misreading of the Report.

The UNESCO Report does not address the issue of when and how best to introduce children to bilingual education. Later studies that focused specifically on the pedagogical and psychological aspects instead of the sociological and political have shown that children are quite capable of learning multiple languages at the same time. Even more remarkable is that the earlier they are exposed to a second language the more facile they would be with that language. They would also learn that second language much faster; hence the introduction of a second language even at preschool.

The acquisition of bilingual ability at an early age confers other significant cognitive advantages. These have been documented by clinical studies with functional MRIs (imaging studies of the brain). Malaysia should learn from these more modern studies and the experiences of more advanced societies, not from the UNESCO studies of backward tribes of Asia.

The other basis for the cabinet's decision was 'research' by local half-baked pseudo academics with a political agenda. They should be embarrassed to append their names to such a sophomoric paper. The quality is such that it will never appear in reputable journals. As for the Ministry's own internal 'researchers,' remember that they came out within months of the policy's introduction in 2003 documenting the 'impressive' improvements in students' achievements!

The one major entity that would be severely impacted by the cabinet's decision is the universities. Yet Vice-Chancellors of local universities have remained quiet and detached in this important national debate. They have not advised the cabinet nor lead the public discussions. That again reflects the caliber of leadership of these major institutions.

Had the cabinet considered the possibility that the original policy (of teaching STEM in English) was sound but that the flaws were with its implementations, then measures other than rescinding it would be the appropriate response. This would include recruiting and training more English-speaking teachers and devoting more hours to the subject.

What surprised me is that when Mahathir introduced the policy in 2003, he was supported by his cabinet that included Najib, Muhyiddin, Hishamuddin, and over a dozen of current ministers who now collectively voted to reverse the policy. Likewise, the policy was fully endorsed by UMNO's Supreme Council then. Like the cabinet, many of those earlier members are still in that body today. Yet today the Council also voted to disband the policy. Muhyiddin, Hishamuddin and the others have yet to share with us why they changed their minds. The conditions that prompted the introduction of the policy back then are still present today. The current reversal would not change that.

Najib, Muhyiddin, Hishamuddin *et al.* are "*lallang* (a tall weed) leaders," they bend with the slightest change in wind direction. Unlike Margaret Thatcher's famed resolve of "This lady is not for turning," with Najib, Muhyiddin, *et al.*, all you do to make them undertake a U turn would be to blow slightly in their faces. Blow a bit harder and they would scoot off with their tails between their legs. These leaders will never lead Malaysia forward much less to greatness.

This reversal would not solve the widening achievement gap between urban and rural students. The cabinet has yet to put forth new ideas on ameliorating that problem. So, just as ancient Chinese women were physically handicapped because of their bound feet, rural or more specifically Malay children would continue to be intellectually handicapped by their warped and small minds, the consequence of this policy shift.

Perhaps that is the real objective of this policy reversal, the shackling of the intellectual development of the young so they would forever be dependent on their 'leaders.'

Test Scores, Meritocracy, And A Dysfunctional Education System

July 5, 2009

Three recent and unrelated news items reflected Malaysians' distorted views on merit and the nation's dysfunctional education system. Malaysians believe that merit is measured only by test scores. As for the flawed education system, its current minister is seeking UNESCO's help while his immediate predecessor commissioned the World Bank. As in the past, there will be an expensive and voluminous report, and that will be the end of it.

The first news item was the rooky law lecturer from a local public university who flunked over 97 percent of her students; second, the tragic death of a college dropout at Universiti Teknoloji Malaysia's (UTM) campus dormitory in Johor Baru; and third, Prime Minister Najib's announcement of special 'merit' scholarships.

That Universiti Sains Islam Malaysia (USIM) law lecturer was smug in announcing that only 4 out of her 157 students passed her test. She is now a *cause celebre* among those who have legitimate misgivings of the nation's education system. However, I would gently suggest instead that perhaps teaching is not her calling. That assessment would change of course had she approached her dean early in the academic term to discuss her classroom problems.

For her to realize only at the end of the year that nearly her entire class was not prepared to undertake rigorous law studies is incredulous. She must have been totally out of touch with her class. If what she claimed were true, that should have been obvious within the first few days and weeks, not at the end of the year.

The second, the death on UTM campus, was tragic in many ways. This, together with the recent snafu over processing applicants at the supposedly 'apex' Universiti Sains Malaysia, reflects the quality of local public universities' management. Her and her baby's bodies were not found until two days later. Where were her dorm mates? Were they deaf and blind? This is a pathetic reflection of the campus social environment.

The university released a statement that she was a fourth-year unmarried 'dropout' who had been renting a room from the university. How cold and callous a statement. There was no mention of condolence to the poor victim's family. I wonder if the campus Imam had performed the funeral rites on her and comforted her grieving family. More than likely, he too had condemned her for her sins. If I am wrong in my assumption, I unreservedly apologize to the Imam.

A fourth-year student does not 'just drop out.' She must have had other than academic difficulties, most likely her pregnancy. That undoubtedly was a mistake, but not a reason for dropping out. The university could have granted her leave of absence. To expel someone at that level is uncalled for.

Nor should the UTM victim pay for her one mistake with her life, as well as that of her innocent baby. That she felt isolated and without any help right on campus is an indictment of her university. The campus should not have punished her or aggravated her problem by not offering her medical care and counseling services. The campus environment must be supportive such that students like her could readily seek help.

The university should provide adequate sex education and the necessary medical services. This is not just to prevent unwanted pregnancies but also the spread of sexually transmitted diseases. The moral qualms of the officials should not blind them to the needs (health and otherwise) of their students.

The third news item was the giddiness that greeted Prime Minister Najib's announcement of special scholarships based only on 'merit.' This response was most pronounced from those who felt that awards where Malays would predominate, as with JPA (Malay initials for Public Service Commission) scholarships, would, by definition, lack 'merit.'

Najib's announcement followed an earlier controversy where students with 21 A's in the SPM examination were denied the honor in favor of those with only 10 or 11 A's. Never mind the absurdity of sitting for so many subjects. 'Merit' to these folks is a simplistic concept, something that can readily be measured by a paper and pencil (or pen) test. If that were the case, there would be no need for selection committees or interviews, just use computers to select the candidates.

These folks would be bewildered if told that even top universities have large admissions departments to look out for potential talents that could have been missed from just looking at their test scores alone. For its part, JPA has not seen fit to learn from the great universities on how they select their candidates, like having them write personal essays. With JPA scholarships, I would have eligible candidates write personal essays in both Malay and English, in addition to separate interviews conducted exclusively in Malay and English.

One company has interviews with a twist. A day before the interview, the candidates were assigned a real-life problem. During the interview, the candidate would discuss his or her approach to solving it. It is a revelation to see how candidates approach a problem.

Those who view merit strictly as test scores obviously do not have the humility or capacity to understand the limitations of those tests. There are at least three variables to a test. One is the test itself, its validity and reliability. Meaning, does it really measure 'merit' (however we define the term) and are its results reproducible? Then there are the students. The third would be the teacher and her teaching. The students may be intelligent, willing, and capable, but if their teachers' skills are wanting, the results would also be poor.

It was presumptuous if not outright arrogant for that junior law lecturer to assume that she was a superb teacher and that the fault was with her students. Even if she were to be a superb teacher (or others have convinced her that she was), she still could not attribute her class failure entirely to her students. She may have been inept in designing effective test questions. The only way for her to prove that her tests were valid would be to administer them to two control groups: one would be those who should pass her examination (positive control) as with a senior law class, and the other would be where you expect them not to do well (negative control), as with non-law students.

If the first group excelled on her test while the second did poorly, then she could rightly conclude that her examination questions were valid. Short of that she was unjustified in assuming that her students were all duds and that her teaching and tests were superb and thus blameless.

If as she claimed that her students were totally unprepared, a good or at least diligent teacher would have changed her emphasis and approach to bring them up to par. There would be no point piling on materials that the students could not absorb. If need be, she could have alerted her dean on the need for remedial instructions. Perhaps she could have asked the dean to put the entire class in a year of preparatory instructions.

Any of or all these approaches would have been more productive. Had she done so she would have won the eternal gratitude of her students. She would also make a national contribution by producing a class of competent lawyers. More importantly, she would not have been fired. Instead all she achieved with her strutting was to brand her entire class as failures, a stigma that will tag them for the rest of their lives. In the process she had also branded herself a failure as a teacher.

On many American campuses, even at the most prestigious, there are preparatory summer classes before the new academic year where students could enroll to better prepare themselves. Many students, even bright ones, avail themselves to such programs. Even top MBA programs have similar summer programs so students could brush up on their mathematics, for example. Then there are special courses tailored to the unique needs of the students, as with "Physics for Poets."

It is amazing how once you have correctly identified the problems it would be remarkably easy to craft the needed solutions. On the other hand, if you fail to identify or comprehend the problems clearly, then you are more likely to seek gimmicky solutions. Najib Razak's plan for 'merit' scholarships is one such example.

Najib was admitting that the existing program was based on other than merit. I wonder how those current JPA scholarship holders feel about that? The awards they had worked so hard for had been trashed by no less than the Prime Minister.

Like that bewildered USIM law lecturer, Najib Razak is confused on the meaning of education and learning, as well as that of merit, tests, and test scores.

Abolish Overseas Undergraduate Scholarships

May 31, 2009

Every year at about this time, Malaysians go through their regular spasms of indignation over perceived unfair distribution of scholarships for studies abroad for those with the Sijil Persekutuan Malaysia (SPM), the Year 11 national examination. This being Malaysia, such controversies inevitably and quickly acquire ugly racial overtones, no matter how 'objective' or 'sophisticated' the arguments put forth.

I suggest that Malaysia discontinue all public scholarships for undergraduate studies abroad. That would at least remove yet another source of racial disagreement. The fewer such contentious issues, the better it would be for the nation.

Instead, public scholarships for studies abroad should only be given to those pursuing higher degrees. As for the handful of the brightest students who have secured undergraduate admissions to the most competitive universities, rest assured that there would be no shortage of sponsors outside of government if they need financial aid.

If Malaysia still has leftover funds after funding those pursuing higher degrees abroad, then divert them towards strengthening local undergraduate programs. They are desperate for funds.

A candidate with only the SPM regardless of the number of A's obtained could secure a place only at a third-rate institution in America. We do not need to send students there. On the rare occasions when they do end up at a good university, they would still have to spend a year or two doing preparatory courses (essentially Sixth Form).

Cheaper To Hire American Professors

This may surprise many, but it is less expensive to hire a professor from America than to send one student there. Let me go over the arithmetic.

The average American professor earns about US$100K annually. Pay her that amount to teach in Malaysia. With that pay, there would be many takers. Out of that she would spend about US$40K for local living expenses. At that level (about RM140K) she would have a lifestyle that would be the envy of her former colleagues in America. She would also spend about $10K for transportation, another $10K for her driver, for maid and gardener, and $5K for local holidays. Then there would be the local income tax of about $20K. At the end of the year she would be lucky to have $15K left to remit home.

The rest ($85K) would be spent locally to benefit the area satay sellers and apartment owners, among others. Imagine the local multiplier effect of that spending.

Contrast that to sending one student to America at an average cost of US$50K per year. That whole sum is lost from the country, with no local spin-off or multiplier effect. In terms of actual foreign currency loss, it is about three times more expensive to send a student to America than to hire an American professor to come to Malaysia ($50K versus $15K).

That extra expense would have been worthwhile if we were to send students to the MITs and Harvards of America, but we are not. This is true especially of MARA students, and only slightly less so with Petronas.

Imagine if local universities were to have a critical mass of American faculty members. The first impact would be felt at the faculty level. Those local faculty members would now have real competition and new academic role models, scholars instead of politicians in academic robes. One reason the National University of Singapore had a quantum leap in improvement was its recruitment of many foreign professors back in the 1970s, despite opposition from the locals.

Malaysian universities need a generous infusion of foreign academics as there is a limited local supply. Even the so-called top tier universities have fewer than half of their faculty members with terminal qualifications.

For the students, they would now have not the typical aloof and imperious Third World professor but a more approachable and less formal teacher. Lastly for the university, it would end up with a scholarly-productive faculty. That incidentally is the only way for the university to ascend the academic scale.

Sending a student abroad would only benefit him; the nation would gain only later, and only if he were to return. If he were to abscond, the country could never recoup the loss. On the other hand, that one professor would directly and immediately benefit local students, the university, and thus Malaysia.

Malaysia sends about 2,000 new students abroad a year at a cost of RM350 million. For the four years they would be abroad, the total budget must be in the range of RM1.4 billion (350 x 4). Compare that to the 2009 operating budget for all local public universities of RM14.1 billion!

Fallacious Arguments on Meritocracy

I am surprised how otherwise intelligent Malaysians would suddenly have an almost religious faith in the validity of the SPM as a measure of merit. One needs only peruse the examination, as well as the syllabus and textbooks on which the examination is based on, to be disabused of this misplaced confidence. If you need further affirmation, just sit in one of those classes and see what the teachers' expectations are of their students.

SPM measures how faithfully (and fast) the students could regurgitate what the teachers had imparted to them in class. It is an excellent surrogate indicator of a student's memory, hard work, and obedience to authority figures. The first two qualities would get you far anywhere. I am uncertain of the value of the third. While it will get you far in the Third World and authoritarian societies, I am certain that it is not an attribute that Malaysians should hold at a premium if the nation were to progress.

Malaysia needs her young to be able to think critically, solve problems, and communicate effectively. Those unfortunately are not the skills being taught or tested for SPM.

Nobody even questions the ridiculousness of a student sitting for 20 subjects! A matriculating American high school student sits for only seven, at most. The American standardized test, SAT I, covers only three: English, mathematics, and writing skills. Even top American universities require the SAT II (or subject SAT) in only three subjects, while students sit for at most five.

Seven subjects should be enough for SPM. Focus more on content. The International Baccalaureate, now recognized as the global standard for matriculation, offers only six subjects, while its middle school program (equivalent to SPM), 8.

Minister of Education Muhyiddin's proposal to reduce the SPM offerings to 10 subjects represents the usual seat-of-the-pants decision rather than the result of serious policy deliberations. He only adds to the muddle. Why not 12 or 8?

Even SAT, which has been the most evaluated test, is not the end all and be all in terms of student evaluation. Harvard and other top universities could easily fill their slots with class valedictorians and perfect SAT scorers, but they do not. These institutions recognize that no one test could be valid for all students. And on any one test, its discriminatory value diminishes rapidly at the extremes of the curve.

Yet we have those who would ascribe miraculous powers to SPM such that someone with 20 A's should automatically get a scholarship over another with only 13 or 9! They are ascribing to the SPM a degree of precision it does not deserve. The SPM has yet to prove itself a valid instrument in the first place.

These misplaced discussions on merit remind me of two items. I am told that in the old cemeteries of Beijing, the civil service examination scores of the ancient Mandarins were chiseled onto their tombstones! Nobody bothered to find out how well those Imperial civil servants were at solving the problems of the Empire. The second was a delightful essay, "Lost in the Meritocracy" I read in *The Atlantic* (2005, now available in a book form) by the writer and critic Walter Kirn. His thesis is essentially that these tests and others really measure how well you could outwit the test designers!

Back in my days in high school when examinations were essays rather than the SAT-style multiple-choice fill-in-the-blanks type, success was measured on how well you could "spot" the questions, which of course is a variation on the same theme—to outwit your examiners.

The controversies over SPM are symptomatic of a much more serious problem with the school system. These arguments over scholarships based on SPM are but distractions to addressing these other more fundamental issues.

Enhance, Not Abolish The Teaching Of Science And Mathematics In English

May 8, 2009

Minister of Education Muhyiddin Yassin is doing Malaysia a great disservice in further delaying the critical decision on the teaching of science and mathematics in English (TSME, or its Malay acronym, PPSMI —*Pengajaran dan Pembelajaran Sains dan Matematik Dalam Bahasa Inggeris*) in schools. His indecision compounds the uncertainty among educators, parents, and students.

He should be exploring ways to enhance the policy, not end it. He should focus on finding ways to get more competent teachers, explore innovative teaching techniques, and provide inexpensive textbooks. He should be busy eliminating such expensive but ineffective teaching gimmicks as the "computerized teaching modules" with their laptops and LCDs that our teachers are unable to handle. Those machines are now either stolen or crashed because of viruses and dust.

Malaysian students have not changed from 2003 when the policy was first introduced. Whatever the rationale was for adopting the policy back in 2003, it is still very much valid today.

Today's many critics of the policy are latecomers. Where were they when the policy was first mooted six years ago? These critics have yet to answer the basic question on whether the policy itself is flawed or that the deficiencies are with its implementation. They are unable to answer this important question as they are entirely confused over the issue. Their opposition is based more on emotions than rational thinking.

Consider the joint statement of the five National Laureates in Literature. First, the facts they cited were erroneous. Stating that most Nobel Prize winners are from non-English-speaking countries is not only incorrect but missed the essential point that most of those luminaries are English literate. Consider the Scandinavian countries. Their students are fluently bilingual if not multilingual, with English being the most common second language. Malaysia should emulate the Scandinavian countries and ensure that local students are fluently bilingual.

The National Laureates's concerns are grossly misguided. No one is questioning the status of the Malay language, or its importance in nation building. *All* subscribe to that. It is unclear from their statement whether they are against local students learning a second language or against English as that second language.

Those luminaries went on to make the totally irrelevant point that Mandarin would soon replace English as the most widely spoken language. Having made that observation, they failed to follow up on it. Should we substitute Mandarin for English? Even China is now encouraging, no, forcing her students to learn English.

These laureates and other critics missed the essence of the current policy, which is to enhance our students' ability to read and understand English. It is not the policy's intention that we should learn English at the expense of Malay. In short, the policy aims to expand our students' intellectual horizon, not curtail it.

The laureates' muddled thinking produces their muddled conclusions.

In truth, it is too early to pass any judgment on the wisdom of the policy. Any policy, especially one pertaining to education and social matters, takes time to discern its effects. To evaluate this policy credibly, one would need to let at least three to five cohorts of students finishing the program. Consider that Malaysia is only now recognizing the damaging effects of the educational reforms introduced in the 1970s!

Yet "researchers" from the Universiti Perguruan Sultan Idris (UPSI) confidently declared the policy "ineffective" barely four years after the policy was implemented. Earlier, just a few months after the policy's adoption, a Ministry of Education's "study" pronounced the remarkable "improvement" in test scores of those students taught under the new program. Who do these folks think they are kidding?

I could not get a copy of the Ministry's paper, but I have the UPSI professors' draft on which the minister depended heavily for his decision. Suffice to say that the paper would never appear in the pages of refereed journals, except perhaps the Ulu Langat Bulletin of Education. If I were an academic, I would be embarrassed to append my name to such a shoddy paper.

This policy of teaching STEM in English would not have triggered its many belated critics had the leadership showed more resolve and greater commitment. They became vociferous and assertive only when former Minister of Education Hishamuddin misguidedly re-opened the issue. Why he did it is best left for him to answer, but I venture that the then looming UMNO leadership contest had plenty to do with it. Old Hishamuddin needed to display his nationalistic manhood once again, especially after the spectacular flop of his earlier unsheathing of the *keris* incident.

Flawed Implementation

I have not seen any change in the Ministry of Education operations since or in response to the adoption of the policy. I would have thought that at least there would be a dozen English-medium teachers' training colleges by now to provide for the necessary trained teachers. The local universities too should be expanding the number of classes in science and mathematics taught in English so there would be an ample supply of graduate teachers competent to implement the new policy.

Similarly, the ministry should have by now commissioned textbook writers and publishers. Failing that, I would have expected these officials to be contracting with established foreign publishers to buy their texts.

None of these measures were taken. That reflected incompetence or lack of commitment to the new policy, or both, and at the highest level. The fault then lies not with the policy but with those entrusted with the awesome responsibilities of implementing it.

Those Malay language nationalists and other strident critics of TSME fail to recognize one glaring reality. That is, the current educational policy is failing the students and the nation. Those who can or have other options for their children have already abandoned the system. We see this especially among non-Malays. Increasingly, more and more Malays are also following suit. That leaves those poor village folks who have no other choice; they are trapped in the current system. And they are almost all Malays. They are the ones left out, victimized by their own kind, the language nationalists on one side and the incompetent education bureaucrats on the other.

If not for the public sector and the various GLCs acting as employers of last resort, graduates of the current educational system would be without jobs. There is a limit however to the government's capacity as employer of last resort. Malaysia is already way beyond that.

For a society to advance, it must first come to terms with itself. A major part of that exercise involves recognizing its weaknesses, for unless that is acknowledged, then that society could not even begin to overcome them. Malays must recognize that our major problem is that we are not competitive, not even in our native land let alone the global arena. A major contributor to this sorry state is the defective education system that continues to produce graduates who have abysmal language and mathematical skills, as well as being science illiterate.

Malays have completely indoctrinated our young and ourselves with a "zero-sum mentality." That is, learning another language could only come at the expense of our own. Worse, we have gone further and mentally programmed our young that fluency in another language is not an asset but an expression of hatred for one's own. In so doing we exposed our own collective limited intellectual capacity, and an inability to expand it. That is the sorry part and root cause.

Malays only delude the young by appealing to their base emotions. Exhortations of *Ketuanan Melayu* would never make them competitive or guarantee them a place under the sun, not even in Tanah Melayu. Unless Malays are competitive, we cannot survive, let alone be Tuan. On the other hand, when we are competitive, we would be Tuan even in lands other than Tanah Melayu.

The other part of the exercise involves our willingness to learn from others, especially those more advanced. The ancient Arabs learned from the Greeks, the medieval Europeans from the Arabs, and the Japanese from the West. It saddens me that Malay luminaries by their actions and words are sending the wrong message to our young. That is, we have nothing to learn from others.

Malay leaders are too preoccupied with their own short-term political survival and gamesmanship instead of leading the nation forward. As a result, Malaysians, especially the young and future generations, would bear the burden of these leaders' follies. I see few signs, much less hope, for the situation to change soon.

Invest In Our People

March 1, 2009

Millions of Chinese had a rude awakening when they returned last month from celebrating their Lunar New Year in their villages. They discovered that the jobs they had in the cities before they left only a few weeks earlier had now disappeared. Tragic though that may be to them individually, the aggregate loss pales in comparison to that suffered by their government through its massive investments in the stocks of American companies and other paper assets like US bonds and Treasury Notes.

If only the Chinese government had invested in its people, imagine the good that would do to them, and to China. If their government had spent the funds to build better schools, Chinese schoolchildren would not have dangerous physical facilities that collapse with the slightest tremor. Had those funds been used to build affordable apartments, the Chinese people would have been better housed. That would at least help alleviate their miserable existence.

The Chinese people suffered twice. First, they worked incredibly hard under intolerable conditions and insufferably meager wages so the West could enjoy inexpensive consumer goods. Then the foreign currencies earned by their government from the exports created through their hard work vanished with the downward spiral of Western economies.

When Western consumers could no longer afford to spend, the Chinese were forced to work under even harsher conditions so the products they make could be sold cheaper still. This is just a modern twist to the old "coolie" concept. In the early part of the last century, millions of indentured Chinese were brought to America to work on the gold mines and railways. Today the coolies remain in China; America brings in only the products of their hard labor.

China is not alone in engaging in this folly of investing abroad instead of in their people, so is the rest of Asia. Singapore lost a hundred billion dollars on its American investments. On a per capita basis, Singapore's loss is massive and dwarfs that suffered by China.

Granted, Singaporeans live in a different universe from those folks in China, at least with respect to the creature comforts of life, though not in personal freedom. That notwithstanding, imagine how much better off Singaporeans would be if only their government had invested in them instead of being enamored by the fancy financial papers hustled by those Ivy League-educated white boys on Wall Street.

A Singaporean friend who owns a subsidiary in Silicon Valley lamented that the secretary to the head of his American company enjoys a lifestyle far better than his: larger home, a decent car, more social amenities, and better opportunities for her children. Meanwhile back in Singapore my friend make do with one of the pigeon-holes of a home in those monotonous urban high-rises, and his children spending what little spare time they have in "cram schools."

On another level, had Singapore invested those billions in nearby giant Indonesia instead of faraway America, imagine how much good it would do to the poor Indonesians. More pragmatically, a developed Indonesia would be a more high-value market for Singapore's products and services. Besides, imagine the gratitude and goodwill created through such investments. You cannot put a monetary value to that. Indonesia desperately needs those investments; America could easily do without Singapore's dollars.

Malaysia Fortuitously Spared

It is fortunate that in the current global crisis Malaysia is spared this tragic fate of losing its investments abroad. This is not the result of any brilliant foresight on the part of the nation's leaders, rather the consequences of the harrowing experience with the Asian economic crisis of 1997. For one, Malaysia has not yet fully recovered from that trauma and thus does not have the extra cash to be investing in any new and exotic financial instruments concocted in the West, those acronym-filled papers that are the "assets" of what former Finance Minister Tun Daim Zainuddin derisively termed the "cowboy economics."

For another, the capital controls implemented by Mahathir, though now largely dismantled, have left a deep impression on Malaysian economic managers, immunizing them against future meddling in such poorly understood foreign "investments."

That has not always been the case. Prior to 1997, agencies of the Malaysian government were active players on the London Stock Market, as well as the London Metal Exchange and the Foreign Exchange Market.

It was at the London Stock Market that Malaysia executed its famous (or infamous, to the Brits) "Dawn Raid" on September 1981 that effectively nationalized the huge British plantation company, Guthrie. That was hailed as a brilliant move that also satisfied Malaysia's national pride. It proved that we natives were fast learners and could be just as agile as those pros in the City, a much-needed confidence booster for those who require it periodically.

Malaysia's brash attempt to corner the world's tin market at the London Metal Exchange also involved mega sums. This time however, there was no rush to accept responsibility for this squandering of citizens' precious funds. There were other colossal losses, including Bank Negara's forex debacle, as well as the now defunct Bank Bumiputra's many expensive foreign misadventures.

I could only imagine the immense good had the Malaysian government invested those precious funds on its citizens instead. Although average Malaysians have it considerably much better than the average Chinese, nonetheless the quality of life could always be improved.

Contrary to the soothing but misplaced assurances from her leaders, Malaysia cannot insulate herself from the current global economic storm. There is no "comfort zone." Yes, Malaysia was fortunate enough not to have been entangled in those highly deceptive newfangled financial instruments with such fanciful acronyms. However, when your biggest trading partner and consumer of many of your commodities is in economic difficulties, rest assured that you too would be roped in.

Invest In What You Know

Like other countries, the Malaysian government had also introduced its own economic stimulus to deal with the crisis. Malaysian economists too have read Maynard Keynes and understood the rationale for counter cyclical public spending in a downturn.

Understanding the concept is one thing, translating it into reality in the local context is entirely another matter. The challenge is to make sure that the economic stimulus does indeed work, meaning it does spur the economy, and that the investments are indeed investments, meaning they would produce returns in excess of the capital expended.

At the height of the dotcom boom, the legendary American investor Warren Buffet was asked why he was not investing in that sector. He answered, "I invest only in things I know!"

I live in California and know that the real estate dynamics in San Francisco is radically different from that of San Bernardino, so I invest only in my community. I can at least follow the trend. Yet we have bankers in Singapore and Beijing pretending to be knowledgeable about real estate in the entire United States. That is the only explanation for their readily investing billions in securitized American mortgages!

Follow Warren Buffet's maxim: Invest only in what you know. What do Malaysian leaders know? For one, more than any Western banker or Nobel prize-winning economist, they know Malaysians, their daily needs and living conditions. Invest in them! For another, the economic "multiplier" of such spending is considerable; there is no such local multiplier effect when you invest in foreign stocks and other paper assets.

Malaysian leaders are aware of the deplorable conditions of local schools especially in rural areas. They also know that these children risk their lives daily in crossing rickety bridges to get to their schools. When they return home, their houses are flimsily built and in an unhealthy environment. They also have poor access to healthcare. So why not invest in building new schools, bridges, clinics, and affordable public housing?

It is well known that those rural children could not get good teachers. Why not invest in teacher training and provide greater incentives for teachers to serve in rural areas?

The beauty of such investments in human capital is that they generate values and returns way over and above the money, resources, and other efforts put in. The benefits are also enduring, and indeed "recession-proof." Should there be an economic downturn, the superb education those children had received would still be with them, as would their good health. A populace that is healthy and well educated, and thus productive, is the best weapon against a downturn.

In the last budget, and in the proposed additional stimulus, considerable sums were devoted to investing in the local stock market and in furthering the government's already considerable involvement in the private sector. Come another recession or a market misjudgment, such "investments" could easily evaporate. Think of the colossal loss with Bank Bumiputra, the various State Development Corporations, and the myriad GLCs. All they could show for their investments were some old tattered letterheads. They have not learned any useful lesson from those earlier and costly debacles.

Let the investment bankers, brokers, middlemen and paper shufflers invest in exotic financial assets; governments should invest in their people, and in infrastructures that would enhance their lives. Those are the only investments that are properly the purview of governments, not company stocks, foreign bonds, or fancy derivatives.

Investing in your people is also the only effective way to prepare them for the increasingly competitive world. More significantly for leaders, that would also ensure that come election time when citizens would make decisions about their future, these leaders would not be rudely awakened to find themselves without jobs.

English-Medium Islamic Schools

December 7, 2008

The Minister of Education will soon decide whether to continue the teaching of science and mathematics in English in Malaysian schools. That decision will not materially change the continuing decline in educational achievements of Malays.

This harsh reality is the consequence of national schools—the default choice for most Malays—being abysmal failures. Most non-Malays as well as affluent Malays are fully aware of this and have long ago abandoned the system. Ask where Najib Razak and Hishammuddin Hussein send their children for their education!

In today's economy, the most advantaged are those with high science literacy and mathematical skills, as well as being fluent in more than one language, with one of those languages being English, the language of commerce and science.

The next most advantaged would be those fluent only in English. The least advantaged would be those who are literate in only one language, and that language is other than English. This unfortunately is the fate of Malays today.

While one could attain high levels of science literacy and mathematical skills without knowing English, that is true only if one's primary language is Japanese, German, or any of the other already developed languages. It is not true for Swahili or Urdu. It is not true for Malay, no matter how passionately the language nationalists assert to the contrary. Even with those Germans and Japanese, the crucial point often overlooked is that they are also literate in English. Japanese children learn English right from kindergarten.

These educational deficiencies of Malays are long standing and most critical as well as most difficult to overcome with rural Malays. The cultural, intellectual, language and other ambience at home and in the community are not conducive to these children lifting themselves out of their trapped environment. They need help. To help them Malay leaders must be daring and innovative. Resorting to pat answers would not do it.

English Schools in Rural Areas

Earlier I had proposed setting up English schools in the kampungs. That would make sense as those Malays are the ones with the lowest proficiency in English and thus would benefit the most from such an initiative. With their already high usage of Malay at home and in the community, these pupils would not likely "forget" their native tongue if they were to attend English schools.

This is not a novel or risky social experiment, rather the resurrecting and improving upon an old successful one. That was how Malays of my and earlier generations received our education. As Tun Mahathir noted, we have not become any less Malay for the experience. Nor have we degenerated into "brown Mat Sallehs," the expressed mortal fear of the language and other nationalists. Indeed, that was how those ardent defenders of Malay language as Nik Safiah and Hussein Ismail received their education and enhanced their intellectual development. Now they want to deny today's young Malays–their grandchildren–the very same opportunities that they had enjoyed and benefited from.

While my proposal would be an improvement over the present system, there are problems with its implementation. Politically, there could be similar demands for such schools to be set up elsewhere, especially in areas where the background level of Malay in the community is low. Then we could potentially end up with the situation akin to the bad old colonial days where students would be fluent in English but at the expense of their proficiency in Malay. That would be unacceptable as Malay is now the national language. Further, that would divert resources and personnel away from rural areas, where the need is most acute.

Then there is the ire of the nationalists. They would go ballistic seeing those village children heartily singing *Baa Black Sheep* instead of *Nyet Semut*, fearing the cultural and other "polluting" influences on the young. That those children would continue singing our melodious Malay lullabies at home would not reassure these nationalists.

A more practical problem would be in getting good teachers to serve in rural areas. This could be alleviated through generous incentives like higher bonuses and providing them with living quarters. Not readily surmountable would be that such schools would necessarily be small; hence their academic offerings would be limited.

English-language Islamic Schools

To bypass these problems, I propose setting up English-medium Islamic schools. I am not suggesting anything radical here, merely expanding on an already successful experiment. I refer to the International Islamic University (IIU); extend that concept down to the school level.

Like IIU, these Islamic schools would use English as the medium of instruction, be open to all, and teach religious as well as "secular" subjects. These schools could be set up anywhere, not just in rural areas. Those in the major towns could be big enough to offer a varied and rich curriculum.

IIU already has its own Islamic School, using English as the medium of instruction. Unfortunately, its curriculum and pedagogical philosophy are more madrasah-like, the antithesis of a modern educational institution even though the school prepares its students for the GCE "A" examination. The emphasis at that school is on students learning the rituals of Islam and memorizing the Koran. I would prefer that those be done outside the classroom.

The Islamic school I have in mind would be modeled after the many excellent Church-affiliated ones in America. Their academic standing is such that they are the first choice for many non-Christians, including Muslims. These schools are first and foremost academic institutions, concerned primarily with education. They are interested in making their students better citizens, not on producing future priests or on proselytizing.

These schools matriculate their students to competitive universities to become engineers and doctors. Only a tiny fraction, if any, would end up in the clergy. Likewise, my vision of Islamic schools would produce Malaysia's future scientists and scholars. These schools are not meant to produce converts to Islam or turn their students into ulama.

There are now many such Islamic schools in America, and their numbers are growing such that the University of California, Irvine, offers a teachers' credentialing certificate in Islamic Education. Ultimately these schools would lead to the establishment of an English-medium Islamic University modeled after and of the caliber of a Georgetown University. Meaning, it would offer solid liberal education in a rigorous academic environment with an Islamic ambience.

A more local but historical model for my proposed Islamic school would be the old missionary schools. They did a credible job in educating many Malaysians, including the present Minister of Education Hishammuddin. Just substitute their Christianity for Islam.

While English would be the medium of instruction, Arabic (and with it *jawi* script) would be taught as a second language. Islamic Studies would be taught in English, but the emphasis should be on teaching it as an academic subject, not as theology.

In a typical seven-period school day, one period would be devoted to Arabic and another to Islamic Studies. The remaining five would be for regular or "secular" subjects, including English, science, and mathematics. Science and mathematics would be taught as per the current understanding, and not as some presumed "Islamic" variant. The curriculum must include the performing arts, and the extracurricular programs robust and varied to include sports.

The emphasis should be on solid liberal education and critical thinking. Literature for example would be taught not only as a means of learning the language but also to develop the students' critical faculties, as per Louise Rosenblatt's "Literature as Exploration" philosophy. Students would be discussing Shakespeare's sonnets as well as Rumi's rhymes.

Using English would go a long way in disabusing Malays of the negative psychological connotation associated with learning that language.

Malays should no longer view English as the language of colonials and infidels but as a necessary intellectual tool. For another, such schools would truly educate their students, teaching them to think critically as well as imparting to them modern skills and knowledge. Far too often what goes on in existing Islamic schools is nothing more than indoctrination masquerading as education.

Properly executed, these schools would attract students from abroad, especially the Middle East. These schools could be viable business investments as well as contribute to making Malaysia an educational hub.

Since these schools are open to all, they should get state support. There is precedent for this; the old Christian missionary schools also received governmental funding. Additionally, such schools should also get a generous slice of the huge *zakat* and *wakaf* endowments. Impose a surcharge of RM100 for every Hajj and *umrah* ticket towards funding these schools.

My version of the Islamic school is different from the current Sekolah Kebangsaan Agama (SKA). Apart from differences in admission policy and language of instruction (SKA admits only Muslims and uses Malay), there would also be profound differences in mission and teaching philosophy. SKA aspires to nurture future *pendakwah* (missionaries), and like IIU's version, is more *madrasah* in ambience and philosophy than a modern educational institution.

My proposal transcends politics; it would also be a splendid way to initiate conversations between Malay leaders in the various parties for the betterment of the community. This dialogue is desperately needed as Malay leaders are determined to go their separate and divisive ways. They seem intent on erasing any commonality of objectives in the relentless pursuit of their political goals.

English-medium Islamic schools may prove to be the effective avenue to propel Malays up the educational ladder. The Islamic imprimatur sells with Malays. Malay language nationalists would not dare oppose such schools even if English were to be the medium of instruction. Capitalize on that! These schools could be the salvation for Malays, just as Catholic schools were for impoverished and marginalized Irish immigrants in America at the turn of the last century.

These are the issues I expect Hishammuddin and his senior officers at the Ministry of Education to deliberate on, not flip flopping on major policies. That they are not doing so is a gross dereliction of duty. It is the young who would bear the terrible burden of their negligence.

Continue Teaching Science And Mathematics In English

July 1, 2008

The government's decision to revisit (and most likely do away with) the current teaching of science and mathematics in English is an instructive example of how an otherwise sensible policy could easily be discredited and then abandoned because of poor execution. Had there been better planning, many of the problems encountered could have been anticipated and thus avoided, or at least ameliorated. The policy would then be more likely to succeed, and thus be accepted.

Only a year ago a Ministry of Education "study" pronounced the program to be moving along "smoothly," with officials "satisfied" with its implementation. Now another "study" showed that there was no difference in the "performance" (whatever that term means or how they measure it) between those taught in Malay or English.

The policy was in response to the obvious deficiencies noted in students coming out of national schools: their abysmal command of English, and their limited mathematical skills and science literacy. They would carry these deficits when they enter university and onto the workplace.

The results were predictable—unemployable graduates, the vast majority being Malays. That created tremendous political pressure on the government to act as employer of last resort and making the civil service bloated and inefficient, burdened by these graduates' deficient language and mathematical abilities.

This longstanding problem began in the late 1970s when Malay became the exclusive language of instruction in public schools and universities. Overcoming this would be a monumental undertaking.

The greatest mistake was to underestimate the magnitude of the task, especially in overcoming the system's inertia. Today's teachers and policy makers are products of this all-Malay education system. Change would mean repudiating the very system that had produced them, a tough sell.

In their naivety, ministry officials convinced themselves that such enormous obstacles as the teachers' lack of English fluency could easily be overcome by enrolling them in short *culup* (superficial) courses that were in turn conducted by those equally inept in English. Or by simply providing these teachers with laptops programmed with instructional modules!

Even with the best talents devoted exclusively to implementing the policy, the task would still be huge. With Hishammuddin Hussein as Minister of Education shepherding the change, well, an insightful innovator or an effective executive he was not. Being simultaneously an UMNO Youth Chief, he was also distracted in trying to pass himself off as the champion of *Ketuanan Melayu*.

These factors sealed the initiative's failure. The tragic part was that the burden of that failure would fall disproportionately on the rural poor, meaning Malays, a point missed by these self-professed nationalists.

A Better Way

Teaching science and mathematics in English would solve two problems simultaneously. One, considering the critical shortage of textbooks, journals, and other literature in Malay, teaching the two subjects in English would facilitate the acquisition of new knowledge by the students. With the exponential growth of new knowledge, it would be impossible to keep up solely through translations, even if the entire national intellectual resources were to be devoted towards that endeavor.

The other objective was to enhance the students' English fluency. If that were to be the only consideration, there are other more effective ways of achieving it, like devoting more instructional hours to the subject or teaching in English another language-heavy subject like history.

If as the recent Ministry's "study" indicates, there is no difference in performance between those taught in Malay or English, that would favor continuing the program because of the twin benefits discussed earlier. Changing course midstream would not only be disruptive but also counterproductive. The educational system needs predictable stability and incremental improvements, not disruptive U-turn and faddish changes, especially in response to political pressures.

A more important point is this. Altering a politically pivotal and highly emotional public policy requires careful preparation and deliberate execution. If I were to implement the policy, this is what I would do. Lest readers think that this is hindsight wisdom on my part, rest assured that I had documented these ideas in my earlier book, long before the government even contemplated the policy.

Being prudent, as we are dealing with our children's and nation's future, I would begin with a small pilot project, analyze the problems, correct the deficiencies, and only then expand the program.

First, I would implement the policy initially only at primary and selected secondary schools, like our residential schools. The language requirements as well as the science and mathematical concepts at the primary level are quite elementary, and thus more readily acquired by the teachers. And at that level the pupils would not have to unlearn much as everything would still be new.

In schools where the background English literacy level of the pupils is low as in the villages, I would have the pupils take English immersion classes for a full term or even a year. We had earlier successful experiences with the Special Malay Classes of the 1950s and Remove Classes of 1960s. This strategy has also been tried successfully in America for children of non-English-speaking immigrants.

Another would be to bring back the old English schools in such areas. As the Malay literacy level in the community and at home is high, these pupils are unlikely to "forget" their own language.

At the secondary level, residential schools get the best students and teachers. The program could be more easily implemented there as the learning curve would be steep, and mistakes more readily recognized and corrected. Once the kinks have been worked out, expand the program.

Second is the issue of teachers. Malaysia has two large untapped reservoirs of talent—recently retired teachers trained under the old English-based system, and native English speakers who are either spouses of Malaysians or residents of this country. Given adequate compensation and minimal of hassles *vis a vis* work permits, they could be readily recruited.

I would add other incentives especially if they were to serve in rural areas where the need is most acute. In addition to the greater pay, I would give them first preference for teachers' quarters.

A permanent solution would be to convert some existing teachers' colleges into exclusively English-medium institutions to train future teachers of English, science, and mathematics. As the present teacher-trainees have limited English fluency, I would begin admitting them right away in January following their leaving school in December of the preceding year.

From that January till the regular opening of the academic year (sometime in July), these trainees would undergo intensive English immersion classes where their entire 24-hour day would be consumed with learning, speaking, thinking, and even dreaming in English. With the subsequent three years of additional instructions exclusively in English, these graduates would then be fully fluent in English.

With such quality programs, these graduates would be in great demand within and outside their profession. With their heightened English facility and mathematical competency, their educational opportunities would also expand as they could further their studies anywhere in the English-speaking world. With such bright prospects, these colleges would have no difficulty recruiting students.

As for textbooks, there is no need to write new ones. The contents of these two subjects are universally applicable. Meaning, those textbooks that are written for British students would be just as suitable for Malaysians, so we could select already available books. With its purchasing clout, the government could drive a hard bargain with existing publishers.

Ministry of Education officials, including and especially Hishammuddin, would do well to heed these factors when they review the current policy. Continue with the policy, correct the evident errors, and strengthen the obvious weaknesses. The success of this policy would also mean success for the students, and Malaysia. That is a worthy pursuit for anyone with ambitions to one day lead the nation.

Greater Scrutiny Needed For UM/PPC-MINT/Glomac Venture

February 24, 2008

The proposal by University of Malaya's governing board to let a private entity, PPC-MINT-GLOMAC, develop 27 acres of campus land deserves greater scrutiny. The university's press release of February 9, 2008 did not contain enough details for the public or government to make informed decisions.

I am supportive of universities going into partnership with private entities to develop campus assets, real estate, and others. That would conserve the universities' limited financial and other resources which they could then focus on purely academic matters. Creatively and properly structured, such partnerships would benefit the university and its community, the government and thus the public, as well as the participating private companies.

Handled less competently and it would result in the rapacious stripping of valuable public assets to benefit only the lucky few. Malaysia has plenty of such examples, with the boondoggle Port Klang Development Project being the latest and most expensive. Taxpayers would be left holding the tab; it is criminal that such scarce funds be squandered.

According to the press release, the university would stand to collect at least RM312M or RM200M plus the anticipated profit from the project, whichever is higher. Profit figures are tricky; they can be subjected to highly "creative" accounting. Enron posted record profits the year before it filed for bankruptcy.

At the other end, it is the job of smart accountants to "reduce" profits (at least on paper) especially when reporting to tax agencies. A quick and dirty maneuver would be to inflate your expenses by paying your executives, consultants, and directors outrageous compensations. Another would be to "expense" what otherwise would be considered as capital expenditure. Meaning, charging the expense in one year instead of spreading them over many.

Also not stated in the proposal is whether those profits would be a one-time payment as when the developers would sell their finished projects, or a steady stream with the developers maintaining and operating their projects. The latter would produce a smaller initial payout, but the university would benefit from the steady and predictable stream of income in the future.

One significant financial improvement would be to tie the payments not to profits but revenues. Top Hollywood stars know only too well the difference when their compensations are tied to profits, as in the old days. Today they all opt for a share of the revenue, not profits.

Another improvement would be not to sell but to lease on a long-term basis (with renewal options) the land to private developers. Those are valuable real estate; the value could only go up in Klang Valley where land is scarce. By leasing instead of selling, the university would not lose future gains in value.

In a subsequent separate statement, UM's Deputy Vice-Chancellor Amin Jalaludin indicated that the university would maintain ownership (title) of the land, suggesting a lease arrangement. If that were so, then the university owes the public a duty to declare the terms and details of that lease.

Non-Financial Considerations

While financial considerations are important and a major determinant as to the viability of the project, an equally if not more crucial consideration is to ensure that such a development and partnership scheme would enhance or further the goals and activities of the university. On this important point, both the university and developers are curiously silent.

For one, what does the university intend to do with the money it would get? If the funds were to go into the general revenue for running the campus, then the future benefits would be minimal and impact not noticeable. If the university were to dedicate the new money for specific projects like funding a new center for science research, expanding the library, or making the campus wireless, that would be much more meaningful and the impact more lasting and readily appreciated. With the benefits so tangible and visible, that would encourage further similar beneficial partnerships.

The developer was not forthcoming on what it wanted to do with the precious property. The company's development plans should interest the university and the public. If the developer was planning for a convention center, then that would be positive as it would complement the university's goals. The university could use the facility for its convocations and for hosting conferences. The same benefit would accrue to the university with the building of a Research and Development Park.

If the developer were to build exclusive high-end condominiums, that would not add value to or enhance the university's goals or benefit its community. For one, none of its professors could afford to buy or live in one of those units. However, if they were to be modest and affordable, that would alleviate the campus housing problem.

In addition to the financial arrangements, the university must also get a clear commitment from the developer and impose restrictions on the use of the property. These should be the minimal factors for the university's governing board members to consider. Anything less and they would not be fulfilling their fiduciary and other responsibilities. Minister of Higher Education Dato Mustapa Mohamed must ensure these conditions are met before approving the venture.

Financial Autonomy To Universities A Good Start

February 17, 2008

The decision by Minister of Higher Education Datuk Mustapa to grant financial autonomy to public universities was a good start. He should not stop there; he should also push to extend academic, management, and other freedoms. Malaysian universities would forever remain trapped in mediocrity if they were to remain under the clutches of the civil service.

University of Malaya Law Professor Azmi Sharom said it best, "If we love our universities, we must set them free!"

It showed how cumbersome the administrative machinery of the government in that a simple decision as this would take months if not years to implement. It would involve among others changing the various laws and regulations, right down to employment and procurement practices.

With the general elections looming, there was no assurance that Mustapa would remain in his present post. His successor may make yet another policy U-turn, an affliction that have plagued the education system. Even if Mustapa were to keep his present position, there would be no guarantee that he could overcome powerful forces resisting the ceding of control of the universities.

Yet those administrative changes, difficult though they may be to execute, would be the easy part. Much more challenging and trickier would be to adjust existing mindsets. Brought up under the present system, local academics and university administrators have long internalized the ethos and culture of the civil service. They would be incapable of leading or even adapting to the changes.

Making Public Universities Accountable

Public universities are tax supported; as such they must be accountable to the body politic, meaning the government of the day. However, there are other more effective ways to hold universities accountable without directly micromanaging them.

The matrix of the civil service is the very antithesis of academia. In the civil service, following established orders (*"Kami menurut perentah"*–We await directives!) is valued and is the ethos; in academia, you question established wisdom and assumptions.

The currency of the civil service is the size of your department as measured by the number of subordinates and budget allocations; with academics, the number of publications and frequency of citations.

Meritocracy as practiced in the civil service is a different concept from that in academia. To have the Director of Public Service Department decide who should be promoted Dean or Professor would be a recipe for disaster. That is the current problem with Malaysian public universities.

The government could exert effective influence more through the twin macro levers of the governing boards and budgetary process.

Appoint competent individuals with integrity who share the government's broad policies and philosophy to the governing council of universities. If it were a choice between someone competent but does not share your political views versus someone who shares your views but otherwise incompetent and corrupt, opt for the former. It is easier to convert someone to your viewpoint; more difficult to change or improve on someone who is incompetent and or corrupt.

The other powerful lever would be the budget, both operating and capital. With operating budgets, the government could tie them to the universities meeting certain prescribed goals. If they were to exceed the target, they would get bonuses; if they fail, they would be penalized financially.

These goals could be tied to government policies. For example, the government's oft-stated goal is to increase the number of Bumiputras enrolled in the sciences. Universities that meet or exceed that target would be rewarded financially. With the policy of encouraging graduate studies and research, why not reward those universities who award doctoral degrees (especially in the sciences) and whose faculty members publish scientific papers?

As for capital budgets, the government could underwrite 90 percent of it, to start new programs or buildings, with the universities funding the remaining. That would encourage universities to seek funds from other than governmental sources.

We should be careful that such incentives be not too generous otherwise that would divert those vice-chancellors from being academic heads to glorified fundraisers, the plague on many American campuses.

With greater management autonomy, each university could find its own unique and ingenious ways of meeting its own needs. On many American campuses, private developers lease university land to build student residences and faculty housing. Companies like Marriott provide food services on many campuses. Such initiatives would free up scant academic resources. We could then send the Deputy Vice-Chancellor responsible for student housing back to the lecture halls instead of wasting his time in making sure that students are being well fed and housed.

Such innovations are just the beginning; we would see many more if only we dare liberate local campuses.

Dispense with MOHE

By liberating the universities, the government may find that it does not need a huge bureaucracy to run them. It could then dispense entirely with the massive Ministry of Higher Education (MOHE) and divert the considerable savings to fund campus libraries and research laboratories. We could hire a Nobel laureate to teach at one of our universities for the money we pay for MOHE's Secretary-General, or the many Directors-General. Imagine the good such appointments would do!

This is one reason why I am skeptical that Mustapa's grand scheme of liberating local universities would not be vigorously pursued. It would mean one fewer Secretary-General and many more Directors-General out of their jobs! Then there are their deputies and assistants!

California has an extensive system of quality universities and community colleges, yet it has no Ministry of Higher Education. The state government exerts control through two main powerful levers. The first is via the budgetary process and the other through its nominees on the universities' and colleges' governing bodies. Unlike in Malaysia, professors and other university employees are not part of the state civil service and thus not bound by its rules and regulations.

Malaysia would do well to learn from and emulate the Golden State.

I cannot imagine any faculty member of the University of California feeling intimidated by the state's highest civil servant or Secretary of Education (equivalent to Malaysia's Minister of Education). In Malaysia, the Vice Chancellors of her public universities would even without prompting kowtow to the lowest civil servants at the Ministry of Education.

Stated in a different manner, those professors and scholars who have any sense of professional pride or academic integrity would never rise high in local universities.

The central question policymakers should answer is this: How to make local universities serve the needs of the nation? We would do this best by liberating them so they could find their own path to excellence.

Endless, Meaningless Reforms

The Havoc Education Reforms Inflict: *Education Blueprint 2013-2025*

I: Transparent, But Not Bold Or Comprehensive

September 16, 2012 (*First of Five Parts*)
Education reform is inflicted upon Malaysians with the regularity of the monsoons. Like the storm, the havoc these "reforms" create lingers long after they have passed through.

Education Blueprint 2013-2025 identifies the main problems and challenges at both systemic and individual levels but fails to analyze why or how those came about and why they have been let to fester. The recommendations are based more on conjecture rather than solid data; more towards generalities and the stating of goals rather than on specifics on how to achieve them. On the positive side, the goals and milestones (at least some of them) are clearly stated in quantifiable terms, so we would know whether they would have been met or not.

Despite extensive public participation and the inclusion of many luminaries (including foreign ones) on the panel, the report has many glaring omissions. It fails for example, to address the specific challenges facing Islamic and rural national schools. A major deficiency as the constituents there are Malays, a politically powerful constituency. Those schools perform at the bottom quartile, dragging down the system. Improving them would go a long way in enhancing the system. Another is the failure to analyze and learn from earlier reforms.

This *Blueprint* does not live up to Najib Razak's hype of being "bold, comprehensive and transparent." That is not surprising as the panel is dominated by civil servants. They have been part of the problem for so long that it would be too much to expect them to magically be part of the solution now.

Predictability of Education Reform

It is a Malaysian obsession to reform its educational policy with the political season. Every new minister feels compelled to undertake one, as if to demonstrate his political manhood. Now it is Muhyiddin's turn.

Five years ago there was Hishammuddin with his *Langkah Ke Arah Cemerlangan* (Steps Towards Excellence). Five years before that under Musa Mohamad was *Pembangunan Pendidikan 2001-2010: Rancangan Bersepadu Penjana Cemerlangan Pendidikan* (Education Development 2010-2011. Plan for Unity Through Educational Excellence). Notice the long pretentious titles and frequent use of the word "excellence."

Meanwhile generations of young Malaysians, especially Malays, continue to pay the price for the follies of these reforms, the most disruptive being the one in the 1970s that did away with English schools. Someone finally wizened up and brought back the teaching of English, albeit only in science and mathematics. Then just as Malaysians were adjusting to and recovering from that reversal, a new leader who thought himself smarter changed back the system!

This latest reform released on September 11, 2012, could prove to be the 9-11 of Malaysian education. The destruction may not be as dramatic visually and physically as the other 9-11, but the wreckage would be just as real and massive, with the havoc remaining long after to haunt current and future generations. The damages would be extensive, cumulative, and compounding.

As in the past, this time Malaysians are again promised that this storm of a reform would wash away the metaphorical thick polluted haze that has been hovering over the system. The air would be clearer and fresher. The birds would return to sing. Meanwhile you would have to deal with ripped roofs, flood debris, destructive landslides, and other interruptions.

In compiling this *Blueprint*, the government had sought wide public participation and at great expense. The public in turn responded enthusiastically, reflecting the angst over the system. The panel however did not discern the difference between quantity and quality, duly giving equal time to the bombasts as well as the wise.

The Challenge of Quality

This *Blueprint*, like earlier ones, is already getting rave reviews from the usual quarters. Just as predictably, a year or two from now even before any of the recommendations have been fully implemented, "scholars" from our public universities would declare through their "research" that the reforms have already produced the anticipated improvements!

We saw that when the policy of teaching science and mathematics in English was rescinded. Barely a year into the program Malaysian "scholars" and pundits were already trumpeting the "remarkable" improvement in the science and mathematics scores especially among rural Malay students. With all those great improvements one wonders why Malaysia would need another reform!

This new *Blueprint* was barely released when Muhyyiddin announced a new history curriculum, meaning, one written by UMNO hired hands. So much for the weight given to this reform and its objective of creating students capable of critical and independent thinking!

No one would argue with the *Blueprint*'s objectives of improving access, quality, equity, unity, and efficiency. Consider quality; it is uppermost in everyone's mind. The government proudly parades the success rates at its national examinations, as with the accelerating number of A's scored. Yet when assessed by such external yardsticks as TIMSS and PISA, Malaysian students scored poorly. As the report acknowledges, they are at least two to three grades behind their counterparts in South Korea, and fast declining.

The panel glosses over this glaring anomaly and fails to draw the only and important conclusion: What and how we teach as well as how we test are substandard. Malaysia is doing both wrong!

If your home thermometer says you do not have a temperature but at the hospital you register a high fever, then you should get rid of your thermometer lest you would be misled you again in a very dangerous way. If Malaysia aspires for her students to be in the top third in PISA and TIMSS, then she should first dispense with the current curriculum and testing as they do not correlate (in fact inversely correlated) with those international measurements.

Consider another objective, to have Malaysian students be bilingual in Malay and English. I agree with that; the problem is how to achieve it. The panel addresses the issue generally, but the kampung boy in Ulu Kelantan faces vastly different sets of challenges in learning English *vis-a-vis* the diplomat's son in Bukit Tunku; likewise a Tamil girl on an estate school in Ulu Tiram learning Malay to a penghulu's daughter at a national school in Ulu Trengganu.

As the challenges are radically different; so too would the solutions. For vernacular schools especially in areas where Malay is not widely spoken, devoting more hours to Malay language, and having bilingual (Malay and the vernacular language) teachers would be the more appropriate approach.

In the kampungs, not only is English not widely used, there is also active antagonism to using and learning it. This is not a problem unique to the kampungs. In Western Canada there is similar resentment to learning French despite it being Canada's second official language. To overcome this and compensate for the low level of French usage in the community, some schools have total immersion classes where pupils would spend their first three or more years in classes conducted entirely in French. As the program is voluntary, it is politically and socially palatable. As parents discover the many advantages, the enrollment soars.

A similar solution could be employed in the kampungs. Have English immersion classes for the first few or better yet throughout the entire primary school years. Introduce Malay only at Form One. Go beyond and have secondary schools that would teach half the subjects in Malay and the other half in English. Science and mathematics would be the ideal subjects to teach in English. Such a school would produce fluently bilingual graduates.

Aware of the political sensitivities Malays have towards learning English, I would make the program entirely voluntary, like those French immersion classes in Western Canada. Kampung Malays are as rational as those Anglophone Western Canadians. Once those Malays see the advantages of being proficient in English, they would flock to enroll their children in those immersion classes.

Such schools could be the innovation worthy of emulation by other nations who similarly aspire to have their students be bilingual. Such Malay-English bilingual schools are much easier to set up than Arabic-English or Mandarin-English ones as Malay and English share the same roman script.

This was how my contemporaries and I learned English back in the 1950s. English usage was even much lower then, in fact non nonexistent at my home and community. As such I advocate bringing back those

English schools, but site them only in areas with low level of English and high Malay usage, as in the kampungs.

If Malaysia were to bring back the old English schools unmodified (as the parent-group PAGE is advocating) and locate them in the cities where the usage of Malay is low, then we would only resurrect the old problem where students would ignore Malay. Similarly, Malay immersion classes could be introduced to enhance the proficiency of non-Malay students, especially in communities where the usage of Malay is low.

The panel highlights the many islands of excellence in the current system. There certainly are, as with missionary and independent Chinese schools. As they are already doing a superb job there would be little need to reform them. Instead the government should support them so they could enhance and replicate their successes.

I would impose only one condition for that generous public support, and that is the enrollment must reflect the general Malaysian society. Such a policy would also further one of the stated goals of the Blueprint: to enhance unity among the young.

II: Quality Schools Begin With Quality Teachers

September 23, 2012 (*Second of Five Parts*)
In the 1950s, the headmaster of my Tuanku Muhammad School, Kuala Pilah, lived in a palatial bungalow up on the hill, next to the residence of the District Officer. Two decades later, his local successor was renting a modest house from my father, a retired Malay-school teacher. As for that hilltop house, it is now occupied by a civil servant.

In the 1960s when the then Minister of Education visited Malay College, he was noticeably deferential to its colonial leftover headmaster. Today, the threat of a visit by a lowly ministry functionary would throw the headmaster and his senior staff into a tizzy.

Those are the realities of the teaching profession in Malaysia today. The folks that produced *Education Blueprint 2013-2025* see the world of Malaysian teachers differently. They brag about having 38 applicants for every teaching slot, way over the eight in Finland. The Finns are acknowledged as having the best schools and teachers.

What gives? Just a few lines away and easily missed by careless readers, the *Blueprint* reveals that over a third of those applicants lacked even the minimal (and unbelievably low) current qualifications. Imagine! The perception students have of the teaching profession is this: If you are not qualified for anything else, apply to be a teacher.

The panel wants to tighten the qualifications so only those in the top third could apply. Great, but how? As a mental exercise, I wonder how many of the current applicants would qualify if the proposed higher standards were to be applied. If the panel had done so, it would realize the magnitude of the problem. They would then be dissuaded from resorting to simplistic solutions as merely raising the entry requirements. The challenge is not with imposing tighter criteria (that could be done with a directive) but enticing those top students to be teacher-trainees.

The panel's approach to the teacher issue is reflective of its collective muddled thinking. Its members are unable to look at data critically or know the limitations even when those figures appear to defy reality and common sense. They are easily mesmerized and be taken in by such silly statistics as over 38 applicants per teaching slot.

Yes, there is a glut, but only from those in Malay and Islamic Studies. They are unemployable elsewhere. The critical shortage is in science, English, and mathematics (STEM). The focus should thus be on this critical and difficult challenge instead of searching for an overarching solution to all problems, or ones that do not even exist, as with Islamic Studies teachers. Some problems could be solved just through less meddling from the ministry.

Consider another set of figures cited in the *Blueprint*: Malaysian teachers have comparable pay to and are treated like their peers outside the profession. Again, the reality is far different, as attested to by that headmaster renting my father's house. Salary figures alone do not tell the whole story, as with that bureaucrat's house on the hill in my old hometown.

As the *Blueprint* does not provide actionable recommendations to address this critical shortage of STEM teachers, I put forth mine. First, I would double their stipends during training. To help defray the costs I would simultaneously reduce the stipends for the others, especially those in Malay and Islamic Studies. We already have a glut of them. If that would not attract enough top candidates, I would sweeten the deal. Guarantee them scholarships to pursue a degree upon graduation from teachers' college. That would also encourage them to enhance their qualifications to enable them to enter university.

If that would not still do it, then select from the next tier of candidates—those just below the top third—but put them through six months to a year of rigorous "prep" where they would undertake intensive classes in the three subjects. Those who do well would then continue. Pay them during this "prep" year.

Those chosen may not be in the top third as per ministry's criteria, but then as noted earlier, local examinations do not correlate well with international tests. It may well be that those *not* currently in the top third by local criteria may be the truly smart ones.

Another factor to attracting top candidates would be to have superior teachers' colleges. It is a sad commentary that despite the demonstrated critical shortage, only one of the 27 teachers' colleges is devoted to training science teachers and one for international languages but not English exclusively. It is no better at the universities; not one public university has a dedicated Department of English. That reflects the gulf between intent and action.

The ministry's perennial training mode is "crash" or short-term *culup* courses of a few weeks or even days. It proudly proclaimed to have "trained" thousands of such teachers. Ever wonder why Malaysian students have abysmal results or why the talented are not attracted to teaching?

Convert a dozen existing colleges into exclusively English-medium for training STEM teachers. This should have been done earlier in preparation for the switch in teaching science and mathematics in English. Had that been done, the initiative would have been more likely to succeed, and those children would have been spared yet another disruptive switch.

Making those colleges all-English would also help attract top students. Those smart students know that furthering their education in English would expand their career, intellectual, and other horizons. Look at the earlier experiences with Kirby and Brinsford Lodge graduates.

To attract top candidates, you would also need first class physical campuses and facilities, meaning among other things, not only air-conditioned lecture theaters but also residence halls. I would also give trainees free I-pads or laptops. I would pamper them beyond their college years, as with extra allowances. If they were to serve in rural areas, they would get additional allowances that could effectively double their pay. Beyond that I would ensure that they would get the top priority for coveted on-campus quarters and government houses generally.

These tangible recognitions would be far more effective than such silly things are *Tokoh Guru* (Champion Teachers) awards and other public ceremonies. If the government were to recognize outstanding teachers and educators in its civil award lists, that too would help.

The measures proposed here would produce not only competent STEM teachers but also truly be bilingual ones. And bilingual teachers would produce bilingual students, another stated goal of the *Blueprint*.

I applaud the *Blueprint* for advocating greater autonomy and authority for headmasters. However, it would be difficult for them to exercise both when those bureaucrats at the ministry are paid and treated so much better. The Minister of Education in the 1960s was deferential to Malay College's Neil Ryan not because he was the headmaster rather that as an expatriate and was thus paid much more than the minister! That was also the reason why Ryan did not *kowtow* to those politicians and bureaucrats.

While issues of pay, autonomy and respect are important, those are not the main considerations in opting for teaching. As a former teacher, and as my parents who were longtime teachers demonstrated, the greatest satisfaction would be to see the sparkle in your students' eyes when they learn or discover something new, and the reflected glory you quietly savor on seeing your former students reach great heights. As a physician the best that I could do for my patients is to restore them to their pre-illness state. For a teacher, there is no limit to the potential achievements of her students.

It is this professional satisfaction that drives teachers. Before they can get to savor that, they first must be treated as true professionals.

Training competent teachers takes time; meanwhile we have an immediate problem in the classrooms with respect to STEM teachers. As for English teachers, Malaysia used to have a big pool of them, but we squandered that precious resource. Attempts at enticing them out of retirement have been marked by incompetence and outward antagonism by those in charge. The reason is obvious. Those retired teachers would put their present colleagues to shame. Instead of encouraging them, current headmasters are intent on imposing obstacles.

There is another large pool, the native English-speaking spouses of expatriates and Malaysians. They can be trained "on the job" in the manner of the old "Normal" teachers. Malaysia needs to be flexible and innovative in recruiting teachers.

One of the *Blueprint*'s consultants is the former South Korean Minister of Education. I am surprised that he did not recommend for Malaysia to import STEM teachers as South Korea and other (especially Asian) countries are doing. Thailand demonstrates that you do not have to pay exorbitant expatriate pay to recruit them. Malaysia has a small program undertaken jointly with the Fulbright Foundation. I see no reason why Malaysia could not do it independent of American agencies.

Teachers do not operate in a vacuum; good teachers need good schools. My greatest disappointment with this report is its lack of ideas on revamping what is obviously a failing system—national schools (more on that later). Non-Malays have already abandoned the system; now Malays too are joining them. This failure mocks the *Blueprint*'s claim to be transformational.

The only innovative idea was liberalizing local enrollment in international schools, but that was already done long before this report. That measure is only the "letting out of steam," to satisfy the elite.

In an earlier book, *An Education System Worthy of Malaysia* (2003), I proposed charter schools and the decoupling of the identification of vernacular schools with race. Charter schools would get the same financial and other governmental support as national schools but would be free of ministry's control, especially with respect to the curriculum and medium of instruction. The only stipulation is that their enrollment should reflect the general society, and their graduates be fluent in Malay and English. How that is achieved is left to the genius of the school's management and teachers.

The other is to disconnect the present identification of vernacular schools with race. Make Sekolah Jenis Kebangsaan China less a school for Chinese, more one using Mandarin as its medium of instruction and catering to all Malaysians who desire such an education. These schools would have to make serious efforts at attracting non-Chinese especially Malays, as with having halal canteens and teaching Islamic Studies in Mandarin, as they do in China. Along the same vein, I see no reason why there cannot be Sekolah Jenis Kebangsaan Arab, Inggeris, or even Swahili supported by the government, provided that those schools attract a broad spectrum of Malaysians.

Having students of all races study and play together would advance the *Blueprint*'s unity agenda far more effectively than all the other measures combined. As a bonus, diversity in the classrooms enhances the students' learning environment.

For Malaysia, there is another and very crucial reason for encouraging diversity in the classroom. If we continue with the present trend of self-segregation, then Malaysia could end up like Northern Ireland. That wretched community has a well-educated populace; alas it is deeply and viciously divided. Malaysia had a taste of its own Northern Ireland not too long ago; Malaysians have no wish to repeat that bitter, bloody experience.

III: Quality, Efficiency, Efficacy, And Trimming Of Fat

September 30, 2012 (*Third of Five Parts*)

The one diagram in the *Blueprint* that best captures what is wrong with Malaysian education is Exhibit 6-4, the ministry's organizational staff structure. It is described as rectangular; it is more a fat Grecian column. That diagram is the best graphic representation of data in the entire document; it captures and demonstrates well two salient points. One, there are as many Indians as there are chiefs in the organization, and two, the attendant overwhelming administrative burden at all levels.

"Malaysia arguably has one of the largest central (federal) administrations in the world, relative to the number of schools," says the *Blueprint*, quoting a UNESCO Report.

We do not need those highly paid international consultants to remind us of the bloat. The gleaming tower that is the Ministry of Higher Education in Putrajaya is emblematic of that. It reveals the government's perverted priorities. That edifice shames that of the Department of Education of the US, or any First World country.

By any measure, relative to the economy, population, or total budget, Malaysia funds its education system generously, much more so than countries like Finland and South Korea. Yet Malaysian students and schools lag far behind. The answer lies in that Exhibit 6-4. The bulk of the resources do not end up in the classrooms.

It reflects the panel's commitment (or lack of it) to enhancing the system's efficiency that the post-reform chart looks only slightly tapered at the top. It needs to be sharply pyramidal to tackle the current bloated rectangle.

Efficiency is one of the *Blueprint*'s six goals. Briefly though not inaccurately defined, efficiency is output relative to input. If I expend "x" amount of resources (time, money, effort) and produce "y" amount of intended results, while my colleague expends twice as much, then I am twice as efficient. However, if he produces other than the intended results, then he is not being efficacious quite apart from being not efficient. His producing all those unintended and unwanted products reduces or interferes with his output of the desired ones. Efficiency is doing things right; efficacy, doing the right thing.

Malaysian education is both inefficient and inefficacious. It is not efficient because despite the vast resources expended it produces far too few graduates who are bilingual, science literate, mathematically competent, and capable of critical thinking. It is not being efficacious because the graduates produced are not the types desired, meaning, they are unilingual, unable to think critically, and good only at regurgitating what has been spoon-fed into them.

Another manifestation of this inefficiency is the computer initiative. Rwanda could provide each child with a laptop at a fraction of the Malaysian price. Malaysians are not being as efficacious as Rwanda where its laptop program teaches not only the children but also spills over to their families. In Malaysia, those laptops end up either being "lost" or gathering dust in the school's storerooms. Malaysian teachers have not been adequately trained to use them; besides those computers belong to the school and not given to individual teachers. There is no pride of ownership, and opportunities for them to learn are very constricted.

Pursuing efficiency, we have two ministries (one for higher education), each with its own overpaid minister, deputy ministers, KSUs, DGs, Deputy KSUs, Assistant Deputy KSUs, and hordes of directors. With the government's stated goal of autonomy to universities, all you need then would be one person to write the checks perhaps once a semester. You do not need a ministry, much less a grand one. That expensive edifice and bloated administrative staff divert resources that otherwise could have been channeled to the classrooms and teachers.

Peruse the organizational structure of the Ministry of Education (MOE); dozens of divisions could be chopped off. Why does it need a separate division for *matrikulasi*; it is nothing more than Sixth Form. The purpose of decentralization and devolution of authority to the periphery is, among others, to reduce the central bureaucracy, not to lighten the load of those already under-worked civil servants at headquarters. If schools truly have autonomy then all you need is one person at headquarters to write the big check every month, term, or year.

Bureaus like Textbook, Translation, and Dewan Bahasa could be privatized with the resources saved diverted directly to pay writers, translators, and publishers, the actual producers of goods and services. Then there are the corporate and international relations offices. Get rid of them. The only important relationship MOE should cultivate is with parents and teachers.

Spin off the Examination Syndicate. Such bodies in America like the College Board (responsible for the Scholastic Assessment Test, SAT) and American College Testing (ACT), as well as those responsible for graduate and professional studies like GMAT (business school) and MCAT (medical school) are private.

Yet there is not a word in the Blueprint on streamlining the ministry, reducing the bloat, and getting rid or at least privatizing those peripheral services.

Malaysians, individually and as a society value and respect education. Malaysia willingly expends resources on education but are unwilling to expend the extra effort to ensure that that those funds would be spent wisely. MOE's budget fails on this critical scrutiny.

MOE, being part and parcel of the massive Malaysian bureaucracy, is also afflicted with rampant corruption, blatant cronyism, embarrassing incompetence, naked nepotism, and a distorted sense of meritocracy. The last scandal (at least one that was exposed) was in 1960 under Rahman Talib when RM100 million in school construction funds were "unaccounted for," the euphemism for "missing" or siphoned off. That may seem small change by current standard of greed, but after factoring for inflation and devaluation, it would be a billion in today's currency.

This *Blueprint* ignores this blight of administration in MOE. In an earlier book I cited the example of the bloated cost of a MARA residential college where through competitive bidding we could get three such schools for the price of two. If competitive bidding were to be standard practice, then not only would we get more for our money but also our schools would have roofs that would not collapse, thus endangering the children.

Najib and Muhyiddin did not demonstrate their ability or willingness to take on local UMNO warlords. On the contrary, both are central to the corrupt political patronage system that plagues Malaysia, including its education portfolio. Expect the bloat and inefficiency in MOE (and the rest of the government) to continue.

As for efficacy, the *Blueprint* does not even comment on whether the recent rescinding of the teaching science and mathematics in English advances the goal of producing bilingual and science literate graduates. There is no recommendation for increasing the number of hours of instruction in English or mandating a pass in the Malaysian University English Test (MUET). The more hours and the younger you are exposed to a language, the more proficient you would be, and faster. Making students pass a test would motivate them to study for it.

In the 1950s the government mandated all civil servants to pass a test in Malay to impress upon them its importance. That prompted many especially non-Malays to take private lessons lest they would be bypassed in promotions. This *Blueprint* does not mandate teachers and headmasters demonstrate their competence in English.

As for developing "critical, creative and innovative thinking skills," the government could begin by abolishing that indoctrination center, Biro Tata Negara (BTN). The resources saved could be diverted to schools. Both Najib and Muhyiddin are ardent defenders of BTN; that reflects their veneer of commitment to nurturing independent critical thinking.

Quality is linked with efficiency, efficacy, and the trimming of an organization's fat. Malaysia must strive high; surpassing a low bar is no achievement. It would give only a false sense of it. On a recent visit to China, Muhyiddin declared that we have done well with "93 percent of Malaysians able to attend schools and most of them could read, write and count." Malaysians deserve better and should demand more.

The goal should be for Malaysian children to attend not just any school but one that would teach them to be fully bilingual, science literate, mathematically competent, and be able to think critically. Malaysia should be haunted by the fact that 40,000 of her graduates are still unable to find jobs at a time when Malaysia has millions of foreign workers. That tells us that it is not a problem with the economy rather with the quality of those graduates.

The focus must be on quality and not on years spent in schools. Instead of extending mandatory schooling to 11 years (the *Blueprint's* recommendation), I would focus first on providing universal preschool and kindergarten especially in rural areas. If you want to teach kampung kids English, starting them in immersion classes at preschool would be the most effective way. Insights from modern neuroscience support that contention.

Further, a year of preschool costs considerably less and is far more consequential to a child's future than an extra year at high school. As the Jesuit wisdom would have it, "Give me a child until he is seven, and I will give you the man."

Without quality, Malaysian schools would degenerate into nothing more than human warehouses for the young, and her teachers but glorified babysitters. The nation would have wasted all those precious resources, but the most precious of all are those young minds. They would be better off out of school and learning the more important lessons of life in the real world instead of being bullied by their peers and indoctrinated by the system. Then when they failed, they would be tagged forever as losers, turned into caricatures of their race, and made to bear the burden of ugly stereotypes.

That thought should haunt anyone given the awesome responsibility of educating the young and those tasked with reforming the system.

IV: Roar Of An Elephant, Baby Of A Mouse

October 7, 2012 (*Fourth of Five Parts*)
Education Blueprint 2013-2025 lacks clear authorship. The document carries forewords by Najib, Muhyyiddin, and the Ministry's Secretary-General as well as its Director General, while the Appendix credits a long list of those

involved in this "robust, comprehensive, and collaborative effort," but the Blueprint itself is unsigned and with no documented authorship.

It is also impossible to tell who oversaw this whole reform effort. According to the complicated box-chart diagram, the entire endeavor was anchored in a 12-member "Project Management Office" (PMO) that reported to the Ministry's Director-General; as well as to an 11-member "Project Taskforce" that in turn reported to Muhyyiddin. Both the PMO and Taskforce are manned exclusively by ministry officials. Then there are the local and international panels of experts.

Such a convoluted arrangement could easily degenerate into a morass when no individual is tasked to be in charge. Every military operation needs a commanding general; every orchestra, a conductor. That is the greatest deficiency with this reform exercise—no one was in charge, likewise with the writing of the report.

This is typical of the Malaysian civil service's "management by committee" mode. As a result, it would be difficult to heap praise, or in this case, lay blame. That no one was in charge could be gauged by the final product. For a report that claims to be comprehensive, aimed no less at transforming the system, it is disjointed and lacks a central theme. It heaps praise on the system's "remarkable achievements" for the past 55 years. If that is so, why reform it? The *Blueprint* embellishes how well Malaysian students had performed on national examinations over the years, and then cites the PISA and TIMSS reports that indicate otherwise.

There are also many technical but irritating deficiencies, as with the lack of references. The Appendix makes only general references to reports from such bodies as the World Bank, OECD, and UNESCO. Those are relatively easy to trace. However, when it quotes studies done by experts from local universities, there are no specific references, leading one to suspect that those studies are not of publishable quality.

Those aside, my greatest disappointment is the *Blueprint*'s failure to address the system's obvious and critical weaknesses that demand immediate attention: rural schools; the religious stream; and vocational education. All three regularly perform at the bottom; improve them and you improve the system's overall performance. For another, the students affected there are mostly if not exclusively poor Malays. This failure to address their problems is made more incomprehensible and inexcusable because those involved with this reform, from Muhyyiddin on downwards, are mostly Malays. While today they may live in plush bungalows at Putrajaya, scratch a bit and the "kampungness" would ooze out of their pores. During Hari Raya they all flee *en mass balek kampong*.

Surely on one of those trips they would hear and see the plight of the children of their cousins and other relatives. I too was once one of those children. On visiting my kampung recently, I was painfully reminded of my earlier challenges. Only now they are worse.

At least when I was young I could dream that if I were to do well in school, I could escape my kampung. Today even if those children were to excel, their opportunities would be severely limited because of their limited command of English.

Then there is the problem of school transportation. During my time there was a bus service, erratic though that was. Today there is none. Those children depend on fellow villagers who happen to have a car. If perchance he is sick or slept over that morning, then those children that he normally packs into his tiny Kancil would miss school.

The biggest school expense my parents faced was for our bus fares. It still is for those village parents. American schools are required to provide free transportation especially for rural students. During colonial rule, schools had hostels to cater for those from remote areas. If we have more such facilities, then those students would not have to cross rickety bridges over dangerous rivers to have an education.

The wonder is that chronic absenteeism and academic underachievement are not worse with kampung kids. The *Blueprint* does not address this. A simple solution would be to have specific transportation allocation for each school for those pupils who live far away. The headmaster would then issue vouchers to be redeemed by the student and the village taxi driver. Better yet, the school could contract directly with individual village car owners and taxi drivers. There are other possibilities; all you need is for someone to first identify the problem and then diligently think about solving it.

The panel should be less enamored with advanced countries like Finland and South Korea, and instead learn from such poor countries as Mexico. The problems of our kampung children are closer to those of Mexico than South Korea. Mexico's *Progressa* program *pays* poor rural families for their children to attend school. The scheme extends to healthcare, as with immunizations. The money typically goes to the mothers.

The program has been modernized such that there are no transfers of cold cash as in the past, rather direct deposits into bank accounts. Yes, bank accounts for poor illiterate villagers! That would also bring them into the modern economy, quite apart from bypassing petty local civil servants.

The poor are identified through direct surveys, so even those who do not register or are distrustful of governments would not be missed. The program is divorced from the ruling political party; hence no associated corruption and leakage. The initiative has been effective in targeting the hard-core poor, and with low administrative costs.

Progressa reveals the close relationship between health, poverty, and educational achievements, and that all three could be simultaneously addressed effectively with a social initiative that is low cost, highly efficient, and remarkably efficacious. *Progressa* underscores the wisdom of former US Surgeon General Jocelyn Elders, "You can't educate a child who is not healthy, and you can't keep a child healthy who isn't educated."

Then there are the dilapidated rural schools; many lack power and potable water. Supply those schools with power and those children could use computers and two-way videoconferencing so that one teacher centrally located could serve several classes from different schools. This is useful for small schools as they can be combined on-line. Similarly, the shortage of teachers for specialized subjects like music could be overcome by sharing one teacher rotated among many schools in one district. Both strategies are used in rural America.

As for vocational education, Malaysia cannot be an economic power unless she has well trained and skillful workforce for manufacturing as well as for the service sector. For Malays, the only way for signs like "Mahmud Motor Repairs" and "Halimah Hair Saloon" to appear on Main Street would be to train these skillful workers. Again, Malaysia does not have to re-invent the wheel. Germany provides an excellent example of industry/school collaborative apprenticeship programs.

As for religious schools, they share all the challenges of national schools, only worse. Physically, the standard of hygiene of their canteens is substandard while their hostels are death traps, lacking basic safety features as sprinkler systems. They lack even mosquito nets.

Beyond the awful facilities, the religious stream faces an even far more daunting challenge. Its educational philosophy, pedagogical approach, and learning psychology are archaic, misguided, and simply wrong. This is an affliction peculiar not only to Malaysia but all Muslim countries, and from the highest institutions like Al Azhar to the lowest local Al Arqam preschool.

Abdullah Munshi best described the approach and philosophy of a modern education: It should treat the human mind as a knife to be sharpened. Current Islamic educational philosophy on the other hand considers the human mind a dustbin to be stuffed with dogmas.

The possibilities with a sharp knife are limitless. In the hands of a skillful surgeon, it could cure cancer; in a talented sculptor, an exquisite work of art. With a dustbin all you could get out of it is what you put in, nothing more. That assumes nothing gets stuck or crushed at the bottom.

A sharp knife in the hands of a thug is a lethal killing weapon. This is where religious education comes in so that when we send our young abroad to study nuclear engineering, they would come home to manufacture nuclear medicine instruments, not build dirty nuclear bombs.

What goes on in those religious schools and universities is indoctrination masquerading as education. The emphasis is on mindless recitations and the quoting of earlier scholars and luminaries. The strength of your argument is not based on logic or data but the pedigree of your quoted authorities. Religious education as presently practiced entraps rather than liberates Muslim minds.

The irony is that modern education has all the hallmarks of early Muslim practices and philosophy, at least until the so-called "closure of the Gate of Ijtihad" in the 12th Century. Many would attribute the decline of the Muslim world since then to this closure of ijtihad and with that, the closing of the Muslim mind. Those longing for an Islamic Renaissance would do well to first critically examine current religious education.

The other irony is that only in America and Singapore, two secular countries with Muslim minorities, have Islamic schools been modernized. *Blueprint 2013-2025* does not even address religious education in Malaysia.

Religion is now a major influence in national schools, one reason why non-Malays have abandoned the system. Removing religious studies from national schools, as some are advocating, is not the solution. Then we would be back to my childhood days where I was put in the hands of the *pondok ustads* in afternoon schools. The only way I survived that intellectual dissonance was to strictly compartmentalize my mind between my morning secular school and afternoon religious one. Sooner or later I had to reconcile the obvious contradictions. We should never burden young minds with such heavy dilemmas; instead, we should guide them in reconciling the two and thus benefiting from both.

The young should be taught early that there is no contradiction between secular and religious knowledge, and that the division between the two is false and artificial. Keeping religion in our national schools would best demonstrate that unity of knowledge. Metaphorically put, modern education sharpens the knife while religious education guides one to use it as a surgeon or sculptor would, to good purpose. I do not suspend my rational capacity on reading the Koran or listening to a sermon, and I do not shelve my religious convictions when I conduct scientific experiments or operate on my patients.

Before Malaysia could bring religious studies into national schools, the manner, objective, and philosophy of teaching would have to be revamped. Religious studies should be taught as an academic subject, not as theology.

After discussing these major deficiencies, it would seem petty if not anti-climactic to cite the *Blueprint*'s other omissions, which pale in comparison. However, I will include two. Though seemingly minor, they reflect the panel's lack of diligence and failure to critically analyze data.

The *Blueprint* quotes at length in the text and appendix both TIMSS and PISA. Malaysia paid considerable sums to participate in those studies. They are well designed and tested a broad spectrum of students to get as representative a sample as possible. The reports however present a composite picture of the nation.

As is obvious, there are vast differences between the students at Penang's Chung Ling versus Kelantan's Madrasah Al-Bakriyyah, between SMK Ulu Temiang versus SMJK (Tamil) Ulu Tiram. Those differences are in the data of TIMSS and PISA but buried deep. Malaysian scholars and policymakers have not analyzed them.

In America, Singapore, and elsewhere those statistics are pored over, with reams of papers published. Not so in Malaysia. That is surprising as the data are in the public domain. Had that been done, the disparities within Malaysia would have been shocking. Perhaps that was why the panel contends itself only with the composite findings.

The one chapter missing from this Blueprint would be, "Lessons From The Past." There is no attempt at critically looking at past reforms, their successes and especially their failures. If you do not examine them, you would not likely learn from them. You are more likely repeat those same mistakes. Then when the next Minister of Education arrives, he too would once again embark on another "bold, comprehensive, and transforming reform."

If I were to be tasked with this awesome responsibility of reviewing our education system, I would approach it differently. And that's the focus of the last part of my commentary.

V: When You Are Part Of The Problem

October 14, 2012 (*Last of Five Parts*)
The greatest weakness of this reform effort is its exclusive dependence on in-house or MOE staff, the very personnel responsible for the current rot with Malaysian schools. These individuals have been part of the problem for so long that they cannot now be expected suddenly and magically morph to be part of the solution. That would take an exceptional ability to be flexible, innovative, have the willingness or at least capacity to learn, and give up your old ways. Those are the very traits not valued in or associated with the Malaysian civil service.

The *Blueprint*'s local consultants included Air Asia's Tony Fernandez, Khazanah's Azman Mokthar, and Sunway's Jeffrey Cheah, presumably representing the three major communities. These individuals were already busy with their businesses. Unless they took time off from their considerable corporate responsibilities, they could not do justice to this important national assignment.

The international consultants were equally impressive. Here I wonder how much time they spent talking to teachers, students, and headmasters. Another significant flaw is this: With the possible exception of the Canadian consultant, the others are from systems not burdened with the Malaysian dilemma of low educational achievements identifiable with specific ethnic or geographical groups. In Ontario, Canada, only the

Toronto School System which is separate from the provincial has significant experience with the "Malaysian" problem. That Canadian was with the Province of Ontario with its relatively homogenous student population.

Many of those impressive consultants were conspicuously absent during the many public sessions leading one to conclude that they were more window dressing.

As for the public meetings, there were few formal or well thought out presentations. Far too often those meetings quickly degenerated into "bitch" sessions, or to put it into local lingo, *cakap kosong kopi-o* (coffee shop empty talk), with a few vociferous and frustrated individuals hogging the discussions. Worse, there were no records of those hearings for preview, except for those amateurish low-quality recordings posted on social media. Consequently, opportunities for learning from those sessions were minimal.

The reform has its own website (myedureview.com) and uses social media extensively. The dialogues there were no better; the comments were un-moderated and simply the spouting of anger and frustrations. As for the few serious ones, the panel never engaged their contributors. The cyber forums, like the public hearings, gave few insights; the signal-to-noise ratio was low. There was no shortage of passion and strong views, reflecting the angst Malaysians have of their school system.

A Superior Approach

There is a better approach. To begin with, dispense with the current or past personnel of MOE; they are or have been part of the problem. Consider that the most consequential reform in medical education, The Flexner Report of 1910, was produced not by a doctor or even an educator but an insurance salesman! It still is the foundation of modern American medical education to this day. In Malaysia, the Razak Report of 1956 transformed Malaysian education, yet its author was no educator or teacher.

The only qualification I would seek in those undertaking reform would be a respectable education (meaning, they have earned rather than bought their degrees), a proven record of success in any endeavor, and the necessary commitment, especially time, intellect, and energy. Meaning, these individuals would have to take a sabbatical from their regular duties. I would have no more than five members, with one designated as leader.

I would give them a generous budget to hire the best independent professional staff, from clerks to answer the phones efficiently to IT personnel to design and maintain an effective website, to scholars, statisticians, and data analysts. The budget should also provide for travels to visit exemplary school systems elsewhere. I would also have those panelists spend most of their time talking to students, parents, and teachers rather than ministry officials.

The panel should have the necessary resources to hire consultants from countries with demonstrably superior school systems. I would choose two in particular–Finland and America. Both have experiences in dealing with children of marginalized communities – Finland with its new immigrants, America its minorities. Yes, American public schools do not enjoy favorable reputation but there are islands of excellence for Malaysia to emulate.

I would avoid consultants from Korea and other East Asian countries. One, their societies are ethnically and culturally homogenous; they have no experience dealing with diverse groups; the Malaysian dilemma is alien to them. For another, while the Koreans regularly excel in international comparisons, they do not think highly of their own cram-school-plagued system. Those who can, meaning the rich, avoid it.

I would also look beyond the advanced countries to, for example Mexico for its *Progressa* Program, and Rwanda with its ambitious and successful One-Laptop-Per-Child (OLPC) scheme. If poor Rwanda could have such an imaginative initiative, Malaysia could do even more. That poor country demonstrates that an enlightened government approach could bring down prices. It could acquire computers for under RM500 per unit! It could do that because the program is under the management of competent and honest foreign experts, not local inertia-laden bureaucrats and corrupt politicians on the take. Rwandan leaders are self-confident and fully aware that they lack local expertise; they are not hesitant in calling in foreigners and do not worry about being "neo-colonized" or whatever.

Rwanda offers many other useful lessons. Foremost is that children from even the most physically and socially challenged environments could leapfrog the technological gap. That is pertinent for Malaysian children in

Ulu Kelantan and Interior Sarawak. For another, reform in the classrooms could spill into the wider community, spurring further changes and developments there. Those Rwandan children dragged along their parents and grandparents into the digital age. Those elders are now open to the wider world; consequently, they demand more of their leaders, like their villages having electricity so they could use their computers. They view those machines as agents of liberation and emancipation; now they can find out the price of the commodities they sell and the goods they buy directly from the market instead of being captive to the middlemen.

The only time I would call for ministry's input is to have the staff enumerate the problems and challenges faced under the current system. That would also show whether they were indeed aware of those problems and whether their assessments matched those of parents.

I would arrange the public participation component differently and encourage input from all, individuals as well as groups. The initial submissions however would have to be in writing. That would force presenters to think through their ideas. For groups I would stipulate that their report be accompanied by an attestation that it had been endorsed by their executive committees or general membership.

All submissions would be in Malay or English, with a translation in the other language. For those exceeding 500 words, there would have to be an accompanying executive summary not more than 200 words, again in both languages. All these submissions would be posted on the panel's website, with readers free to post their comments. Those comments as well as the original submissions would have to be edited (again by the panel's professional staff) for clarity, brevity, and accuracy, as well as to avoid embarrassing grammatical and spelling errors. That would lend some gravitas to the website as well as provide useful learning opportunities for those who surf it. The website as well as other media outlets must reflect the professionalism and excellence of the reform effort.

I did not get this impression on reading the *Blueprint* or perusing the reform's website.

The panel would then select from those submissions the few that are worthy for further exploration in an open public hearing. The purpose of those structured open hearings is to give the panel opportunities to elucidate greater details from the submitters, and for them to expand on their ideas. Those hearings are not meant to hear from new or on-the-spur commentators. Such a format would cut out the grandstanders. Again, those proceedings, their transcripts as well as the video and audio recordings, would be posted on the website.

Only after all the public hearings have been completed would the panel gather to write their final recommendations, with freedom for each member to produce his or her own separate or dissenting comment. That is the only way to be credible.

The current process produces nothing more than a sanitized press release of MOE, embellished with the imprimaturs of those impressive corporate and international consultants.

Measures of Success

There are only four reliable indicators of success with education reform, and all could be readily measured. The simplest would be to stand at the Johor causeway on any school morning and count the number of school children going south. Trend those numbers. If five years hence that number were to dwindle, then you know that Malaysian parents have confidence in their local schools.

Perhaps those chauvinistically inclined have already concluded that regardless how good local schools are, they would still go south. If that were so, then I have two other trends to monitor. One, visit the top universities abroad and survey the Malaysians there. How many (or what percentage) came from Malaysian national schools? In the 1980s I could count many; today, hardly any.

Another would be to trend the number of Malaysians enrolled in local international schools. Now that quotas for local enrollment have been lifted, that number would be inversely related to the level of confidence the elite has of local schools.

These statistics are easily collected and trended; you do not need fancy "labs" for that. PEMANDU should assign a junior staff member to collect those data.

Approach reform thoughtfully, both with the process and the people selected to lead it. The full consequence of the changes put today would not be felt till decades or even generations later. Malaysia is only now realizing and paying the price for the educational follies of the 1970s.

As a youngster my father would admonish me whenever I did something sloppily. Not only had I wasted my effort, he reminded me, now somebody else would have to undo what I had done before he could do it the right way. Triple the work and effort!

These reform efforts consume considerable human, financial and other resources. They also distract everyone, from politicians and ministry bureaucrats to parents, teachers, and most of all the students.

As such reform must be done right. You do that by first selecting the right people.

Reforming Education

I: Overview

March 25, 2012 (*Part One of Six*)

Deputy Prime Minister and Minister of Education Muhyiddin Yassin promised to release his "thorough review" of schools by yearend. I hope that he, his officials, and the slew of expensive consultants he hired would pay attention to the unique challenges facing three groups of students: those in kampung schools, the residential schools, and those university-bound with their post-Form Five dilemma.

There is no shortage of reviews, thorough and otherwise, of the Malaysian education system. Unfortunately, just as the recommendations of one new policy were being implemented, there would follow, just as surely as a burp after a *roti canai* breakfast, a stunning reversal soon after. Unlike a burp where only stale gas would be expelled, with a policy reversal the whole earlier content would be vomited out. It is enough to keep the heads of our pupils and teachers spinning, further distracting and confusing them. A prime example would be the many switches in language used in the teaching of science and mathematics.

In addition to the confusions and distractions from these frequent policy reversals, kampung pupils are further burdened by a triad of formidable obstacles that have remained unresolved for decades despite the multitudes of reforms. As these pupils are Malays, these frequent reversals should concern UMNO, PERKASA, and other champions of *Ketuanan Melayu*. On a more general level, Malaysia cannot become developed if a major segment of its population—its rural youths—are deprived of quality education. That is quite apart from the racial implications.

It is pathetic if not reprehensible that after nearly three years as Minister of Education it is only now that Muhyiddin is aware of the glaring achievement gaps between rural and urban schools. He discovered this from perusing the results of the recent Sijil Persekutuan Malaysia (Form Five) examination. Muhyiddin's ignorance is even more incomprehensible considering that he is the product of a rural school. That could only indicate sheer bumbling incompetence, gross dereliction of duty, or just simply dumb with the associated inability to learn.

As usual, his answer to the crisis was a promise to develop a "ten-year master plan" to "transform" (that favorite word again!) rural schools. By the time that committee is formed he would be busy campaigning or scheming to take over Prime Minister Najib's job, and those kampung students would be back to where they are today—being ignored.

The challenges confronting these kampung students are many and obvious. One is their persistent low English proficiency; two, their less-than-conducive intellectual environment at home and in the community due to poverty and associated factors; and three, inadequate schools and less-than-superior teachers.

The government cannot easily ameliorate their poverty and lack of intellectual stimulation at home and in the community. The authorities however, can compensate for those deficiencies by improving the other two factors. That is, enhance their English fluency specifically and give them superior education through better schools, enriched curriculum, and competent teachers. That will be the pupils' sure ticket out of poverty. From there they could then change for the better their families' and communities' intellectual and socio-cultural environment. This has been proven in different societies and at different times.

Those who harp on changing culture as the effective route towards improving educational achievement or ameliorating poverty have it backward. This does not mean that familial and social factors are unimportant in a child's education; they are. Nonetheless it would be much easier to improve the child's education first. The results and impact of that would also be more readily apparent and measured.

Enhancing English Proficiency

There are two immediate and practical reasons for improving the English proficiency of kampung kids. One is to enhance their employability. The most advantaged in this world are those who are at least bilingual, with one of the languages being English.

For kampung youths, there is another equally compelling reason for enhancing their English fluency, and that is to increase their self-confidence. This is a major handicap for them. Increase their proficiency in English and watch their confidence grow. This is more effective than repeatedly reveling in our imagined glorious past during Hang Tuah's time or proudly proclaiming our special status under the constitution.

This special aura associated with the English language is attributable only in a small part to our colonial legacy. English is today effectively the global language of commerce and science. Ignore that reality at your peril. Even China is recognizing this, even though Mandarin is being spoken by more people in the world.

Enhancing English fluency cannot be achieved through endlessly exhorting the young to "study harder" or haranguing them on the importance of that language, but by increasing the hours of instruction in that language and providing these pupils with competent teachers.

That was one reason for the earlier policy (now reversed) of teaching science and mathematics in English. We could just as easily increase the number of hours devoted to English or teach other subjects with high language content such as history or Moral Studies in English. Elsewhere I suggested teaching Islamic Studies in English, or even establishing English-language Islamic schools. English-language Islamic schools would break a major psychological barrier for Malays to learning English: its negative association with Christianity, again a legacy of colonialism.

In Japan, English is taught throughout the entire school years right from pre-school, yet its students remain hopelessly crippled in that language, as with our kampung students. The reason is clear. Both the Japanese and our kampung students have little opportunity to exercise their English skills at home and in the community.

Native English-speaking pupils in Western Canada learning French, the country's second official language, face the same challenge as that language is not widely used in the community. One solution is French immersion classes, during holidays or the first few school years.

Malaysia could adopt a similar approach in the kampungs by having kindergarten and the first few years of primary school totally in English. As the usage of Malay is high at home and in the community, and as these students are also Malays, it is unlikely for them to forget their native tongue. This was how Tun Razak learned English prior to his enrollment at Malay College. This was also the basis for the Special Malay Classes during colonial times and the Remove Classes of Tun Razak's policy. They were all effective.

This was also how Malays of my generation learned English. We were, in a manner of speaking, in total immersion classes throughout our school years. Bringing back these English-medium schools to rural areas would be a good solution.

Malays like me certainly did not lose our native language skills because we attended English schools. Peruse the many seminal contributions to Malay literature from Malays who were educated entirely in English. Pendita Za'aba and National Literary Laureates Shahnon Ahmad and Muhammad Haji Salleh are shining examples.

II: Reforming Education: Providing Competent Teachers

April 1, 2012 (*Second of Six Parts*)
The special challenges with kampung pupils and their schools are with attracting teachers, specifically to teach English, and on improving the physical facilities.

Malaysia had a deep reservoir of English-speaking teachers trained under the old all-English system. They are now retired. Given attractive incentives they could be enticed to teach in rural schools. Today there are only half-hearted attempts at attracting them, with the efforts left to local headmasters. These headmasters, brought up under the existing system, are only too aware of their own limitations in English. They are not about to be welcoming of or risk having their own inadequacies exposed by these hitherto senior English-fluent teachers; hence the failure of the current policy.

To overcome this entrenched resistance, you would have to impress upon the headmasters that their ability to recruit these retired teachers would be a major factor in their (headmasters') promotions or bonus payments. We should also insist that future candidates for headmasterships, as well as other promotions within the ministry, be based on demonstrated competence in English. That is an effective way of conveying the message on the importance of English. For those retired teachers, a call back to teach would be an opportunity to not only augment their pension income but also re-ignite their intellectual and professional passions and challenges.

Another source of teachers would be born English-speaking expatriate spouses of Malaysians. Malaysia has plenty of them. The issue of working visas is administrative, and solvable. They may not be trained teachers but given some brief training as with the earlier "normal-trained" teachers, they would be able to handle their classes. Their limited teaching skills would be more than compensated by their enthusiasm and English fluency. They would also bring much-needed attitudinal and cultural changes to the class. They would expose our kampung pupils to a different way of learning as well as speaking English. You can be certain these teachers would not be indulging in "Manglish" or "rojak" English, not to mention their improving our students' accent. These teachers with their different cultural and personal experiences would open the world to these kampung kids. That would be reason enough to recruit these teachers.

For those spouses of expatriates, this would also be a splendid and quick opportunity for them to learn and adapt to local culture and society.

The last and most expensive recourse would be to import teachers from English-speaking countries. The least expensive (in fact cheaper than hiring locals) would be to recruit from India and the Philippines. Some of my best and most inspiring teachers in high school were from India. That was then, however. Today I am uncertain whether bringing in teachers from those countries would serve Malaysian students well.

Another source, though not as cheap, would be Eastern Europe, specifically Poland. They may not be born English speakers but thanks to their superior education system they have acquired near-native fluency in that language.

Japan imports thousands of young Americans under its JET (Japan Exchange and Teaching) Program; likewise China, Thailand, and South Korea. Malaysia cannot match what the Japanese and Koreans are offering, about US$45K annually, but then living costs in Malaysia are considerably cheaper. Thailand has no difficulty getting foreign teachers for about 30K bhat (RM3K) per month. Malaysia could easily better the Thai pay. Foreigners, especially Americans and Brits, would have minimal difficulty adjusting to our roman script as well as other aspects of Malaysian society.

Thailand attracts essentially two groups of teachers: one, fresh graduates on a year or two hiatus before entering graduate or professional school; and two, seasoned mid-career teachers. Again, America provides a deep reservoir of both. Many Americans, especially those bound for graduate and professional schools (and thus among the brighter ones), take time off after graduation. These are the students who sign up for such programs as the Peace Corp and Teach For America. Malaysia cannot match what Teach for America could offer in terms of salary but could more than compensate for that deficiency with the adventure, experience, and exoticness.

As for mid-career teachers, there are plenty of them who have become disillusioned with the highly bureaucratized and increasingly alienating and violence-plagued American public schools. With their pensions vested and their children now grown up, a Thai or Malaysian pay would nicely supplement their retirement income, especially if living quarters were provided. In my view these are the teachers Malaysia should actively recruit; they would transform local students and schools.

Many rural schools have teachers' quarters. Most are occupied by religious teachers which Malaysia has a glut. There is no need to attract or cuddle them by providing them with housing. Reserve that for foreign teachers and those teaching science and mathematics.

Currently Malaysia brings in scores of American "teaching assistants" under the Fulbright Exchange Program, a government-to-government initiative. I fail to see why Malaysia cannot recruit American teachers directly and independent of the US government, unless of course those Fulbright "teaching assistants" are funded by the Americans.

Do not post those foreign teachers in isolation but group them, preferably three to five to a school. If they were to be alone at a school, their influence would be minimal and be diluted; it would be difficult for them to make an impact. In a group they would support each other and would serve as a critical mass to effect changes in attitude and culture among their students. That is quite apart from reducing the "foreignness" they would feel.

I had one such wonderful Canadian mathematics teacher at Malay College, Mr. Neil Brown. He was taking a few years off before pursuing doctoral work at Cambridge. He was an effective teacher; our class set a national record for the number of A's in calculus, but his impact outside the classroom was minimal. The local teachers dismissed him as a "hitchhiker." If Malay College had a few more such teachers at the time, they would have triggered a cultural change among both teachers and students. Their local colleagues would not be so disparaging of them. The locals might have even learned a thing or two from them.

This is what China is doing today. On a recent trip to Beijing I was surprised that the plane was full of teachers, lecturers, or professors on their way to teach at various levels in China. I recently read the memoir of one such teacher where she related how touched (and scared!) she was in that her students would more readily confide their problems to her instead of the local teachers. She soon found out why. Those students did not trust their local teachers. To them, their local teachers were but agents of the party or state.

A similar sentiment or mindset exists among Malaysian students. When I addressed Malaysians here in America, I was always conscious, as were the students, that there were representatives of the state, or more specifically UMNO (they are the same anyway), in the audience keeping an eye over the students. Not that it bothered me, but it certainly did some of the students. There were also representatives from the religious department, more for policing than spiritual guidance.

Their intimidating presence affected not just the students. A British educator posted in Malaysia once confided to me that his local colleagues and superiors were none too pleased with him when he included some of my essays for his students' reading assignment! It is such instances, more than anything else, that poison the learning atmosphere of Malaysian classrooms.

In recruiting these foreign teachers, I would look for additional skills that they would bring, as for example their ability in drama, music, and fine arts generally, as well as in sports so they could coach their local students.

Improving rural schools must begin with the teachers. Knowing the inadequacies of the education system generally and the teacher training program specifically, Malaysia would have to wait a very long while before she could get better trained local teachers. In the interim Malaysia should adopt the measures suggested here.

It reflects the national priorities that Malaysia has a cabinet level decision-making mechanism to import maids but not to bring in skilled teachers.

III: Reforming Education: Challenges Of Rural Schools

April 8, 2012 (*Third of Six Parts*)

Finland demonstrates the crucial importance of having professional, well-trained teachers. That is only one part of the solution. Provide these teachers with superior school facilities, as those Finns are doing, and only then could Malaysia expect miracles from her students. Kampung pupils are provided with neither. And we expect miracles from them. When they do not deliver, as you would expect, they would be blamed and bear the brunt of the negative stereotypes and presumed deficiencies of their race and culture.

What a terrible burden we impose upon our fragile young!

The first and immediate issue is the deplorable physical conditions of kampung schools. Many are unsafe, from roofs collapsing to unhygienic canteens. At first glance this is purely an engineering and public health issue, respectively. Meaning, get competent engineers and builders to design and build structurally safe schools, and have public health inspectors to check on the canteens.

Like everything else in Malaysia, the corrosive effect of political corruption intrudes everywhere, even and especially on school contracts. The roof contractors and canteen operators are at the end of a long feeding chain, after the economic parasites that are the corrupt politicians have had their fill. Then we wonder why school children are burnt to death from unsafe hostels. There is no money left for a sprinkler system or fire alarm.

It is a complex and systemic problem, and school contracts are only a small and not even the most lucrative part. So do not expect remedies any time soon, certainly not from the government as these corrupt politicians are it.

It is fortunate that in Malaysia the various professional bodies still retain some semblance of autonomy. One solution would be for them to hold those professionals accountable. When roofs collapse for example, the engineers and architects responsible should be hauled before their respective professional boards to be disciplined. Revoke a few professional licenses and that would send a clear and effective message. It would not stop political corruption but at least that would keep the professionals honest and, well, professional. The Watergate scandal of the Nixon era saw many lawyers disbarred, with salutary effect on the others.

A more direct and practical solution would be to stop building schools and focus instead on having factory-built modular classroom units. Put a few of these together, and with additional units for administration, teachers' lounge, and multipurpose use, and you have a school. The only local tender left would be to prepare the site to put these units, grade the school field, and pave the driveway. The monetary value of such tenders would be so small as not to interest the local political warlords.

With portable generators these units could be air-conditioned and equipped with satellite dishes. Then those children would no longer be disadvantaged, at least with respect to digital connectivity.

Put these modular units under shady trees and you lessen their cooling bills. With cool classrooms you could extend the school day and year. Those students would rather remain in class rather than be out in the heat of the day. I would use the afternoon for fine arts as with music lessons, "prep" time, and sports so that when these students leave for home it would be only to play with their friends, and to sleep. All their schoolwork and more would have been done at school.

I would lengthen the school year from the current 180 to 210-220 days, to match the Japanese. This is one area to "Look East." I would also provide lunches and mid-morning and mid-afternoon snacks to ensure that the pupils would get adequate nutrition. It is hard to get the attention of a hungry kid. Meaning, hard to educate them.

Next to nutrition is health. You cannot educate a child who is unhealthy, and you cannot keep a child healthy who is uneducated. During my primary school days in the early 1950s, there was a dental clinic at my school, and we had regular checkups. Indian and African school children are today regularly de-wormed. That is one intervention that contributes most to their improved school performance and reduced absenteeism.

Worm infestation was endemic during my youth as kampung kids were essentially *kaki ayam* (barefooted) at home and in school. Today with a better economy, they wear shoes. However, now with frequent floods, worm infestation may again be a major factor. We need solid data for if indeed this is a major problem, it can be readily and cheaply remedied through regular supervised deworming.

Enrich the curriculum with music lessons and singing classes. That would boost the pupils' confidence and spill over to their academic performance. This has been demonstrated in rural Venezuela with its highly effective El Sistema program, and has been successfully replicated in inner-city schools of New York. Singing is also the best way to learn another language. I learned English through singing Baa Black Sheep, as well as taking part in debates, speeches, and class plays. Those activities would not and could not be readily tested at the end of the year, but they contribute immensely to learning.

Kampung schools are also small; we should exploit that advantage and not let it be a liability or an excuse for not doing anything. For one, the teachers would get to know the students and their families well. Learning and other problems could be spotted earlier, and effective interventions instituted sooner. Rest assured that there would be no bullying or other anti-social behaviors as they would be spotted much earlier before they could get out of hand. America's Small School Movement championed by Deborah Meier is premised precisely on these proven advantages.

There are definite challenges to small schools especially when they are scattered in rural areas. Again, here we can learn much from America with her experiences in Midwestern rural states. A solution to the availability of teachers, more so the specialists as with music and "Special Ed" teachers, would be "clustering," where a group of four or five nearby schools would share a teacher.

Another would be the virtual classroom where you could have one room specially wired so students could be connected digitally to a teacher elsewhere. Technology could alleviate many of the problems associated with the isolation of rural schools.

Malaysia has a definite advantage in that even though her rural schools are scattered they are not as widely spread out as in America; thus travel or transportation would not pose a major problem. Malaysia also does not have America's problem of declining enrollment in its rural schools. It is increasing, which makes solving these problems even more pressing.

For those who think that my proposals as unduly expensive, consider the price for not providing kampung children with superior education. That would trap or condemn them to perpetual poverty, with dire consequences not only for them but also for the rest of Malaysia. A large component to the Bumiputra/non-Bumiputra gaps in educational achievement, as reflected in the recently released SPM results, is the consequence of this urban/rural divide.

In responding to these and other myriad problems, Minister of Education Muhyyiddin could not venture beyond the banalities. I wish he and his officers would tackle head on the specific issues raised here. You do not need to convene yet another expensive commission or blue-ribbon committee. Malaysia already has plenty of those. The problems are obvious; so too are the remedies. With some political resolve and concentration of effort, plus a wee bit of intelligence and imagination, you could go a long way in ameliorating these issues.

IV: Reforming Education: Enhancing Residential Schools

April 15, 2012 (*Fourth of Six Parts*)
Malaysian residential schools get the top students, have the best teachers, and consume more than their fair share of resources. Yet their aggregate performance has been underwhelming. When I visit top American campuses, the Malaysians I meet there are from other than our supposedly elite residential schools. That is the most telling indicator.

Residential schools cater only to Malays. Malaysia's oldest, The Malay College Kuala Kangsar, only recently (June 2011) started its matriculation program, the International Baccalaureate. Despite the luminaries on its board and the institution's special status, it took a full decade to implement the program. Imagine the glacial pace at lesser institutions!

Prior to that, the students had to go elsewhere for their matriculation, reducing the school (and others like it) to nothing more than a glorified middle school, and an expensive one at that.

This has not always been the case. Up till the late 1960s, MCKK still had its Sixth Form. For over the past 40 years the institution had been emasculated academically; the same with Tunku Kurshiah College and other residential schools. What a colossal lost opportunity for Malays, one that could not be quantified. My surprise is that Malay leaders, especially the PERKASA types, are oblivious of this loss.

The issues with residential schools are two—reducing costs and enhancing output.

Reducing Costs

The comparable cost for private schools in Malaysia ranges from about RM25-45K annually for tuition, plus another RM15-20K for full boarding per student. The facilities (academic and non-academic) at MCKK and other government residential schools are nowhere comparable to such private ones like Tuanku Jaafar College, so I would put a lower figure, conservatively at RM40K per student. That is still at least 8-10 times more expensive than the regular public day school.

The government bears the entire cost regardless of the families' economic status. One quick way to reduce cost would be to have parents bear some of the costs based on a sliding scale, depending on income and assets. Beyond a certain level they would have to pay the full cost; below that, nothing, the students are effectively on full scholarship. With the extra revenue the schools could enhance their curriculum and facilities.

The immediate impact would be to discourage well-to-do Malays from enrolling their children at these schools, preferring the much superior private ones instead. That would free up more slots for children of the poor.

Another would be to make these schools only partially residential, restricting boarding facilities only to those from out of town. Yet another way would be to limit intake from within the state or adjacent ones, thus reducing transportation costs, although that is only a minor component.

With the increasing urbanization of Malays, I would build these schools in the cities to cater to poor urban families. Then with most of the students coming from nearby areas, that would obviate the need for full hostel facilities.

Increasing and Enhancing The Output

As these residential schools get the best students, at a minimum their students must qualify for university; anything less would be a failure both for the students as well as the institution. It would also be a loss for Malays.

These schools must be challenged and compared with the best in the region, and not to SMK Ulu Kelantan. If today MCKK were to be compared with Kolej Tuanku Jaafar or KYUEM, the results would be embarrassing.

The most effective way of reducing cost and at the same time increase the output would be to eliminate the lower forms. Focus only on the last four years. That means taking in students after Form Three. Resources and facilities currently devoted to the lower forms could now be diverted to the all-important upper forms.

MCKK takes in over 100 pupils at Form One, but five years later fewer than 50 would be in its IB program. I would rather get rid of Forms One to Three and double up on the IB class. That would boost both the quality as well as quantity of the output.

One way of enhancing the quality would be for these schools to offer specialized programs. Some schools could emphasize the sciences, others foreign languages, performing arts, or sports. Or these schools could admit only boys (as with MCKK) or girls (TKC). The government recently started one specifically for the children of FELDA settlers. There could be one catering only to children of Orang Asli, or those who would be the first in their family to enter college.

I would have the headmastership of these schools be a terminal appointment. Let it be the job he or she will retire in (contingent upon performance). That would be the incentive for the individual to strive for a significant legacy. During the tenure, superior performance would be recognized by increasing the pay, and not, as is the current practice, by being promoted and transferred out.

It is a crying shame that Malay College had nearly twice as many headmasters during the past 47 years when locals took over than in its first 60. One local headmaster stayed barely a few months, just enough time to put an entry on his resume, before being promoted to be a functionary at the ministry. Then we wonder why MCKK has slid so far behind.

Other schools trumpet their students being accepted to top universities, but MCKK and other residential schools are still obsessed with and fixated over their students' SPM scores, with their graduation exercises ("Speech Day") attended by sultans and ministers. That, more than anything else, reveals the standards as well as aspirations of these students, their teachers, and Malay society.

The government is building many more residential schools. Each new one merely replicates and is being run like existing ones. There is little innovation—in curriculum, management, or philosophy. They repeat the same mistakes and call that experience!

V: Reforming Education: Post-Form Five Options

April 22, 2012 (*Fifth of Six Parts*)
In reviewing the recent SPM results, Education Minister Muhyiddin did not once pause to ponder what those nearly half a million 17-year-old Malaysians were doing since they sat for their test last November [2011]. These were the youngsters infesting the shopping malls, roaring around on their motorcycles, or otherwise getting into mischief. For over six months they would be unable to plan for their future. They could not even enjoy their break as their future is uncertain. The government's myriad post-SPM programs like Sixth Form, *matrikulasi*, polytechnic institutes, and teachers' colleges depend on the SPM scores, and therefore do not begin selecting their candidates until the middle of the year following their SPM examination.

This long period of uncertainty and inactivity during a critical period in a teenager's development is unhealthy. The expression "an idle mind is a devil's workshop" is never more true than for teenagers. Even if they could ward off the devil's machination, with the long hiatus would come considerable attrition of knowledge and good study habits, a critical handicap for those aspiring to go to universities.

Those parents who can afford it, and or who are not in the habit of depending on the government, enroll their children in the many excellent private programs in January following their SPM examination. Then when the results come out in late March or early April, they would apply to the various government programs which are far cheaper. If they were accepted, the switch would relieve of a great financial burden. If they are not, they would continue with their private program.

The monetary savings, even though considerable, are but a minor advantage. The far bigger benefit is that should they be accepted into the government's Sixth Form, *matrikulasi*, or any other public post-SPM program, they would be at least six months ahead of their classmates who had been idle. This academic advantage is even greater when you factor in the attrition of knowledge and good study habits of those who had been idle. This six-month advantage is almost insurmountable in an otherwise 12- or 18-month program (as with Sixth Form or *matrikulasi*), and would remain when these students go on to university.

Most Malay families cannot afford private programs, have not planned for the six-month hiatus, or have long been dependent on the government. Their children are typically idle after their SPM as there is no government program that starts in January. Come June, those who had excelled in their SPM would then be accepted in the government's many university "prep" programs. Then they wonder why they could not keep up with their non-Malay classmates who had been diligently studying in private programs for the past six months. Unaware of their already significant academic disadvantage from their being idle, these Malay students would then readily succumb to ugly racial stereotyping of the "dumb Malay." I meet many of these students here in America and feel sorry for the terrible burden that they bear.

Their burden is no less heavy should they enroll in local public universities. Then their Malay Vice-Chancellors and Deans would berate and chastise them for not "measuring up" to non-Malays, thus aggravating and confirming the ugly racial stigma. If only those officials had been diligent and studied the problem and listened to those students, those officials would not be so quick to resort to such counter-productive and offensive racial stereotyping.

As with the problems of kampung and residential schools, the solutions here are as simple as they are obvious. Again here, as the burden falls primarily on Malays, it is critical that we solve those issues.

One solution would be to begin the various post-SPM programs like Sixth Form in January, as in the old days. Have a special entrance examination in September, in time for the results to be ready by early December. There could be another intake in late March or early April for those who were unsuccessful at the earlier entrance examination but had excelled at their SPM. This would be a separate class, with abbreviated holidays to make up for lost time.

For those who enter in January, there would be a first term examination in early March. If they were to pass that, then no matter how poorly they performed in their previous SPM, they would remain in class and not be expelled, as was the practice in the 1960s. That would motivate them to pay attention to their first term and its tests.

Malaysia should have the original full 24-month pre-university program instead of the present highly truncated one. The objective is to not only prepare students well for university but also to cover much of the first year's work. Only then could we justify a three-year baccalaureate program. The added costs for starting Sixth Form in January would be minimal. After all, the teachers are already being paid. What are they doing from January to June?

Fully resurrecting Sixth Form in its original format without addressing its many shortcomings would be no advance. The old Sixth Form was too selective; fewer than 10 percent of my classmates made the cut. Related to this was the second problem; the not unexpected overrepresentation of students from the superior and better-equipped urban schools. As the urban/rural divide then also paralleled the racial one, it did not take long for the issue to be exploited by chauvinistic politicians. The third issue with Sixth Form was its narrow and rigid curriculum. It still is that.

The first problem could be solved by expanding Sixth Form. That would also be cheaper than expanding *matrikulasi* or the various universities' "foundation studies." Both in turn are of several orders in magnitude cheaper than the current idiotic practice of sending students abroad after their SPM to pursue essentially Sixth Form work.

If *matrikulasi* were to be continued, restrict the intake to students from kampung and other schools too small to have their own Sixth Form. *Matrikulasi* should supplement not replace Sixth Form, as was the original intent. I would have the universities run its own *matrikulasi* or have it subsumed under their Foundation Studies program. Each university would then design its own curriculum and introduce innovations and other unique elements with the idea of the government adopting some of the more successful ones nationally into its Sixth Form. Such a program would also be a resource to the universities' education faculty and teacher-training program.

Broaden the Sixth Form curriculum from the current five subjects to seven. Eliminate General Studies and have all students take Malay and English. Malay or English Literature would be separate subjects. Arts and Islamic stream students would have to take as electives a laboratory science and mathematics, together with their three Arts or Islamic Studies core subjects. Science students would take an Arts elective, mathematics (preferably calculus or statistics), and their three science subjects. Teach science and mathematics in English and abolish the current Islamic stream's Sijil Tinggi Agama Malaysia (STAM). Its curriculum is narrow and rigid; STAM does not serve the students or Malaysia well.

Introduce Islamic Studies as an elective for arts and science students. It would not be taught as a religious subject but as an academic one, covering Islamic thoughts, philosophy, arts, and culture but minus the religious rituals and Koranic recitations. The course would treat Prophet Muhammad, pbuh, as a great historical figure. Such an orientation would attract those non-Muslims with the intellectual curiosity to study Islam without fear of being treated as potential converts.

Instead of tinkering with the Sixth Form examination format, as with making the term examinations count towards the final as per the current proposal, I would retain its present form as a comprehensive terminal examination and use that as well as the student's year's Grade Point Average with equal weightage for university admissions and other academic purposes. This is the practice in America.

Malaysians currently pay too much attention to SPM. It is after all a middle school examination. When the results are released, there would be a national outcry over alleged unfairness in the awards of scholarships. Those SPM students who were awarded the scholarships could not enroll directly to a university or even a community college; they would have to undergo the equivalent of matriculation or Sixth Form first. So why not wait until those students are accepted to top universities before awarding them their scholarships? Besides, at this stage in Malaysia's development, the nation should be focusing on graduate, not undergraduate and certainly not scholarships for matriculation.

Do away with undergraduate scholarships except for those accepted at top universities. By this I mean the Berkeleys and the Ivy League category. I certainly would not award scholarships for colleges in India, Indonesia, the Middle East, and Eastern Europe.

Malaysian university-bound students should have solid 13 years of rigorous schooling. Do away with the present six months of idleness following SPM. Expand and diversify the paths towards university admissions beyond SPM, as with accepting IB, GCE A Level, and other foreign matriculation examinations.

VI: Reforming Education: Futility Of The Exercise

April 29, 2012 (*Last of Six Parts*)
There is another group, also exclusively Malays, that is being poorly served by the current system. These are students in Islamic schools. These schools see their mission as primarily producing ulama and religious functionaries; they are more seminaries. Their intent is indoctrination, not education. They are more the local version of Pakistan's madrasahs and Indonesia's *pesantrens*.

I would prefer that Islamic schools in Malaysia be more like America's many faith-based and church-affiliated schools. They regularly outperform public ones. They are also cheaper and produce their share of America's future scientists, engineers, and executives. Religion is only one subject in these schools, not the all-consuming curriculum. As a result, those schools attract many non-Christians. Contrast that to Islamic schools in Malaysia.

If Malaysia were to serve those four groups of students well, that would go a long way in ameliorating the "Malay problem." It would also be much more effective than squandering billions on GLCs, greedily hogging the constitutionally guaranteed special privileges, or incessantly spouting *Ketuanan Melayu* (Malay hegemony) slogans.

The converse is even truer. If these students were to be ignored, then it would not matter how much resources we devote to GLCs, how jealously we guard our quotas of public goodies, or how loudly we proclaim our superiority, those would all be for naught. Worse, if we do not serve these students well, that would be bad not only for them but also for Malays and Malaysia. What is self-evident is that we do not need yet another commission or a blue-ribbon committee to start addressing these pressing problems.

It is a uniquely Malaysian obsession to reform its education policies with every political season. Every new Minister of Education feels compelled to do it, perhaps to show off his political manhood or display his presumed take-charge talent.

I wish the old wisdom—the more things change the more they remain the same—were true. At least then we could be comforted that the system would maintain its old quality and standards. The reality is far different. Each reform brings with it a new low. For Malaysian education, the more things change, the more they change ... for the worse!

Malaysia needs a stable predictable education policy. Changes brought on today would not manifest their results until decades or even generations later. The nation is only now bearing the follies of the "reforms" instituted in the 1970s. Predictability and stability of policies would also encourage investments in the system. Textbook writers and publishers are more likely to invest their intellectual and financial resources if they were to be assured that the medium of instruction of our schools would not be changed on a whim. Likewise, investors would be encouraged to set up private schools and colleges if they were assured that the government would not change polices regarding enrollment, curriculum, or language of instruction with every election season.

Malaysia has had far too many of these reforms, reviews, blueprints, White Papers, and Royal Commissions. Now in her 65th year of independence, only Education Minister Muhyiddin is smugly satisfied with the results, declaring at the recent National Higher Education Carnival that the young are receiving better education than those in America or Britain. Wow! Talk about detachment from reality!

There was not even a hint of embarrassment on his part when he asserted that. Then with unconcealed smugness he added, "For those who have come to me complaining about our education system, it seems the [World Economic Forum Global Competitiveness] Report contradicts their claims."

"Carnival" accurately describes the event where he spoke, for that is exactly what Malaysian education is, with Muhyiddin the carnival barker. He obviously missed the part of the Report that read, "… Malaysia will need to improve its performance in … higher education and training (38th), improving access … in light of low enrollment rates of 69 percent (101st) and 36 percent (66th) for secondary and tertiary education, respectively." Those figures are national averages. If you were to dissect further, specifically with respect to Malay *vis a vis* non-Malay performance, the statistics would be even uglier for Malays.

Muhyiddin is beginning to believe his own spin. What or who he believes is not my concern except that the young of Malaysia (especially Malays) are bearing the heavy burden of his folly. He promised, or more accurately threatened, Malaysians with yet another "comprehensive" reform aimed at "transforming" the schools. Do not expect much; after all we are already the best. Such hubris!

This "comprehensive" review would once again consume the attention of the minister and his officers, distracting them from their day-to-day responsibilities. Resources would again be diverted to the hiring of expensive foreign consultants. Routine but important matters would be ignored and pressing problems deferred until after the "comprehensive" review. Meaning, they would once again be left to fester.

Do not expect much with this planned review. The education establishment, like the civil service generally, is insular and in-bred. There is little, in fact no infusion of fresh talent at the upper levels, apart from recycled ones from quasi private and other governmental entities. Those currently at the top, having been brought up under the present system, would find it difficult to fault it. That would be tantamount to criticizing themselves. I do not expect them to raise fundamental questions or challenge basic assumptions; they are more prone to "group think."

There should be a moratorium on these distracting and resource-exhausting reviews. There are already stacks of reports gathering dust in the ministry's archives. Their authors are merely recipe writers; they consider their job done with the writing. They are not interested in finding out the fate of their recommendations. I doubt those ministry officials have even read them!

A vast universe separates a fancy recipe from a delicious morsel. Metaphorically speaking, whether Malaysian students remain starved, flabby, or well-nourished depends less on the glossy pages of the recipe book, more on the ingenuity and skills of the chefs. They will determine if or when those students get fed, and whether with junk food or nutritious meals.

I would prefer that Malaysian educational chefs—the minister, his officers and policymakers—focus on a few recipes at a time instead of trying to remodel the entire kitchen. Study the issues thoroughly, learn from the experience of others, and then try them on small portions. Monitor the details of the ingredients and the cooking, carefully sample the results, and then once successful and with the kinks straightened out, adopt the recipe for national use.

A good recipe begins with fresh crisp ingredients; thus, I would begin with getting solid reliable data. I have difficulty getting such simple statistics as how many students at MCKK could bear the costs, how many would be the first in their family to enter university, or how many come from families where no one could speak English. Those are important details if we are contemplating the changes I am recommending here. Similarly, there is no solid data on what Malay students do in the six-month hiatus following their Form Five. That problem cries for attention.

Consider the abysmal level of English among Malay students. I have yet to come across a study on the challenges and obstacles they face in learning the language. There is no survey for example on assessing the English fluency of their teachers. If you do not know the problem, you are not likely to solve it. Worse, you would then think that you have already solved your problem, tempting you to brag and thus bring embarrassment to yourself.

Consider this glaring fact. With Malaysia in desperate need of English teachers, there is not a single all-English teachers' college. Few local universities have dedicated Departments of English. The government for its part awards far too few scholarships to pursue a degree in English. That is the measure of the "diligence" in "solving" the problem of English fluency among students.

It is precisely this paucity of good data, rigorous analyses, and plain rational thinking that prompts local officials to make ad hoc decisions and carry out their usual seat-of-the-pants solutions. It is also this mindset that leads the Minister of Education to make such outrageous claims as Malaysian schools being the best. And they believe their own spin!

Even if the minister's preposterous claims were true, there would be very little pride if those students in the kampungs, the residential as well as religious schools, and those left in limbo after their Form Five—all Malays—were to remain trapped as they are now.

The purpose of my exercise is not to pontificate on the issues or belittle those charged with solving them. It is also not my intention to imperiously diagnose the malady and then dogmatically impose my prescription. My intent is to ignite a much-needed debate. Only then could we appreciate the issues in all their varying facets and myriad complexities. That is the only basis upon which to craft a sensible and workable solution.

I am appreciative of those who have highlighted facets that I am not fully aware of and brought forth aspects that I have not considered. An American scholar suggested that I am underestimating the fear of Malay language nationalists (and Malays generally) to any prominence given to English. That the fear is irrational makes it even more formidable.

To my suggestion in my earlier book that Chinese schools should be identified less with race and more with its medium of instruction, meaning, a school using Mandarin instead of one appealing to a particular race, an activist with the Chinese school movement responded that it would be too much of an emotional burden, bordering on being irrational, for them to do that.

There is one group that surprised me for its lack of engagement—those who have spent their careers in Malaysian public education. I do get the occasional response, invariably from those who have retired! Recently someone important in the government kindly forwarded my essays to senior officials in the Ministry of Education. They responded by duly thanking me for my "interesting" ideas. Nothing beyond!

In the 1980s the Ministry of Education sent many of its senior officers on a *culup* or crash summer course at Stanford. I managed to interest a few of them to visit the area's best private and public schools. A few hours before the appointed time however, they called to cancel as they were going shopping instead! Then apparently mistaking my reason for the meeting, one of them assured me should I have a nephew or niece applying for a residential school back home, to let him know as he could "facilitate" it!

Trying to engage local public officials is like dropping smooth pebbles into a lake; there is hardly any ripple.

With today's digital revolution, Malaysians are better informed; hence the derision that greeted the minister' pronouncement on the supposed superiority of local schools. Malaysia has a long way to go, Muhyyiddin! In trying to delude us, you succeed only in fooling yourself.

Yet Another Report On Reforming Higher Education!

December 21, 2007

It is a sure sign that local leaders are way over their heads (or refuse to make the tough decisions) when they start calling in expensive international consultants. This is the case with Higher Education Minister Mustapa Mohamad's commissioning (together with the Economic Planning Unit of the Prime Minister's Department) the World Bank that resulted in its report *Malaysia and the World Economy: Building a World-Class Higher Education System.*

You can be certain that the report, 18 months in the making, was not cheap. That would be just the beginning. Consultants have a knack of making themselves indispensable, so expect even greater expenses when they are called in to help implement their recommendations.

Yet for all the expertise, wealth of data, and impressive comparative statistics presented in this 285-page report, its recommendations are nothing new or original. These include, among others, granting greater autonomy, meritocracy both in admitting students and recruiting faculty, rationalizing the role of the private sector, and emphasis on science, technology, and research.

What Malaysia lacks is the political will to make the tough necessary decisions to implement them. No foreign experts no matter how skillful their powers of persuasion are can help in this arena. The only hope is that with those recommendations now carrying the World Bank's imprimatur, the natives would be more likely to listen.

The World Bank's Report

The Report is divided into two parts. The first addresses or "diagnoses" the various issues like governance and financing, quality matters, graduate unemployment, and the integration of universities with the national innovation system. It begins by "benchmarking" Malaysia against selected OECD and East Asian countries.

No marks for guessing where Malaysia stands, not even in the same league. For example, fewer than half of the faculty at the University of Malaya, supposedly the nation's premier, has terminal qualifications, as compared to over 98 percent at Canada's McGill.

My point in making such obviously glaring comparisons is to wake up Malaysian leaders who are smugly satisfied as they are forever comparing Malaysia with the likes of Zimbabwe.

The Report highlights the universal dilemma of quality versus quantity with the democratization of higher education. One solution would be to emulate California's tiered model. Malaysia has adopted some aspects of this by designating selected institutions as "research universities." Designating alone is not enough and would be counterproductive unless accompanied by other changes, like much greater autonomy and increased funding.

The beauty of the California system is that there are enough commonalities and clearly defined channels to enable students to switch from one system to the other. This flexibility is necessary to accommodate changes in students' plans. Also notable with the California system is that each campus enjoys considerable autonomy, including choosing its own students and faculty. The central office serves only administrative functions like dealing with the legislature and managing the faculty's pension plans.

In Malaysia, the ministry micromanages every campus, right down to choosing the color of the faculty lounge drapes. I wish the Report would emphasize this point.

Problems With International Data

The report is inundated with cross-national statistics. While that is good for comparison and reference purposes, we must first however be assured that we are using the same measuring stick. That is easier said than done.

Take the apparently straightforward data on years of schooling. This seemingly objective criterion is anything but. One does not have to be particularly perceptive to note that nine years of schooling in South Korea would produce a far superior graduate as compared to someone with many more years spent at an American inner-city school. Likewise, comparing nominal figures on expenditures per student; a dollar at the University of Malaya would go a long way as compared to at the University of California.

Statistics could mislead the unwary or uninformed. Then we would be better off without those figures. Even a dead clock tells the right time twice a day; a malfunctioning one, never. Likewise with the data; bad data is more damaging than no data; a bad compass is worse than no compass. With the latter you would not be misled, and you learn to use your senses.

Studies on OECD countries indicate that it is not so much the years of schooling that matter with respect to labor productivity rather the workers' actual language and mathematical skills. Harvard's Robert Barro shows that it is not just any education system that enhances economic development rather one that emphasizes STEM that is crucial.

This is clearly demonstrated in Malaysia. The government's oft stated goal of 60:40 ratio favoring students in STEM remains just that: a goal. More important would be to raise the mathematical skills and science literacy of *all* students. Most American universities require all their students to take a year of science and mathematics.

The Malaysian data indicate that Malays have more years of schooling and fewer dropouts than non-Malays, specifically the Chinese. Yet the economic performance of Malays lags that of the Chinese. The reason is obvious. The education of Malays is heavy on arts and religion; Chinese, science and technology. When Chinese students drop out, they work for their parents' enterprises, be they mom-and-pop retail stores or roadside hawker stalls where they would learn important lessons on economics and life generally far more effectively than at school. Malay students would hang around waiting for government jobs. The only lesson they would learn in such an environment is that the world owes them a living.

There is one comparative statistics worth noting: the tuition fees differential between public and private institutions. In Malaysia it is about ten-fold whereas in America it is about a 3 to 5-fold difference. Narrow this by increasing tuition at public universities, coupled with more generous students' aid. Both would generate more revenue as well as reduce the subsidy for rich students.

Timid Report

The Report soft-pedals two distinct but interrelated crucial issues: one, the dangerous racial segregation of educational institutions at all levels; and two, the intrusive as well as destructive role of politics, in particular language nationalism.

The Report advocates the giving of scholarships for students to attend private institutions as one way of making them reflect the greater Malaysian society. I would go further and make it a condition for granting of permits. I agree. Malaysia should treat private and public institutions equally in the awarding of research funds and other grants. If these institutions are doing good research and performing useful societal functions, what difference does it make whether they are public or private?

Politics underlie most if not all the problems with Malaysian education. While it is impossible to divorce politics (institutions ultimately must respond to the political realities) nonetheless once certain objectives are agreed upon by the body politic, then let the professionals take over and implement them.

Take the teaching of science and mathematics in English together with the general need to enhance the English proficiency of students. This decision was made at the highest political level, yet at the slightest obstacle in implementing, an otherwise sensible policy was reversed. It is such flip-flopping that is so destructive.

The World Bank should have been more forceful in presenting its recommendations and in highlighting what ails Malaysian education. Had the Bank done so, it would have encouraged the many voices for reform from within the country. That might just nudge these politicians and bureaucrats to take the necessary bold steps.

Instead the World Bank Report was just be another expensive exercise, its thick volume being merely a decorative item in the offices of Ministers and policymakers.

For Malaysians, yet another missed opportunity.

Quality, Quantity, And Equity In Malaysian Education

Quality Education And Economic Development

May 9, 2010 (*First of Three Parts*)

In referring to the low quality of the Malaysian labor pool, the New Economic Model Report cites statistics showing that 80 percent of the workers have only SPM level (11 years) of schooling. That surprises me, not the figure rather the fact that the SPM is now viewed as inadequate.

That observation reflects more on the quality of Malaysian education than it does of her workers. Had the education system maintained its quality, meaning, today's SPM be of comparable caliber to the old Cambridge School Certificate "O" Level, then I would argue that Malaysian workers are among the most highly educated.

Members of the National Economic Action Council (they wrote the NEM Report) are old enough to appreciate that when they obtained their O-level certificate, they were in command of the necessary intellectual and other skills to prepare them well for life. The same cannot be said of today's SPM, as the Report clearly implies.

In suggesting that Malaysian workers should have more years of education, the folks at NEAC are falling into the same trap that had ensnared others, of confusing quantity with quality. For if the education system stinks (the Malaysian one certainly does!), then it matters not whether workers have college degrees; they still would not be prepared for the workplace, as attested by the already thousands of unemployed graduates.

As declared in the Center for Global Development's *A Millennium Learning Goal: Measuring Real Progress in Education*, "focus on the real target of schooling–adequately equipping the nation's youth for full participation as adults in economic, political and social roles."

School completion rate alone is an inadequate indicator of this. Likewise, generous funding, low pupil/teacher ratio, and physically grandiose schools and universities do not necessarily reflect quality education.

Consider years of schooling. One can readily appreciate that a year at an Indonesian high school is not the same as at a South Korean one. Even within a country, there are significant variations, as with an inner-city school in South Chicago and one in the heart of Silicon Valley, California. In California, the students are challenged with calculus; in inner city Chicago they struggle with "consumer math."

As for pupil/teacher ratio, South Korean classrooms are more crowded than American ones, yet that does not negatively impact the learning of the Korean children.

Earlier cross-national studies attempting to relate workers' educational levels with a country's economic performance used such readily obtainable data as the level of funding, pupil/teacher ratio, and years of schooling. Even with such crude measurements, economists were able to conclude confidently that workers' educational levels correlate well with a nation's economic development.

That could be the effect and not the cause. It could be that when a country is rich, it could afford to spend more on education, and not that such investments in education make that country rich.

Such studies also expose some glaring anomalies. Latin American countries have universal education, yet their economies have been underperforming. Egypt and South Korea spend proportionately the same on education, with their young having comparable levels of schooling, yet their economies are a universe apart. What gives?

The OECD made a cross-national study of its labor force focusing specifically on cognitive (in particular, reading, and mathematical) abilities rather than years of schooling. As can be appreciated, this was a much more formidable undertaking than merely comparing national statistics that may or may not be comparable. The findings of this much more rigorous study are even more impressive, confirming not only the earlier findings but also explaining the anomalies.

OECD has since refined and expanded its studies to include developing countries. The resulting Program for International Student Assessment (PISA) survey is sufficiently rigorous to conclude that workers' cognitive skills are causally (not just statistically) correlated with economic development across a broad spectrum of countries, from developing to developed ones. Meaning, a country could not develop economically if its workers are cognitively not up to par, regardless of the number of years of formal education.

The relevant cognitive skills relate to critical thinking, language abilities, mathematical competence, and science literacy. It should not surprise us that Indonesia, Bolivia and Peru remain economically backward considering that, as per PISA findings, the average reading ability of Indonesian students was equivalent to that of the lowest seven percent of French students; the average mathematics score of Brazilian students was equal to the lowest scoring Danish students; while the average science score of Peruvian students was equal to the lowest five percent of American students, despite the same number of school years.

Malaysia was not included in the PISA study, but it did participate in the Third (1999) International Mathematics and Science Studies (TIMMS–R) and scored somewhere in the middle, way behind Singapore, South Korea, Japan, and Taiwan. So is Malaysia's economy.

Malaysian leaders and educators do not like to be reminded of this; instead, they would prefer to focus on the fact that Malaysia is still ahead of Indonesia, Bolivia, and Peru.

The American performance in TIMMS was not impressive either. That prompted much soul searching among American educators and leaders. By way of contrast, in Malaysia I have not heard of any official pronouncements or seen academic papers on the subject. The only analyses done on the Malaysian performance on TIMMS were conducted by Malaysian-born American scholars abroad.

America realizes that she would need a skilled workforce to create innovative products and start entrepreneurial ventures that would drive her economic development.

The American performance at TIMMS illustrates another apparent anomaly. While American students lag those of Asia and many OECD countries, the American economy outperforms theirs. At first glance this would negate PISA's conclusion.

Two factors explain this apparent American anomaly. The first relates to the American curriculum and system of teaching. Since this is more important, let me dispose quickly of the second factor, that is, American industries, often supported by public funds, devote substantial resources to training and continually upgrading their workers' skills.

My hospital has a department devoted entirely to the continuing professional education of its nurses, doctors, and other personnel. American editors for example, regularly send their reporters to writing classes and to hear from luminaries in their fields.

For contrast, query any Malaysian civil servant when the last time he attended a course that would contribute to his professional development, and you would draw a blank. The response would be the same if you were to ask what professional journals he subscribes or reads regularly.

Returning to the more important first factor, while it is true that American students do not do well in science and mathematics, they shine in the critical and creative thinking department. These skills are not tested by TIMMS or indeed any pencil-and-paper test. The American curriculum, both at school and college levels, does not emphasize rote memory and regurgitation at examination time. Instead the focus is on critical and independent thinking. It is common for American students to have "open book" and "take home" examinations, a concept incomprehensible to Malaysians. American test questions probe your ability to think critically, not regurgitate textbook or lecture contents.

For those who find an "open book" examination incomprehensible, let me suggest some examples. If *Hikayat Hang Tuah* were a text in an American course, a typical examination question would be something like this:

> *The central injunction of the Koran is "command good and forbid evil." To what extent did the three main characters (Hang Tuah, Hang Jebat, and the Sultan of Melaka) have or have not followed this creed?*

For Shahnon Ahmad's *Ranjau Se Panjang Jalan*, a suggested question would be:

> *Describe three most burdensome ranjau (obstacles) faced by Lahuma (the central character). Imagine yourself the assigned social caseworker. How would you guide him to overcome them?*

Both queries would also be a good intellectual exercise for readers who have read the two great Malay literatures.

Those questions make you think. Further, there is no right or wrong answer. Such exercises in critical and creative thinking are the norm in an American classroom. It is this that accounts for the continuing innovativeness, remarkable resilience, and entrepreneurial vigor of the American economy.

Consider this; the American University in Cairo (AUC), which has an American curriculum and teaching style, has an enrolment of about 5,000, less than one percent of the total undergraduates in that country. Yet at the Egyptian Embassy in Washington, DC, a prestigious posting where only the best would be chosen, 40 percent of the staff are AUC graduates. The Egyptian establishment has rendered its judgment as to the quality of that institution, and by implication, the rest of the country's universities, including its most famous and oldest, Al Azhar.

Undergraduates at AUC are required to take such courses as "The Human Quest: Exploring the Big Questions," where they pursue such queries as, "Who am I?" and, "What does it mean to be a human?"

The Asian 'tigers,' their robust economies notwithstanding, appreciate the value and uniqueness of the American system of liberal education; they strive to make their own more 'American,' quite apart from sending their best students to America and the West generally.

Singapore consciously tries to do this but is burdened by the fact that it relies on current personnel (teachers, administrators, and policymakers) and institutions to effect these changes. As they have been brought up under the old rigid system, they are resistant to change. Never underestimate the power of inertia, systemic as well as personal. It is especially difficult for individuals to change as that would mean repudiating the very system that had brought them to where they are.

South Korea imports wholesale American schools, complete with the teachers and texts. As these schools are expensive, only the children of the elite could afford to enroll. That would be one quick and effective way of changing the whole system as those students would be destined to play key roles and or otherwise be influential in their country.

Japan brings in thousands of young Americans to teach English under the JET program. Although they are primarily for teaching English, nonetheless their teaching methods and styles would inevitably spill over to their 'native' colleagues.

Thailand recognizes the limitations of its current personnel and institutions to effect changes. She attacks the problem frontally by opening its school system to international schools, primarily British and American. Those schools are thriving there. Unlike in South Korea, these schools are more affordable. The ensuing competition from the sheer number of new entries brings down the costs. These schools are now within the reach of the middle class. Such schools would spawn a new revolution in education and other spheres in that country.

These countries realize that they must go beyond the numbers, as with the number of school years or universities, and focus instead on quality. These excellent schools are still far from being the norm; those countries still face the major challenge of access, and thus equity.

Trinity Of Quality, Quantity, And Equity

May 16, 2010 (*Second of Three Parts*)
The UN lauds Malaysia for meeting–indeed exceeding–the Millennium Development Goal of universal primary education. I caution against taking too seriously such praises. The UN works from the base of such countries as Afghanistan and Sub Sahara Africa; those countries should not be Malaysia's reference point.

The dilemma of quality versus quantity is old and familiar. Retired Malaysians wistfully remember the old colonial English schools. Yes, they were good, and when you scored an "A" then, you knew that you were on par with those students in London and elsewhere who also scored an "A." It was the same examination. There was pride of achievement in that.

When you cater only to a tiny fraction of the population, you cannot claim credit for the success. Natural selection plays the major role there.

Beyond the quality-quantity dilemma, those excellent colonial schools exposed yet another problem, that of access, and the attendant problem of equity. Being only in urban centers, they effectively blocked out those in the villages. In a country where the urban-rural divide also paralleled (still does) racial and socio-economic cleavages, that was untenable and a recipe for social disaster.

Malaysia has the added problem of equity to the already challenging quality-quantity conundrum. Again, this challenge is not unique to Malaysia. America too faces its own equity problem, with well-funded suburban schools on one hand and the dilapidated inner-city schools on the other. As with Malaysia, race and socio-economic class compound that gap.

Achieving quality but at the expense of quantity or equity is no victory. Quite apart from the inherent unjustness, it is hard for quality to be consequential in a sea of mediocrity. And if there is no equity in the system, it would not be sustainable.

Equity at the expense of quality is a hollow achievement. That is socialism—yes, we are all equal, but equally poor. As for quantity without quality, that too is futile. Besides, it would be doubly hard and more expensive to remedy a damaged system; better to create a good one right from the very beginning.

Addressing all three would require a prodigious amount of commitment, an awareness of the obstacles, and a healthy dose of humility. The commitment would not only be in resources but also and even more important, leadership and political will.

Resources are necessarily limited; they must be expended prudently. Throwing money at a problem does not solve it. That may spawn even greater problems like graft.

MARA spends billions to educate Malays through its expensive residential schools. The initial idea was great. Gather bright kids from poor rural areas and put them in residential schools where they would get good nutrition, modern living conditions, and superior educational opportunities. The impact would be greater than had resources been thinly spread through village schools, with each getting only a small fraction and not enough to make a substantial difference.

During the first decade or two these schools worked as anticipated despite obvious leakages as with ministers' children also being admitted. One wonders how much more effective those schools would have been had those children of the privileged been excluded.

Good ideas, like good durians, have a definite shelf life. Today with urbanization, there are as many urban as rural poor Malays. As such, fully residential schools make less sense. MARA could instead have day schools in the towns to cater for those poor urban Malays and thus save money in not having to house and feed them. If these schools were to have hostel facilities, limit them to those living far away.

Scrutinize MARA's budget for education; the bulk would be spent on such non-educational items as boarding. Yet in the statistics, those funds would be classified as expenditures on education.

Visit Malay College; the biggest building there is not the library or laboratories, but dormitories. The college will soon open its multimillion-dollar IB center. Again here, the bulk of the space and resources are not for education but to house and feed the students. Imagine if the center were to be a day facility like the old Taylor College, it would be considerably cheaper to build and operate. You could then have three or four similar IB centers for the same cost, and benefiting that many more students, thus achieving both quantity and quality. If we were to spread those centers around the country, that would also increase access, thus enhancing equity.

Malaysia could further increase quantity without sacrificing quality by restricting entry only after Form III. Taking in students at Form I (the current practice) not only wastes scarce resources but is also psychologically unhealthy. Children should not be taken away from their families at such a tender and formative age.

On a smaller scale but in the aggregate quite large, if we restrict admission only to students in the area, we could save considerable transportation costs. At present those 'education' costs are spent on chartering buses to transport students at the beginning and end of the school term. Think of the library books and laboratory equipment that could be had if the money were not spent on those buses and train vouchers!

It would be wasteful to have students from Kelantan attend MARA schools in Johore, while those in Klang Valley at Kota Baru. A generation ago that was a good idea as Malays were parochial then and lacked a sense of national identity. Thanks to today's mobility, that is no longer the case. Why persist on a wasteful practice that no longer serves its purpose?

Enhance equity by restricting admission to only children of the poor or those who would be the first in the family to attend university.

Returning to Malay College, it is a crying shame to see the decrepit facilities. This is true of all the residential schools, even relatively new ones. Some MARA schools are now asking parents to take their children home during weekends to spare feeding expenses!

Query the stakeholders and their reflex answer would be to ask the government for more money. Yet there is one obvious and ready solution. Charge the parents on a sliding scale based on taxable income. Even back in my days in the early 1960s there were quite a few who could afford the full fare. All of Mahathir's children attended these expensive residential schools for free when he was Prime Minister. Worse, he was proud of that fact when he should have been ashamed.

With the extra revenue from charging those well-to-do parents, the school's curricular offerings and physical facilities could be enhanced. More to the point, the thought of having to fork out those expenses might prompt those rich parents to think twice about enrolling their children, thus freeing up slots for children of the poor.

Similar more efficient allocation of resources could be had at the universities. Currently the bulk of the new admittees have only SPM. The university thus wastes academic and other resources catering to those doing essentially Form VI in the first year. If we were to expand Form VI and restrict university admission only to them, the students would not only be better prepared, but they would also get more out of the same number of their undergraduate years.

The universities' *matrikulasi*, foundation, and diploma programs are also a colossal waste as those could be undertaken more cheaply and effectively elsewhere, as at schools and polytechnics. Yes, there was a time when concurrently running the diploma program represented the optimal use of scarce campus facilities, but those days are now long gone. Universities should focus only on academic activities that could not be done elsewhere, that is, education at the undergraduate, graduate, and professional levels, plus undertaking research.

Scrutinize the typical university budget; the bulk (both operating as well as capital) is for non-academic purposes, as in feeding and housing the students, faculty quarters, and vice-chancellor's residence. Today's university is less an academic institution, more a major hotel with long-term 'guests' in the thousands. That is a necessity but there is no reason why such non-academic activities could not be 'out-sourced,' thus freeing the university of the onerous burden. Marriott, the giant hospitality company, feeds and houses students on many American campuses. If Malaysian universities were to do the same, they could then send their deputy VCs in charge of housing back to teaching and doing research.

Malaysian universities also have extensive housing units for their staff. What a waste. Some American universities also provide housing, but short-term to attract young faculty members who otherwise would go elsewhere. In contrast, housing on Malaysian campuses are for established staff members who are not necessarily academics. They would often stay on long after they have retired!

There is waste at another albeit lower (cost-wise) level. I once met a Malaysian dean at a scientific convention in America. He had first class air tickets and stayed at a five-star hotel. Had he traveled economy and stayed at a more modest facility, he could have taken three or four of his fellow faculty members to that meeting. Imagine the good that would do to his staff and institution, and ultimately his students.

His excuse was that as per the civil service code, he was 'entitled' to first class treatment. There we go again, that entitlement mentality! You cannot get rid of it even after you become dean and vice-chancellor.

Effectively addressing quality, quantity and equity would require efficient allocation of resources. That would require another commitment–from the leadership. *That* is the glaring deficit in Malaysia.

Prime Minister Najib exhorts local graduates to discard their *budaya menuggu dan pasif* (culture of waiting and passivity), yet he is blind to the onerous and intrusive rules that govern those students. It is akin to challenging them to explore the wider world but meanwhile keeping them on a tight leash.

Malaysian leaders keep reminding citizens on the importance of English, yet shy away from making that a requirement for university admission. They decry the lack of qualified workers in science and technology, yet when you examine public universities, the bulk of the resources are devoted to other than those fields. To reemphasize, effectively addressing quality, quantity and equity requires commitment of not only resources but far more important, leadership and political will.

Clinical Trials In Educational Initiatives

May 23, 2010 (*Last of Three Parts*)
In addressing equity, the focus and analysis should go beyond providing what would be perceived as "equal opportunities." For if the results do not improve equity, then we should have the humility to examine the premise and be prepared to accept that what we thought of as "equal opportunities" are anything but that.

We may think that making schools "free" would level the playing field, providing for "equal opportunity," but if the results do not show, then we must be prepared to re-examine that premise. It could be that the major constraint is not with tuition fees but transportation and other costs. That was certainly the case when I was growing up. To effectively level the playing field, we should provide for free transportation for those living far away. American schools provide not only this but also textbooks, another major cost item. For children of the poor, schools also provide hot meals. In short, to provide for a truly "equal opportunity" would mean spending *more* on the poor.

In educating children, be aware of the Matthew Effect, that of accumulated advantage. This refers to the biblical verse, "For those who have, more will be given ...." (Matthew 25:29). When we provide so-called "equal opportunity" to children on their first day of school, those who are already prepared (as having been to preschool or have parents with superior education) would gain considerably more than those who are not so advantaged, and this gap would only widen with time. To effectively overcome this would entail giving more to the disadvantaged, for if you continue with your "equal opportunity" you are effectively giving less to the disadvantaged.

The other pertinent observation is that the earlier this added help is given, the cheaper and more effective it would be. It would be much cheaper and more effective to give the extra help at the preschool than at first year in school; at primary than at secondary school, and at school than at university. James Heckman, the 2000 Nobel Laureate in Economics, has written persuasively on the economic advantages of these early interventions, quite apart from the moral arguments.

To apply Heckman's insight to Malaysia, it would be cheaper and far more effective to provide preschools than it is to provide extra *matrikulasi* classes. Having quotas in those *matrikulasi* classes in turn would be cheaper and more effective than to impose quotas later in employment. From another perspective, providing free preschools and serving hot meals at kampung schools would be far more effective and much cheaper than spending billions on GLCs in terms of making Malays better prepared for the private sector and being more competitive.

Apart from the commitment of resources, there must also be the political will. There will be the inevitable obstacles, from the passive and less obvious obstacle as inertia, to more active opposition from those who perceive themselves losing or at least not gaining from the change.

It is to be expected that those who have been brought up under or benefited from the current system to resist change. As such I have minimal confidence with the current personnel and present institutions being able to bring about these much-needed changes. Instead I advocate adopting the Thai and South Korean approaches, that is, wholesale importation of the American school system, its curriculum, textbooks, and teachers.

Begin at the very beginning, preschool, and then work up the system to primary, then secondary, and later, undergraduate level. Once these youngsters are used to active learning and creative thinking at the preschool, they would not tolerate the rote learning and dogmatic style they would get from their teachers in the upper classes. Those teachers would then have to change. It is much easier to instill new values and approaches on a fresh mind instead of having them unlearn their earlier-acquired bad habits later and at an older age.

Admittedly this would be a slower approach, but it would be more enduring and effective.

I would add a twist or two to the Korean and Thai experiments. One is that the student enrollment at these schools should reflect Malaysian society. The other would be that these schools must provide scholarships (full or partial) equal in value to at least 5 percent of their tuition income. The schools could then use those funds to balance the ethnic composition of their student body. Even in ethnically homogenous South Korea, there are already rumblings over the inequity of these private foreign schools, what with the poor being effectively excluded.

When MARA started its *matrikulasi* colleges back in the 1970s, it too adopted the American college semester and other styles. For the most part it was only styles, the superficial aspects not the core. These students had electives and were free from having to wear uniforms. The core ethos remained typically Malaysian—dogmatic instead of inquisitive; indoctrination instead of education. That has not changed.

Consider the Rwandan approach of supplying a laptop computer to every primary school pupil. Those children in turn brought about the changes in them to their families and peers.

The other group I would give free computers to would be the undergraduates. Once they have those laptops and the campuses wired, these students would have access to the libraries of the world and more. They could listen to lectures given at the best universities.

Malaysia has the added problem in that resistance to change in education is often camouflaged under nationalistic flavor. The excuse to rescind the teaching of science and mathematics in English was not based on merit or valid evidence rather on emotional arguments over dubious nationalism. Political will would be needed to overcome such opposition.

This problem is compounded by what economist Timur Kuran refers to as preference falsification, our tendency of saying something publicly what we do not believe personally. Malaysians all abhor corruption, but when stopped by a cop for speeding, their first impulse would be to bribe the policeman. Preference falsification makes problem solving that much more difficult.

Malaysian leaders keep extolling on the importance of Malay, yet they send their children abroad where the medium of instruction is anything but Malay. When I was growing up, my parents who were Malay schoolteachers were under tremendous peer and social pressures to take us out of English schools and enroll us in the then newly emerging Malay secondary schools. If Malay teachers did not support those new schools, who would, was the powerful emotional and nationalistic argument.

Bless my late father, he ignored those pressures. What fortified him, apart from inner conviction, were the actions of Malay leaders. While then Minister of Education Tun Razak was trumpeting the promise and virtues of Malay schools, he was quietly sending his children to Britain for schooling! My father rightly concluded that until those leaders follow their own advice, he would ignore them! My father successfully used that argument on his fellow kampung folks. Today, their children owe him a deep debt of gratitude.

After Tun Razak was Mahathir, the professed champion of everything Islamic. He expanded the Islamic establishment with Islamic schools and universities as well as Islamic 'research' institutes and judicial system. Did he send any of his children to Islamic schools or colleges?

Today, Najib Razak. He extols Malays to be *glokal* (combination of global and local), to be liberated from our affirmative action clutches.

How many of his immediate family members own and operate enterprises free of cozy *san* competitive-bidding government contracts.

The price Malays paid for Tun Razak's preference falsification was a generation of bright young Malay minds sacrificed to the altar of education nationalism. Mahathir's falsification caused another generation to be wasted through the needless pursuit of pseudo religiosity. Malays would know soon enough the price for Najib Razak's present folly.

Preference falsification is pervasive, powerful, and worst of all, pernicious.

An awareness of all these obstacles should be enough to make a diligent leader humble. A healthy dose of humility is indeed what is required when approaching these problems. I do not pretend to know how the initiatives I offered here would work in Malaysia even though they may have worked elsewhere. Ideas that seem brilliant and foolproof in the comfort of the boardroom of a think tank or could withstand the super critical atmosphere of a graduate school seminar room may still flop in the field.

We need to be humble and to think small first. Begin with pilot projects and field trials that are closely supervised, and then analyze the results. When the wrinkles have been ironed out and the necessary modifications made, then only would you expand. Anything less and you would be playing around with precious young minds. That is morally wrong if not criminally negligent. Those precious minds are *not* expendable.

The brilliant young economist from MIT, Esther Duflo [a cowinner of the 2019 Nobel Prize in Economics], suggested that leaders adopt the equivalent of clinical trials before fully implementing any proposal. Clinical trials and double-blind studies are the norms in modern medicine; they enabled physicians to advance from leeches to laser surgery.

Consider policies to reduce school dropout rates and enhance educational performances at primary schools, particularly for Malays. There are many brilliant ideas out there, from the giving out scholarships, as the British did way back when, to paying parents for keeping their children in school as Mexico's *Progressa* program, to the Australian government rounding up children of aborigines and warehousing them into residential schools so they could live and learn in a more "civilized" environment. The Canadians did something similar.

The commonality to all these undertakings, apart from their consequences, expensiveness, and massiveness, is that they were undertaken with the best of intentions. The results are also there and readily apparent, except that few are willing to learn from them. The Canadian government to its credit examined its residential school system for the natives in 1996 and condemned the initiative with such phrases as "an inherent element of savagery," or "kill the Indian in the child." At least the Canadians were honest.

Things need not be that way. Duflo tackled the perennial problem of school dropouts among African children as a research clinician would a disease. She conducted clinical trials. Among the traditional choices were paying parents, giving scholarships, and providing free books and uniforms. Then she added two non-traditional strategies: de-worming the students, as well as informing parents on the value of education. On reflection, both are not that non-traditional. De-worming was one of the recommendations advanced by a Malaysian Royal Commission back in 1960 to explain Malay underachievement in education. As for educating parents, that seems intuitive.

It turned out that the most effective strategy was to educate parents on the value of education, followed by de-worming the pupils. The conclusion: A healthy and physically vigorous kid is more likely to stay in school than if they are lethargic and worm-infested. Former US Surgeon-General Jocelyn Elder intuited this, "You can't educate a child who is not healthy, and you can't keep a child healthy who is not educated."

Traditional interventions like providing extra teachers, school meals, books, or uniforms have minimal positive impact. Interestingly, paying parents has a negative impact, at least with those African children.

Even after such careful trials and subsequent wider adoption level, you should still not rest on your laurels. As mentioned earlier, good ideas, like good durians, have a shelf life. With changing conditions, be prepared to continually tweak the programs and be ready to jettison once wonderful ideas if they no longer work, or that other ideas are better.

Residential schools were once good ideas; likewise, universities' *matrikulasi*. Today, they are resource-wasting endeavors.

Improving the quality, increasing the quantity, and enhancing the equity of the nation's education system are the prerequisites if Malaysia were to have quality human capital, and from that a robust economy.

The Role Of Private Sector In Education

Introductory Remarks

November 29, 2009 (First of Six Parts)

In the proposed Tenth Malaysia Plan scheduled to be unveiled next year [2010], the government would again re-commit to develop human resources through improving the education system. Malaysians have heard all that before, but the twist this time is that the government would actively engage the private sector.

I applaud this. There are many avenues for private sector involvement in education at all levels, either independently or in a variety of public-private partnerships (PPP).

Two points worth noting as Malaysia embarks on this endeavor. The first is that there are already many models of private sector involvement in education throughout both the developed and developing world. There is no need to reinvent the wheel. Instead, study these existing models, ascertain their strengths and weaknesses, and then adopt with suitable modifications the ones that would best suit Malaysian needs.

There is no point in adopting wholesale a system that works well in South Korea or the Netherlands. Their society is different. Theirs is homogeneous ethnically, culturally, and linguistically. Malaysia is diverse, separated by race, culture, language, and religion, among others. Failure to recognize this essential difference would doom any plan.

Second, no matter how brilliant and farsighted Malaysian policymakers are, they cannot anticipate everything. The policies they create could never be perfect. Even when the policy is sound but if the implementation were flawed, that would destroy and discredit the policy. That would make its later resurrection of what otherwise had been a sound policy that much more difficult.

In Malaysia there is a wide gulf separating the formulation and the implementation of a policy. There are many ready examples, the latest being the debacle over the teaching of science and mathematics in English. In the end it is the students, not leaders and officials, who bear the brunt of the poor planning and execution.

It would take more than just a bit of humility on the part of Malaysian leaders and policymakers to acknowledge and then accept this reality. They think they know it all.

When formulating a policy, you would want the greatest possible input from all sources, especially the stakeholders. The best time to do this is after you put forth your preliminary plan. Then post it on the Internet and invite written submissions from all. Go beyond issuing passive open invitations but actively solicit the views of key players like heads of private universities, leaders of industry, local and foreign educators, student and faculty leaders, and yes, even if not especially politicians. Make it clear to all that the plan at that stage is only preliminary and could be subjected to subsequent radical changes.

Post those submissions on the web so others could view them. At this stage the submissions would have to be written to ensure that only those who are serious and willing to put their thoughts on paper would respond. This is also an effective way to weed out those who are interested only in posturing and spouting off.

Asking for submissions before you have a preliminary plan would result only in unfocussed and jumbled submissions, as responders would not have an idea of the scale and scope of your proposed reform.

When all the comments are in, I would invite those with substantive ideas (as judged from their submissions) for direct conversations. Only after all that would I rewrite the policy incorporating the fresh insights and perspectives. That is the only way to garner the widest possible input and tap the wisdom of the crowd. It is also an effective way to make the stakeholders buy into your proposed policy as they had been engaged in its formulation.

Even after all that, be cautious when implementing it. Do some downstream analyses, anticipating possible problems and sources of opposition. If you could anticipate a problem, you are already halfway towards solving it.

Start small, with a limited number of pilot projects that could be easily monitored. It would also be easier to iron out the inevitable kinks, get feedback from the participants, and evaluate the preliminary results. Once all are working smoothly, only then expand the program nationwide. Anything less and you risk jeopardizing your policy.

Malaysia has yet to recognize the full potential contributions the private sector could make to education. There is no coherent policy governing it. What Malaysia has instead is a series of ad hoc rules and seat-of-the-pants policy pronouncements.

Private sector participation could lighten the government's load, thus enabling it to focus on the truly needy and do a better job at that. With its flexibility and responsiveness, the private sector would be in a better position to meet the increasingly sophisticated and varied educational needs of Malaysians. Of greater significance, the involvement of the private sector would provide much needed competition to public education, thus improving services all round. It would also provide students (and their parents) more meaningful choices.

Before that could happen, Malaysian leaders must rid themselves of their entrenched "zero-sum" mentality that views the private sector in adversarial rather than complementary terms. Otherwise all those fancy policy statements and earnest public pronouncements would mean nothing; the reality on the ground would remain unchanged.

Malaysia has seen far too many examples of ill-conceived policies, of sound initiatives incompetently implemented, and privatization projects that benefited only the few at the expense of the many.

Rationale For Participation

December 6, 2009 *(Second of Six Parts)*
Education, or to be specific, the language of instruction in its institutions, is an explosive political issue in Malaysia as in many plural societies. America still grapples with how best to integrate through its schools the children of minorities. Until recently Canada too had to contend with her own English/French language conundrum.

While education can be a divisive issue in a plural society, ironically when creatively handled it could serve as an important instrument for social integration. For Malaysia, it is critical that educational institutions should serve this important function and not be satisfied merely with their traditional role. American public schools have been remarkably successful, at least until recently, in integrating its various immigrants into the mainstream. Perversely, Malaysian schools during colonial rule, specifically the English language ones, were more successful in this integrating role than the current national schools.

Failure in this crucial role would result in a society that is highly educated but deeply divided, another Northern Ireland. The increasing polarization along racial lines in Malaysia today is attributed in large part to the failure of her schools and universities to play this crucial role of social integration.

Education in Malaysia has the added burden of being an important cultural symbol. The emotional and political significance of that cannot be lightly dismissed. Both can be overriding and at times overwhelming.

As such since independence, education has been under the tight control of the central government, with the private sector playing only a peripheral role. Recent moves towards liberalization may have altered the details of the landscape, but the underlying theme remains. The full potential of the contributions of the private sector has yet to be realized.

The move to co-opt the private sector in helping Malaysia become an "educational hub" has less to do with educational objectives but more with economics: the potential foreign exchange earnings from foreign students and reducing the outflow by keeping Malaysian students at home. The discussions rarely if ever were on elevating the quality of education.

Despite the rhetoric, I see no major policy shift. Malaysian public colleges and universities will continue to be under heavy government control, making them unlikely to shine. They will continue to suffer the same sorry decline afflicting all Malaysian public institutions. They will never lead Malaysia to greatness. Recent angst on the state of local public universities supports my contention.

Private schools, colleges, and universities, freed from governmental micromanagement, would be Malaysia's only salvation. Hence the need to nurture them. For them to make their proper contributions they first must be freed from government-imposed barriers. Private institutions do not necessarily need government support–though that would help–rather the policies need to be rationalized so they could play a more positive part.

A major stumbling block is to overcome the current mindset that views the private sector as an unwelcome competitor instead of accepting its legitimate role of complementing public institutions. Malaysian officials still have that old "zero sum" mentality, viewing the private and public sectors as two candles, one trying to outshine the other. They expend their efforts not on making their own shine brighter but on snuffing out the other. As a result, Malaysia has today two dim candles. The challenge is on making both shine brighter so together they would bring more light to the nation.

I liken the private and public sectors to the iconic Petronas Twin Towers, each block enhancing the appearance as well as capacity of the complex. Unlike the Twin Towers, there should be not one but many levels of interconnecting bridges between public and private educational institutions so students could seamlessly move from one to the other.

Rationalizing the role of the private sector is not merely to increase the number of private institutions rather in having quality ones that would meet the needs and aspirations of modern Malaysia.

The increase in the number of private educational institutions that Malaysia has today may not necessarily reflect a healthy development. On the contrary, that may be the consequence of the sorry state of local public institutions. Singapore does not have many private schools and colleges simply because their public ones are so superior. The National University of Singapore and Nanyang Technological University are such quality institutions that mediocre private universities would not have a chance competing against the two; likewise, her schools.

Alberta, Canada has few private schools. Even rich Albertans send their children to public schools. Their public schools are that good!

Malaysia is ahead of many developing countries in recognizing that the government is not the only entity capable of providing public goods and services. That is a recent realization with respect to education.

The advantages to private sector participation are obvious. With it partially bearing the load, the demand on the public sector would thus be lighter, enabling the government to provide even better services. This is especially true for a developing nation where resources are scarce and the demand heavy.

In a developed country the dynamics are different. Their citizens are more sophisticated and likewise their educational needs. There is no way the government could meet them. There the nimbleness and flexibility of the private sector would come in handy.

Malaysia is in between, with a sizable sophisticated population demanding First World level of education for their children. The vast majority still needs the basics. There is no conceivable way for the government to meet these varying needs and expectations even if it has unlimited resources. Nor can these varied needs be satisfied through a rigid single system, as advocated by some misguided souls. Instead what is needed is the flexibility and responsiveness of the private sector to add to the diversity of services and offerings.

Regardless, whether in a developed or still developing country, the entry of the private sector would provide much-needed competition. Properly harnessed, like all competitive situations, that would only improve services all around, including alleviating the urban-rural as well as rich-poor divide.

What Malaysia does not need, and be vigilant to avoid, is for the entry of the private sector to result in increasing social divide and greater polarization.

Malaysia should not expect the entry of the private sector to be welcomed. The public sector has been entrenched and acquired powerful constituencies. The teachers' unions for one would be rightly concerned about loss of job security, among others. Powerful political entities would equate the entry of the private sector to a loss of control. Under such circumstances it would be best not to confront those entities directly but to start afresh somewhere else, as with new schools and colleges.

This is an opportune time to examine and rationalize the role of the private sector in education. In the Tenth Malaysia Plan the government will commit itself to re-emphasizing the development of human capital. A critical examination of the roles and contributions of the private sector should be a major part of that planning.

The Current Situation

December 13, 2009 (*Third of Six Parts*)
Private sector participation in Malaysian education is today limited to the polar ends of the spectrum. At one end the private sector has unbridled access to preschool; at the other, increasing liberalization at the post-secondary level. In between (Years 1-11), private sector participation is limited and tightly controlled.

There is no coherent or comprehensive attempt to rationalize the role of the private sector. The result is a hodgepodge and far from a cohesive pattern. Instead of an exquisite cuisine with the various ingredients contributing to and enhancing the final flavor, Malaysian education is akin to a stew of leftovers, with a few new ingredients thrown in to add a fresh taste. The final concoction is more like dinner at grandma's house on the third day of Hari Raya; not quite rancid yet, but not refreshing either.

Private Preschools and Schools
The result of unfettered private sector participation at the preschool level is unpredictable. Some are superb, with the teachers, facilities and results matching the best elsewhere. Then we have preschools located near dumpsites or busy streets, posing significant dangers to the children. The standard of hygiene is such that outbreaks of foot-and-mouth disease occur with distressing regularity. As for their staff and operators, few are formally trained; none subjected to criminal background checks.

More problematic is that these pre-schools are highly segregated racially, religiously, and socially. Many preach a virulent form of ethnic, religious, and other cultural pride that would be inimical to the development of a harmonious plural society. Because of the government's "hands-off" policy, these sinister developments remain unchecked. That could haunt Malaysia later.

The private sector has a minimal role at Years 1-11. There are a few private religious (mainly Islamic) and vernacular schools but their aggregate contribution is marginal. The exception would be the few excellent, well-endowed independent Chinese schools. There are only about 60 such schools but they send more students to top universities of the world than all the other Malaysian schools combined.

Those independent Chinese schools may be excellent but their influence on the greater Malaysian scheme of things is severely limited because they make no attempt to broaden their appeal beyond their community. The association representing those schools is formidable and among the most powerful, ready, and able to challenge the UMNO ultras.

These private schools receive no formal public funding except at opportune times as during tight election campaigns. Then the government would make a grand show of its on-the-spot generosity. This happens frequently in Penang and Selangor for the Chinese schools, and Kelantan and Trengganu for the madrasahs.

If these excellent independent Chinese schools were to change their mission from being Chinese (meaning, catering primarily to their own community or clan) and instead be one that happens to use Mandarin as its medium of instruction, and then actively seek students and teachers from the other communities, then these schools would be my model for an ideal private school for Malaysia. For that to happen would take a monumental shift in mindset of their leaders. I am uncertain whether they are capable of that.

As for international schools (the other major group of private schools), only Malaysian children who previously attended schools abroad (as with children of diplomats) are permitted to apply. Admission requires the permission of the Minister of Education himself, indicating a high-level decision. Consequently only a few Malaysians are enrolled although the demand is great. This being Malaysia, children of the influential have minimal difficulty securing that permission.

Private Post-Secondary Institutions
A seminal development from the Private Higher Education Institutions Act of 1996 was the setting up of private degree-granting institutions, hitherto the exclusive preserve of public universities. Within the first few years of its adoption there was a mushrooming of private tertiary institutions, with the number zooming to nearly 600 from fewer than 50!

Such explosive development would tax even the most efficient regulatory agency, and Malaysia's is far from being the best. As a result, many of those colleges were nothing more than rented spaces over empty shop lots. They also had the lifespan of fireflies. Many of the permits were granted to those known more for their political connections and financial might rather than academic weight.

Those 'educational' institutions do not serve their students or Malaysia well. They excel only in having the rich part with their money. They are not likely to propel Malaysia into her next trajectory of development. Quite the contrary, they will weigh the country down.

Nonetheless amidst the pebbles there are a few gems, like the local wing of Monash and the University of Nottingham. These institutions have their reputation to protect, and they are precisely the ones Malaysia should encourage and support.

The other noteworthy private colleges are longstanding ones likes Taylor which began initially by catering to the needs of school leavers who could not get slots in public institutions. With the deterioration of public institutions, these private ones with their much-in-demand English instruction expanded to meet the needs of Malaysians.

Thanks to their entrepreneurialism and innovativeness, the likes of Taylor have expanded far beyond their initial offerings of 'twinning' and external degree programs. Today they grant their own degrees, even graduates ones!

Then there are the other major "private" institutions associated with government-linked companies–Uniten (of Tenaga Nasional) and Petronas University are ready examples. They are private in name only, for like their parent GLC, they are under heavy government control.

The major political parties too, UMNO excepted, sponsor their own private colleges. MCA has its Tunku Abdul Rahman College (TARC). The name is its only sop to Malay sensitivity. Meanwhile MIC has its TAFE and AIMST colleges, including (if you can believe it) a medical school! Unlike the Chinese, the Indians love acronyms for their institutions. Like the Chinese, the Indians make no effort to appeal to Malay sensitivity by giving their institutions local-sounding names.

TARC is the oldest, biggest, and most successful. It was MCA's second choice after Malay ultras scuttled its demands for Merdeka University. Unable to grant degrees, TARC initially focused on preparing its students for globally (principally British) recognized sub-professional qualifications. Because of that, and its emphasis on English, TARC graduates are in demand in the marketplace.

It is the supreme irony, one that has not dawned on many, that those Malay ultras had advanced the cause of the Chinese by denying them a university. If those ultras had acceded to MCA's demands of a Chinese-language university, what Malaysia would have today is another of the old Nanyang University, with its graduates well versed in the ways of ancient China but totally unprepared for the modern marketplace. TARC on the other hand produces sub-professionals with recognized foreign qualifications, precisely what Malaysia needs.

Deficiencies of Private Colleges and Universities

Private Malaysian colleges suffer from three major deficiencies. First, with few exceptions, their academic offerings are wanting. Their degrees and diplomas are heavy on such utility disciplines as marketing, accounting, and engineering. As for engineering I am uncertain of the difference between their degree and a technical diploma. In perusing the syllabus, the engineers they produce are but technicians, not educated professionals.

How could these institutions produce educated professionals when they lack a core liberal arts faculty or unit? How can you teach your students English and learn to think critically when you do not have the basics such as an English or Philosophy Department?

To date, no private university has a Department of Malay Studies. I would have thought that having a branch campus in Malaysia would have been an excellent opportunity for Monash and Nottingham to strengthen or establish their Department of Malay or at least Southeast Asian Studies.

Most of these private institutions are nothing more than glorified trade schools, catering strictly to the demands of the marketplace. There is nothing wrong with that, except that is not what a traditional university should be.

The liberal arts may have little marketplace value, but in the end that is what separates the graduates and professionals you produce from mere technicians. What makes the great American universities great, including the highly 'technical' ones like MIT and Caltech, is their strong liberal arts core and commitment.

I would have thought since these private colleges have limited resources, they would husband them and be more focused in their mission. Far from it! They typically have a smorgasbord of academic offerings, from vocational training to secretarial courses, and from diploma to pre-university, twinning, as well as degree and even postgraduate studies. All on the same campus and with the same staff!

Running any one of those programs well would tax even the most talented educator. These private colleges are trying to be all things to all people at the same time, or at least to people who could afford their fees. This miss-mesh strategy is clearly aimed less at improving individual programs, more on maximizing revenue.

Their anemic academic offerings are matched only by their mediocre physical facilities. Many do not have amenities one normally expects of a campus: No auditoria, sports facilities, or students' dormitories. While even the smallest American campus would have a sports team and a string quartet, even the largest private Malaysian universities do not offer these. For these institutions, anything not related to their students passing their final examinations is deemed irrelevant.

The biggest criticism is that these private institutions contribute to the greater segregation and polarization of Malaysians. They are essentially non-Bumiputra institutions; there is minimal attempt at diversifying the student body or faculty. Worse, these institutions justify their stand in arguing that they are only remedying the imbalance of public institutions which are predominantly Bumiputras. To them, two wrongs would make it right.

Diversifying the student body and faculty is a worthy goal in itself; it is not a sop to Malays. How can these institutions, private or public, prepare their students for an increasingly diverse global marketplace when the learning environment is so insular and limited? You would think that with the predominant Bumiputra population, private institutions would strive to cater to this market niche and at the same time expose their students to the predominant culture.

This racial segregation is worse because it is voluntary. There is no attempt at remedying the unacceptable situation. Educators in both private and public sectors are content with the status quo. This segregation does not serve their students; it is also inimical to the healthy development of a plural nation.

Many Malaysian private colleges are satisfied merely in being followers. While it is good for them to have affiliations like twinning and transfer programs with foreign universities, Malaysian institutions must carve their own tradition and path. At present most are content with being 'feeder schools' to foreign institutions.

What is very much needed would be the development of indigenous private schools and universities that would meet the unique demands and challenges of a modern plural Malaysia.

The Experience Elsewhere

December 20, 2009 (*Fourth of Six Parts*)
In envisaging a greater role for the private sector, it is worthwhile to review the experiences elsewhere.

In America, everyone is entitled to free public-funded education from K-12 years. In many states, that is extended to two additional years in junior college. While the government is not directly involved in preschool, there are many public programs for disadvantaged children.

Preschoolers excepted, most (over 85 percent) American children attend public schools where not only is the tuition free but so too the textbooks and transportation. There are also no examination fees. Contrast that to Malaysia where while the tuition is free, there are considerable added burdens of the cost of books, uniforms, non-tuition fees, and transportation.

There is no public subsidy of private schools in America, as in many countries. These schools are thus primarily for the wealthy. However, many of these schools recognize their social responsibility and provide generous scholarships to promising students from poor families. That is also a smart way to widen their talent pool as well as provide diversity to their student body. Many are supported by their sponsoring churches.

In Quebec, Canada, the province subsidizes private schools that meet its standards and prescription. Such subsidies reduce the tuition by as much as 30 percent. It is also an effective way for the province to exert influence over these private schools. It is not surprising that Quebec has a high percentage of its students attending private schools (17 percent as compared to 10 in America).

Chile has a novel system of vouchers. With it a student is free to attend any school, public or private, with the school collecting its revenue through the vouchers of the students it enrolls. The salient point there is that the judgment on a school's quality (and the decision to enroll) rests entirely with the consumer: the students and their parents. Unlike in Quebec, the government exerts no control over these schools. It is sufficiently enlightened to recognize that the best judge of a school's quality is not some central authority but its pupils and their parents. The market will take care of the mediocre schools.

Central to this assumption is that the performances of these schools must be widely distributed so parents could make informed decisions. Another would be no implicit or explicit obstacles to children of the poor from enrolling.

Thailand has another approach towards private—specifically international—schools. Its leaders recognize that the national curriculum is hopelessly out of date, but the teachers and administrators are incapable culturally, intellectually, and politically of changing it as they have been brought up under the system.

Thailand approaches the problem from a different angle by liberalizing the entry of international schools with their own curriculum and free from the controls of the Ministry of Education (MOE). The government still exerts controls but only in areas other than the curriculum. For example, these schools must meet certain physical requirements and be headed by a Thai national.

These schools must also be accredited by a recognized international body. That is smart as there is no way for those bureaucrats in the Thai MOE to competently evaluate those schools.

There are currently nearly 100 such schools in Thailand, not a large number but enough for a critical mass. These schools are not yet within the reach of the middle class, as in Quebec. However, as these students end up at leading universities abroad, and as they are also the children of the elite, they are destined to be future agents of change. They would not be handicapped or trapped by the rigidity and stultifying culture of the current system. The Thai experiment is worth watching.

A slightly different model is South Korea. There are private schools there but except for their being free of government funding, there is not much difference between them and public schools. The same rigidity, mindless memorization, and strict blind obedience to authority exist as in public schools.

To escape that cultural stricture, South Korea allowed many international (primarily American) schools with their independent curriculum and medium of instruction, as with Thailand. Two such schools, Daewon (established in 1983) and Minjok (1993), deserve special mention. Both use English exclusively, designed to prepare the best

Korean students for global leadership. At Minjok the emphasis is on "Teaching-Discussion-Writing," away from the usual memorization and regurgitation that masquerade as education in Asian schools.

The remarkable feat of these two schools is that their short history notwithstanding, they are now the biggest feeder schools for elite American universities. This being Korea however, the two schools still cannot escape their cultural trap. As one former Daewon teacher lamented, one of her students committed suicide on the day her SAT score was released.

Private Universities

Today there are private universities even in the most socialist of countries. Russia boasts more than 200! The most successful model is the American system of private colleges. If you take anybody's list of the top 25 American universities, the vast majority would be private. Private American universities also dominate anybody's list of the top global ones. That is reason enough for Malaysia to look closely at the American model.

First, a clarification on terminology. Those private American universities like Harvard are not "private" in the same sense as IBM or Microsoft Corporation. They are private but not profit making; they do not have shareholders eagerly anticipating dividends. Instead they are non-profit entities, akin tax-wise to non-governmental groups (NGOs). As such they enjoy considerable tax and other advantages. These universities are entitled to research grants from governmental agencies, and their students are eligible for government grants, loans, and scholarships, just like students at public universities.

In return, these universities would have to abide by certain rules, like subscribing to Federal affirmative action rules and non-discriminatory practices in admissions and hiring. It is this unique public-private partnership that makes American "private" universities shine.

There are "real" private (meaning, profit-making and proprietary) universities; DeVry and the University of Phoenix being two of the largest. However, they never appear on anybody's list of top universities. Their student body too is entirely different, made up mainly of working adults rather than those coming straight out of high school. They also do not have the campus associated with a traditional university.

Private universities in other countries are more like America's DeVry than they are with Harvard. In Malaysia's pursuit for private universities, the American non-profit institutions like Harvard should be the model, not the proprietary ones. They have their place and fill a void, but they would never lead a nation to greatness.

Many countries are importing wholesale this non-profit American model by inviting them to set up branch campuses. By far the most successful (that is, with the largest number of campuses) have been the Middle Eastern countries, undoubtedly facilitated by their oil wealth.

There are definite limitations to this wholesale importation concept. Even if I were to transplant *en bloc* Duke campus in Dubai, that university would never be the Duke of Durham, North Carolina. Try bringing a speaker critical of the government to speak on campus at one of the branches of the American universities in Dubai! Those countries that are enthusiastically transplanting Western campuses on their home soil forget one salient element. That is, what contributes to the greatness of Duke include the general social, economic, and political environment of Research Triangle of North Carolina specifically and America generally.

Singapore imported Yale. It did not take long for the faculty to be embroiled in controversies over restrictions on speakers at their campus. Like plants, cloned academic campuses do not necessarily bear the same prized fruits when planted in a different soil and environment.

This wholesale importation is not a recent phenomenon. Early in the last century, Western philanthropists set up the Peking Union Medical College. It quickly achieved its goal of being the Johns Hopkins of China. However, with the Cultural Revolution all that painstaking gains were destroyed. That institution has since regained its original premier status with the return of sanity in China.

Another successful experiment, also led by Western philanthropists, is the American University in Beirut (AUB), established in 1866 at the height of Western imperialism in the region. With its Western curriculum and teaching style, it quickly eclipsed such venerable institutions as the centuries-old Al Azhar. Today with the turmoil in the region, the luster is off AUB, but for a long time it remained the jewel in the crown of the Arab intellectual world.

Malaysia too has dabbled in its own version of wholesale American importation but with little success. The Malaysian University of Science and Technology (MUST) set up in collaboration with Boston's MIT was one. It would take more than just grafting the name of a prestigious American university to make a campus respectable.

A more enduring endeavor would be to adopt the concept of a western liberal education, with the help of proven scholars and educators, and establish your own institutions. The Aga Khan did this, setting up campuses first in Pakistan and then in other Muslim countries. Its success can be gauged by the fact that its medical school, established in Karachi only in 1983, has today acquired an international reputation far exceeding other long-established universities in that country.

What the Aga Khan proves is that what is important is not the building of fancy Western buildings or the pasting of a prestigious name that would make your institution great, rather the adoption of the concept of liberal education, academic freedom, and the pursuit of knowledge.

Malaysian policymakers must keep this uppermost as they examine the various models and envisage a greater role for the private sector.

Pre-Schools And Schools

December 27, 2009 (*Fifth of Six Parts*)
Private sector participation at the preschool level is robust; there is not much more that can be done to increase that. However, the glaring deficiencies must be remedied. One, these private preschools cater only to those who can afford them. No surprise there as they are profit-making ventures. Two, there is minimal regulatory oversight; it is strictly a case of buyer (or more correctly, parents) beware.

Private preschools catering to the poor and disadvantaged are non-existent, except those few set up by religious and charitable entities, as well as public social agencies. The government could increase that number by granting generous subsidies. As an instrument to encourage greater integration of the young, those grants should only be given to those preschools whose pupils reflect the general population. If the subsidies were generous enough, there would be plenty of takers. There could be a chain of brand name preschools set up all over the country catering to the poor and transcending racial boundaries.

There must be greater governmental regulations and scrutiny on these private preschools, and not just to ensure safety. Such issues as adequacy and safety of the physical facility, criminal background checks on the staff, and qualifications of the licensees must be clearly established before these preschools could be set up. The facilities should also be regularly inspected to ensure their compliance.

Private Schools

This remarkable increase in private sector participation in education is a global phenomenon. In resource-challenged Benin, a small West African republic, enrolment in private primary schools increased from 3 to 12 percent from 1990 to 2005, and 8 to 25 percent for secondary schools. That reflects the vast potential for private sector participation even in a poor country.

Private sector participation can take two forms: on its own, independent of the government except for regulatory compliance, or in partnership with the public sector (public-private partnership–PPP). Both would require an official recognition of the fact that while education is a public good, the government is not the only entity that could provide it.

As schools are concerned with the nurturing of young minds–future citizens–permits to operate a private school should not be granted as if one were dispensing licenses to sell ice cream. Even peddlers of ice cream would have to meet certain rules with respect to public health.

Private schools must be subjected to certain rules not only with respect to protecting its consumers (students) but also in serving legitimate national interests. An example of the first would be to require these schools to post performance bonds such that if they were to fail, the students would be compensated for their inconvenience and time loss. Beyond that I do not think the government has any legitimate right to demand that these schools follow the national curriculum or dictate the teachers they employ.

As for serving the national interest, these schools must assume their appropriate responsibility of preparing their students to be citizens of a plural Malaysia. Their students must be sufficiently fluent in the national language, and be familiar with Malaysian history, society, and system of governance. At the practical level, these schools must teach Malay language every school day and at every level. To prevent such classes from being a sham, their students' aggregate performance must match those of government schools. If not, they would risk losing their license.

All the current private schools–international, independent Chinese, and private religious schools–meet these minimal physical standards, except perhaps some of the private *tahfiz* and *pondok* religious schools. This is evident from all-too-frequent news reports of students succumbing to food poisoning or being burnt to death in dorm fires.

The greatest demand in Malaysia is for international schools, in part because they do not follow the national curriculum. That reflects how Malaysians feel about the national curriculum. These schools are still few in numbers and expensive. If Malaysia were to encourage the setting up of such schools, many more would be built. Then the wonders of the marketplace would take over: fees would come down making them affordable to more Malaysians.

As with everything else, we will never know how such a policy would turn out. It would thus make sense to start out small, like giving out permits for about 20-25 such schools initially and then study the results for the first few years.

My hope is that the experiment would be so successful that there would be unanimity to expand it. By that I mean these schools would provide quality education, their students flawlessly fluent in as well as proud of our national language, and their faculty and student body be representative of Malaysian society. The poor would also be sufficiently represented, made possible through scholarships. In short, they would emulate the successful "private" non-profit American prep schools.

Things could of course go wrong. There could be corruption in the awards of these permits. The schools would then be expensive, ineffective, and merely a repository for spoilt rich kids who would be illiterate in our national language and have no appreciation of our history. That would only generate a backlash.

Or these schools could be set up by extremist groups (secular or religious) bent on perpetuating their own brand of intolerance, or consumed on proselytizing rather than educating. That too would not be healthy. If these problems are anticipated, then they would be more likely and easily prevented and remedied.

Public-Private Partnership

The other avenue for private sector participation would be through a variety of public-private partnerships (PPPs). The World Bank recently analyzed the global experience with PPPs. At one extreme is the Netherlands where the government is merely the provider of financing, with the private sector the provider of services. At the other end is Chile with its extensive use of vouchers. In between we have charter schools (America), direct subsidies (Quebec), or where private contractors are engaged to run public schools (America).

Nearly two thirds of Dutch pupils attend private schools, which are either fully or partially funded publicly. This model obviously works for it receives wide support. Dutch students also consistently score at the top in various international comparisons like TIMMS and PISA.

If such a model were to be adopted locally without any modification, there would be the inevitable self-segregation based on class, ethnicity, or religious beliefs. That would not be healthy. There would also be the question of inequity of access based on geography, with the good schools in affluent areas and beyond the reach (physically as well as psychologically) of the poor.

The best for Malaysia would be to have PPP along the concept of American version of charter schools. Charter schools are fully funded by the state but run by private (usually non-profit) entities. The state would pay the school the same amount what it would normally cost for a pupil to attend a government school.

The main barrier to charter schools in America is that such permits are issued by the local public school board. That immediately sets up a conflict of interest because for every charter school it approves, funds would be taken away from the board's budget. Further, to maintain their charter status, these schools would have to satisfy the local school board, which views them as unwelcome competitors.

Malaysia could adopt the charter concept with some adaptations. The first would be that these charters be given only to entities that meet the openly stated criteria put forth by MOE. These should address the financial and academic requirements, specifically the qualifications of senior academic officers like the headmaster. He or she should have a degree from a recognized university and have specified years of relevant experience. I would also put as a requirement that the governing board has significant representation from parents and teachers.

The student body of these schools must also reflect Malaysian society with respect to race and socio-economic class. To minimize inequity of access based on geography, these schools must also have adequate hostel facilities to cater for those who live beyond commuting distances.

The admission policy too must be fair and transparent. Where there are more applicants than space, the school must have a fair method of selection (a lottery for example) to prevent favoritism or corruption. This would also avoid these schools from skimming the top talents. There must be exceptions as with accommodating siblings of present students and children of staff members.

As for the curriculum, the only requirement would be that these schools teach our national language for one period a day at all levels. As with private schools, the students of these charter schools must collectively demonstrate competency in Malay comparable to those attending national schools.

If at any time these schools fail to maintain these standards, they would be given a specified time (three years, for example) to correct the deficiencies, or risk losing their charter.

Schools that do meet the standards would get preferred government funding and credit for capital projects like new buildings and instituting new programs, in addition to their per student grants.

Beyond those guidelines these schools would be free to carve their own path, including the freedom to choose the curriculum and language of instruction. I venture that if there were to be a demand from a broad section of Malaysians for a charter school using Swahili, there will be one.

As with the private school initiative, I would start small, limiting such charter schools to about 15 or 20 each for primary and secondary levels per state. Study the development, and if successful only then expand it. I would also allow for the conversion of existing schools into charter schools, upon petition by majority of teachers and parents.

Malaysia should also be open to other models of PPP. One would be to have private entities (local or foreign) run a national school under a management contract. That would include recruiting the teachers to designing the curriculum, subject to the same conditions as charter schools. The difference is that the contractor would not own the physical facilities like the buildings and land but would lease them from the government.

My first candidate for such private management would be the residential schools. I would invite experienced operators locally and abroad to bid in running such schools. The contract would specify the goals, like the type of matriculation examinations the students would sit, as well as the costs.

Imagine the operators of Exeter running Malay College! We need not go far; we have many existing excellent private schools that could be encouraged, through proper incentives, to run these residential schools.

Another PPP would be the reverse, where private companies bid to build the entire school complete with desks, chairs, and blackboards to the government's specifications and then lease it back to the government. The government would run the school, just like any other government school. Canada's Nova Scotia's P3 is one such program. Such a scheme would lighten the strain on the government's capital budget.

The government, spearheaded by Khazanah, has initiated a PPP with its Trust Schools scheduled to be operational by 2010. It has wisely started with a small pilot project.

There are many commendable features to the concept, principally the granting of greater autonomy to the schools and the possibility of supplemental funding from the sponsoring private entities. However, this autonomy extends only to administrative matters, and a very limited one. For example, the teachers would not be civil servants, thus freeing the schools from the constraints of the civil service especially in critical matters of hiring and firing.

From what I can see from the preliminary design, a private entity would form a non-profit body to run the trust school. So far so good! Then this non-profit body would engage a for-profit "operator" to run the school. This is an unnecessary intermediation, adding another layer of cost structure (the operator is for profit) and administrative hurdle. I do not see why the non-profit entity cannot run the school itself, thus dispensing with the "operator." I can just see it: the awarding of these contracts to the "operators" would be yet another source of local corruption and political lobbying. I can predict who the owners of these for-profit operators would be—companies associated with UMNO chiefs.

More problematic would be that these schools must follow the national curriculum. The central issue is that the national curriculum itself is wanting. This critical point is missed by the originators of the Trust Schools concept. True, these schools are free to add beyond the national curriculum, but that is a meaningless freedom. The national curriculum already consumes the entire school day with little left for anything else.

Similarly, the freedom to prepare students for other examinations (like GCE or IB) is also meaningless as these schools would also have to prepare their students for national examinations. It would be a nightmare to design the curriculum and train the teachers. That is just not practical.

Lastly, the Trust School designers have not addressed the issue of access, specifically equity of access, and increasing racial as well as socio-economic segregation. I would hope that a condition for such schools must be that their students and teachers reflect the greater Malaysian society, and that these schools must have adequate boarding facilities to cater for those who live far away, specifically those from rural areas.

The opportunities for meaningful private sector participation in education, either alone or in partnership with the government, are limitless, bounded only by our creative imaginations and self-imposed limitations.

There is a great pent-up demand for a school system other than what is being offered today by national schools with their stifling culture and outmoded curriculum. We see this in the backlog of applications to international schools, and more dramatically in the daily convoy of school buses carrying our young across the causeway in Johor. Time for Malaysia to address this desperate need by co-opting the private sector.

Private Colleges And Universities

January 3, 2010 (*Last of Six Parts*)
As with schools, opportunities for private sector participation at the post-secondary level are also endless. At one end would be the completely independent proprietary universities free of governmental control except those that govern any private enterprise. At the other end would be the various public-private partnerships.

The advantage of being independent is just that. As Thomas Kealey, head of the only independent private university in Britain, the University of Buckingham, observed, "Every other university ... works solely to government targets. The government gives them money, and therefore they do whatever the government wants. .... [O]ur economic success is determined by our students' satisfaction. The other universities' success is determined by how much they please the government."

Kealey's assertion reveals something else, and that is the basic philosophy of any commercial enterprise: Give your customers (in this case, students) what they want, not what they need. It is not my purpose to challenge the legitimacy of such viewpoints or support the traditional view of the university as a community of teachers and scholars concerned only with the pursuit of knowledge and truth. Both types of institutions have their place.

Just because a college is private and free from governmental funding does not mean that the government can abrogate its responsibilities. They too must come under government purview like other private providers of services including hospitals and restaurants.

The purpose of regulatory oversight is to prevent and weed out fraudulent operators and institutions; that is, to protect the public (consumers) and the industry. Students must be assured that when they enroll in a private college and part with their or their parent's hard-earned cash to pay for the tuition, they are indeed getting an education and not be the victim of a degree mill. There is no way a regulator could prevent an individual with money and eager to burnish his qualification from getting a fake degree from fraudulent purveyors.

Such regulations would also protect the industry. If it were to be infested with shady operators and degree mills, then the industry would suffer. The value and marketability of the genuine providers would decline. This applies to providers of education as well as purveyors of Gucci leather goods. America saw that with its medical schools prior to the Flexner Report of 1910.

This oversight function gets complicated in these days of "non-traditional" learning. The line between a degree mill and legitimate "non-traditional" on-line degree programs can be blurry. A "dissertation" can be nothing more than a few pages of your "life experiences," and heavily coached at that or even ghost written. That these fraudulent operators are becoming more sophisticated is reason enough to remain vigilant.

One way to achieve this would be to have strict definitions of terms and clear criteria. Just as private doctors and lawyers must have certain qualifications and experience before they hang out their shingle, so too private colleges and universities must meet certain published and transparent standards.

Before any institution could grant a degree or diploma, it must satisfy certain academic and non-academic criteria. The former would include the qualifications of its key faculty and academic leaders, entry requirements, and quality of courses. The non-academic criteria relate to the facilities, financial soundness, and the posting of performance bonds.

As for the quality of the academic offerings, these institutions would have to acquire accreditation from recognized foreign bodies or the local Lembaga Akreditasi Negara (LAN).

LAN is not an independent agency; it is just another government bureaucracy. Malaysia needs an independent agency staffed not by civil servants but relevant professionals from both the public and private sectors. That is the only way to enhance LAN's credibility.

Once the regulatory requirements are met, any entity, foreign or local, should be able to set up a private college using whatever language of instruction it chooses.

Private, Non-Profit Post-Secondary Institutions

There is no model of a successful truly private or proprietary university anywhere. As such I would suggest adopting the American model of private but non-profit universities.

Like America, Malaysia should grant private non-profit universities tax-free status: free from income, property, and other taxes, just as with NGOs. Additionally, donations to these institutions should be tax deductible. The government should also treat the students attending these private institutions no differently from those of public ones in terms of eligibility for scholarships and student loans. Likewise, the government should not discriminate the granting of research funds between public and private universities; those should be given to the most competent to conduct the study. These universities should also have access to government-guaranteed loans so they could lower their funding costs for capital projects.

In addition, the government should give direct financial grants to these non-profit universities for specific purposes just as it has done to foreign universities like Cambridge, Ohio University (US), and the Royal College of Surgeons (Ireland).

In return for those privileges, these universities would have to agree to some mutually agreed upon and beneficial goals, like having their faculty and domestic student body broadly reflect Malaysian society. However, there would not be any rigid quota. The university should recognize that diversity in the classroom enhances the learning experience. It would also be a wonderful and effective way of preparing your students for the diverse global marketplace.

In short, these non-profit private universities would be like my proposed charter schools.

My concept could be extended to technical and vocational institutes. I envisage a consortium of construction companies banding together to set up a vocational institute to produce electricians, plumbers, and carpenters. Another would be a group of hotel operators establishing a school to train chefs, tour guides, and hotel workers.

In America there are many bridges between private and public institutions so students could seamlessly move from one system to the other at many levels with minimal loss of academic credit. This would accommodate families that experience unexpected adverse financial conditions making them unable to afford private universities.

On an administrative level, I would not put these universities and institutions under the jurisdiction of the Ministry of Higher Education (MOHE) as that would impose significant conflict of interest. Those folks at MOHE see themselves first and foremost as looking after the interests of public universities. They would see these private universities as unwelcome challenges to public universities.

Instead, these private tertiary educational institutions should be under the Ministry Of Trade and Industry (MITI). After all, the initial idea of having them was essentially economic—to save and earn foreign exchange—the same mission of the ministry. There is precedent for this. The International Islamic University is under MITI. That was also a sneaky maneuver to overcome the government's prohibition on the use of English in public universities. By having IIU under MITI, the university is considered under the law as a commercial enterprise rather than an educational institution, and hence could use English without incurring the wrath of the language nationalists. Brilliant!

Apart from establishing these non-profit universities, there are other avenues for public-private partnerships involving non-academic matters. On many American campuses, the food, housing, and many other non-academic services are run not by the university but by private entities, relieving the university of the financial, human, and other burdens.

Another would be for public universities to employ practitioners from the private sector as adjunct faculty members. That would not only supplement the teaching staff but also bring much needed practical perspective to the teaching. This is standard practice on American campuses. Many have taken this to extremes to the point of exploitation, with the adjuncts doing most of the teaching.

Like everything else, such private-public partnerships could undermine the universities core academic mission. A major concern on American academia today is to what extent these collaborations with private for-profit entities would compromise the intellectual and academic integrity of the research and the institution. In many instances especially with medical research, the findings are often tainted because key investigators are funded by interested commercial parties.

Such conflicts are seen even at such hallowed campuses as Harvard. Recognition of the problem is the first step towards solving or even preventing it.

The Malaysian government tried to loosen its stranglehold on public universities through the exercise of "corporatization" in the hope of freeing them from the tight leash of ministry bureaucrats. The result? Nothing much has changed despite the costs and flurry of paperwork and legal maneuverings. The reason is that the same people with the same mentality remain in charge, only their titles have changed.

Take one example. A few years ago the newly corporatized University of Malaya went into partnership with a private entity to develop part of the campus. It was not to build a new laboratory, convention center, or student residence, but an exclusive gated housing community! Not even under the most generous interpretation could such an arrangement be viewed as advancing the university's mission. The units were so luxurious that that they were beyond the reach of the faculty! Such one-sided arrangements are not the sort of PPP I envisage.

My criticism is not directed at corporatization per se, rather its execution, again illustrating my earlier point about a sound policy having flawed implementation. My proposals as outlined here would entail first a change in the mindset of those in charge.

A vigorous private sector involvement in higher education would lead to greater competition for public universities. That could only lead to their improvement. We already see this. The recent decision by many public universities to improve the English proficiency of their students is directly the consequence of the competition from private universities. Employers (other than the government) are preferring graduates of these private institutions over those from public ones. The latter had to respond.

Such are the consequences of competition. That alone is a good enough reason for the government to engage the private sector.

Affirmative Action – Malaysian Variety

Prize Our Padi, Uproot The Weeds!

September 16, 2018

I applaud lawyer and social activist Siti Kassim for her "Siti Thot" columns and commend *The Star* for publishing them. Writing briefs is second nature to seasoned lawyers, so penning those essays *per se* is not the challenge for her. The courage is with her sharing those views, and for *The Star* to provide her the platform.

Malaysians already know Siti for her many unpopular (at least to officialdom) and dangerous crusades, as with exposing the pathetic plight of our Orang Asli whose God-given human rights are being trampled upon with impunity by the government. For that she had been arrested, with pictures of her clad in orange. Siti is also one of the few brave Malays who dare challenge the Islamic bureaucracy. She and her family have endured many abuses, not just verbal and not just from the uninformed.

Writing in Malaysia is a hazardous endeavor. Ask Syed Husin Ali and Raja Petra. The late Kassim Ahmad paid literally with his life. I respect and admire our Siti Kassims and Kassim Ahmads. They are even more precious as there are so few of them.

Malay-owned media like *The New Straits Times* and *Utusan Melayu* have abrogated their responsibilities to keep citizens informed as well as to serve as effective bulwarks against the excesses of officialdom. That reflects a lot on and is emblematic of what ails Malay society today. Those entrusted with their duties are not up to the task. Worse, they have corrupted their mission. Leaders do not lead but are content with blaming their followers. Teachers do not teach but indoctrinate their students. Ulama are mesmerized with their oratorical prowess and exquisite *tajweed* instead of addressing the pressing problems of the *ummah*.

Islam in Malaysia is a lucrative commodity. It is less a religion, more massive bureaucracy, a government within a government. At least political leaders are answerable to citizens, as Najib and his co-bandits in UMNO are now finding out much to their sorrow. Not so with these Islamist bureaucrats. With their government-issued mansions, generous pensions, and gleaming sedans they are even more insulated from the *ummah*.

When questioned, their haughty response is that they are answerable to a much "higher authority," which means, no one. They are the Vatican of yore. When those nuns and priests were forced by modernity to be answerable to us mortals, many horrible things were exposed. Malays today are repeating that dark chapter of human history.

AIDS, drug abuse, and abandoned babies are rampant in Malaysia. Malays are overrepresented among the marginalized and dysfunctional, but one would not know that from the utterances of these ulama.

To them, anything not invented by the ancient Bedouins are haram; hence their obsession with *ribaa* without understanding what the term meant conceptually and operationally during the prophet's time. As some earlier semi-English literate scholars had translated *ribaa* as interest, Muslims today are consumed in a futile crusade against modern banking. They remain blind to the tremendous contributions to economic growth made possible through credit available through banks and other financial intermediaries.

The reverse is even more true. Put on an ancient Arabic label and bingo, it becomes halal, as with the obscene fees levied by those so-called Islamic financial institutions.

To the ulama, the minutiae of accounting of religious brownie points is more important than justice or the intrinsic virtues of a good deed. So many more *pahala* (merit points) for praying at a certain time and place! Seventy-two virgins for this virtuous act versus another. No mention of the comparable rewards for a righteous female!

As a lawyer, Siti is adept at cross-examining witnesses to expose their lies and inconsistencies. Her columns expose the hollowness and hypocrisy of Malaysian leaders, educators, and ulama. In her "The Real Malay Dilemma," Siti had this to say of those ardent, self-righteous "defenders" of Islam: "… Islam does not need protection …."

Amen to that! I would have also added, "least of all by these jokers in JAKIM!"

An earlier column of hers on education, "…. it's time to talk about the fundamental elephant in the room … when it comes to education reform in Malaysia—the number of hours dedicated to religion … and the influence of religion in Malaysian schools."

That is obvious to many and for so long, but not to these ulama. Nor do they realize that this heavy burden, and the tragic life-long consequences, is being borne by Malays. This cruel reality eludes even our PhD-decorated new Minister of Education.

Heed our kampung wisdom—*Sayangkan padi, cabutkan rumput* (prize your *padi*, uproot the weeds). As a society, Malays have not uprooted our weeds; our *padi* thus does not and could not thrive. Then we wonder at our meager harvest.

In a perverse and bizarre logic, Malays have gone beyond. To quote my late father, far from uprooting those weeds we have *bajakan lallang* (poured the fertilizer on those pesky weeds). On its own, *lallang* is already a tenacious weed, sucking the nutrients out of the soil such that even the lowly earthworms could not survive. What more if we were to *bajakan*!

Siti Kassim is our rare, premium *padi* but the Malay *sawah* (rice field) is already *lallang*-infested. The Ibrahim Alis and Jamal Yunoses have taken over. Worse, we *baja* them.

Siti personifies the Koranic injunction, *Amr bil Ma'ruf wa Nahy an al Munkar* (Command good and forbid evil). And they harass her!

A just Allah endows each community with its fair share of the gifted and talented. What that community does with that divine gift determines its future. It is not enough to pray that Allah bequeaths us with our share of Siti Kassims. More crucial that we value and nurture them. Most of all we must weed out the *lallangs* in our midst—the Ibrahim Alis and Najib Razaks—so our Sitis could thrive and blossom.

Applying Prospect Theory To Ending Affirmative Action

July 20, 2011

An insight of cognitive psychology (that sub-discipline dealing with mental processes like thinking and decision making) is that humans are far removed from the ideal of a rational self-interested *Homo economicus* (Economic man) when making decisions, contrary to the core assumption of traditional economics.

Two factors weigh heavily when we make decisions, given a set of alternatives. One, we are loss averse; that is, we magnify the value of a potential loss and minimize the potential gain even if the two are quantitatively the same. The other is that how those alternatives are being framed would very much influences our decision.

Although these insights refer to individual decision-making processes, nonetheless they can be extrapolated to the societal level, on how we collectively make decisions. This has relevance to the central wrenching issue dividing the Malay community today, on whether to continue or do away with affirmative action and other special privileges.

The example (minus the intricate mathematics and fancy graphs) used to illustrate the Prospect Theory (as this new insight is called) is the potential epidemic of an Asian disease hitting America that is expected to kill 600 people. When asked to choose between an intervention that would save 200 people and another that would have a 1/3 probability that 600 people would be saved with 2/3 probability that no one would, most would approve the first. Both propositions state the same thing. The first framed it more positively with the element of undue certainty thrown in.

There are other variations on the same theme. We willingly drive across town to save $5 on a $15 calculator but not on a $125 suit. The savings are the same—$5 in both cases—but the deciding factor is the framing. Never mind that you spend $10 on gas to drive across town! Marketers make full use of these insights of cognitive psychology when advertising their products; thus retailers' grabbing banners: "Fifty percent savings!"

Returning to the difficult issue of affirmative action, we have made it unduly contentious as we have framed it unwisely. One, we have stated it as taking away special privileges. Being risk averse, we rightly reject that. Two, we have framed special privileges as being part of our character, our right by virtue of being the indigenous people. We forget that affirmative action was instituted for the explicit purpose of overcoming disadvantages we suffered under colonialism. Those privileges were meant to jumpstart our development so we could be on par with the rest of the community.

New Frame of Reference
We can deal with the issue of special privileges more effectively and less acrimoniously by tapping the wisdom of modern cognitive psychology. First, we must reframe the discussion differently, away from privileges and the taking away of those, to the more general but pertinent issue of

enhancing Malay competitiveness; and second, amplify the benefits and minimize or lessen the loss of doing away with these crutches.

By making affirmative action part of the Malay culture and character, we have made it difficult to critically examine it. No matter how noble in intention and beneficial the results, any scrutiny would be viewed as an attack on Malay values, character, and heritage. Those are formidable obstacles.

If we were to focus instead not on special privileges *per se* but on how to prepare Malays for this new highly competitive economy, then we would be on to something. I would eschew any talk of doing away with special privileges; all that does is to inflame passions and further polarize Malaysians. Once Malays are competitive, then the need for special privileges would simply melt away. Then we can talk about ending them more rationally as they would have become irrelevant in the lives of most Malays.

What made affirmative action so highly effective at its inception was its emphasis on education and rural development. Under Tun Razak, schools were literally mushrooming in the villages, bringing both development and education. I vividly recall that in the seven-mile bus ride from home to my high school in town, there were no fewer than seven primary schools being built! In the afternoon when the children were finished, those schools would still be full, this time with adults attending literacy classes.

The emphasis on rural development made great sense. The overwhelming majority of Malays were rural dwellers. Under FELDA, massive land development schemes were initiated, with mass relocations of landless kampung folks, an internal migration of sorts, so they could begin a new life away from the stifling atmosphere of their old villages. Its sterling success in mass relocating poor people remains the only shining example in the world up to this day.

Today the noble mission of FELDA has been hijacked, the entity itself being "corporatized," just another government-linked company (GLC). Tell me, how does the building of a RM 670 million headquarters in the glittering part of KL make those FELDA settlers in Ulu Pahang more competitive? Headquarters are nothing but expensive overhead. Likewise, I fail to see how FELDA's plantations abroad would help the poor people back in my old kampung.

The same questions on the billions spent on GLCs. Najib, like his predecessor Abdullah, could not find a GLC he did not love. He and other Malays accepted that because those expenditures were framed as furthering NEP and not on the more pertinent issue of making Malays competitive. Had we done the latter, then those funds would be better off diverted to making national schools have the best facilities and teachers, and those FELDA settlers have electricity and potable water.

Maximize The Gain, Minimize The Loss

The other insight is on risk aversion. For us to favor a decision, we must be convinced that the promised gains would vastly outweigh the potential loss, and that the majority would benefit while the loss suffered only by a minority, preferably one the majority is not enamored with.

If we dispense with inflated contracts to UMNO cronies and instead get the best price through competitive bidding, then we could build two schools for the price of one. Even if that contract were to be won by a non-Malay or even a foreigner, the benefits would fall on the hundreds more Malay families whose children would now have safer and better schools. The losers would be the handful of UMNO-connected "contractors" and Ali Baba "entrepreneurs." Again, many more gainers with far fewer losers! Besides, those losers are the types the community would have difficulty identifying or sympathizing with.

Had the billions spent on GLCs been diverted to improving schools and universities, as with recruiting superior teachers and professors, thousands would benefit. The losers would be few, those has-been politicians and near-retirement civil servants seeking cushy corporate jobs. Again, those are the people we do not readily sympathize or identify with.

Sell all those GLCs including and especially such jewels as Petronas and MAS. Put the proceeds in a trust fund with the returns to be used exclusively for education and improving the lives of the poor. It is far more important to train young Malays to be pilots, airline mechanics, geologists, and petroleum engineers than for Malaysia to own an airline or oil company.

One big benefit to selling those GLCs would be to eliminate a major source of undue lobbying and influence peddling by politicians and senior civil servants. Currently they, especially the near-retirement civil servants, are preoccupied with ingratiating themselves to their political superiors in the hope of securing a coveted chairmanship of a GLC on retirement from government service. With that no longer an option, these civil servants would then be emboldened to challenge their political superiors should they embark on some silly policies. Were that to happen, Malaysia would have a far superior civil service, and the nation would benefit.

By getting rid of these GLCs, those highly accomplished Malays presently there would be free to sell their talents to the highest bidder and be appropriately compensated. At present they are being unfairly taken advantage of, in fact seduced by such silly sentiments as national service and misguided notions of patriotism.

As for the less talented ones who infest those loss ridden GLCs, well, those companies were not created to be public work projects for them.

The other reality to the discussions on special privileges is this. If today we were to embark on a policy to enhance Malay competitiveness, assuming it is highly effective, it would take a while for its results to be apparent. Further, we do not know nor can predict specific potential winners except for the amorphous "Malay masses" and the aggregate results. Hence there would be no one to lobby or vigorously advocate for those changes.

On the other hand, if we were to terminate affirmative action today, the losers would feel their loss right away. Not being saints, they will fight that, and do so vigorously. They would be the first to be on the streets protesting, as those in PERKASA are doing. That's predictable.

This dilemma is the greatest challenge facing policymakers everywhere, especially in a democratic society. China does not have that problem. It could bulldoze any policy and not have to worry about public protests. That would be great if the country has enlightened leaders. Under Mao, it was a disaster.

It would take an extraordinarily enlightened and farsighted leader in a democracy to achieve this, someone focused on the long term and not on the next election. Such leaders would need to tap the wisdom of others, including that of behavioral economists and cognitive psychologists.

It is unfortunate for Malays and Malaysians that their current leaders are content with parroting the latest buzzwords while their long-term strategy never extends beyond the next party elections. Self-interested they very much are, rational thinkers or wise leaders, they are not.

Old Habits Die Hard With Malaysia's Five-Year Plans

June 30, 2010

The old Soviet Union may have long ago crumbled, but the underlying mindset–the penchant to control and "plan" everything from the center– still has a tenacious hold, and not just on Russian leaders.

Joseph Stalin initiated the first Five Year Plan, incorporating Lenin's New Economic Plan (NEP). However, not many would associate Five-Year Plans with Stalin, as he had acquired other notorieties.

It is ironic that 82 years later, an avowedly anti-communist Malaysia would still embrace Five Year Plans and NEP with gusto. The last Soviet Five-Year Plan was its 12th; the collapse of the Empire took care of the 13th. Even the Communist Chinese have wised up; they now call their "Plan" only a "guideline."

A century hence Malaysia would still be unveiling its latest umpteenth Malaysia Plan (MP). In tone and substance, I predict it would be like the current Tenth MP and all earlier ones. It would boast of the nation's wonderful attributes, and how fortunate Malaysians are to have such farsighted leaders. Then realizing the incongruity of such lavish praises with the need for yet another plan, the report would lament the squandered opportunities of the past.

Then just like the current Tenth MP, it would bravely call for a "transformation plan to become a high income, developed, resilient and competitive nation," and exhort Malaysians to "think outside the box," peppering its report with such phrases as "holistic measures," "development with equity," and other clichés of the time.

If Malaysia were to aspire for developed status–the stated objective of all these Plans–then at least learn from those who are already there. None of them have Five Year Plans. That should be a hint to abandon this whole notion of five-year plans and the attendant "command and control" mindset.

The Straight Jacket of a Five-Year Timetable

There is nothing magical about a five-year time span. At least with a decade, a child becomes a teenager, and a pimply teenager a young adult. Five years? There is no correlate in nature.

Five years would be an eon in Information Technology. Today few remember Netscape, much less use it as a browser. You need a much shorter time span in planning and be incredibly nimble to survive in that industry.

On the other hand, five years is but a fleeting moment with education. Here planning should span decades. Malaysia is only now seeing the follies of the changes instituted back in the 1970s. Likewise with trade and investment policies; investors need a stable environment so their investments would not be subjected to the latest political intrigue or capricious regulatory changes.

Canada best demonstrates this wisdom. It is not surprising that its banks remain robust despite the current global financial crisis. There, legislations governing financial institutions are reviewed only every five years (previously every ten). As a result, its banks and bankers are not seduced by the latest financial fashions and "fintechs" that had snared their hip colleagues in America, Iceland, and elsewhere.

Instead of an all-encompassing five-year plan, Malaysia should opt for a sectoral approach. For education, a ten-year plan would be wise; likewise trade and investment policies. For agriculture, the traditional five-year plan—the time span for a rubber or palm sapling to reach maturity—would be appropriate.

These repeated five-year plans are disruptive. Near the end of the current plan would invariably be consumed with planning for the next, a major distraction from executing the projects at hand. There is no hiatus between plans, and thus no opportunity to pause and learn. The learning curve is flat, the same mistakes repeated umpteen times. Then just as the plan gets going, it would be time for the "mid-term review," an exercise less in reviewing, more excuse-finding.

Then there would be the long lapse between planning and execution. By the time a project is completed, the original assumptions would have changed substantially. Consider the addition to the hospital in Johor Baru where I was attached. It was mulled during the Second MP but did not get funded until the Third. When it was completed in the Fourth MP, it proved hopelessly inadequate with the vastly increased demands.

Now that the Ninth MP is coming to close, I predict that many of its projects either remain incomplete or not yet even started. I once suggested that the sole objective of the next plan should be to complete all those incomplete projects of earlier plans. I did not get praised for that practical suggestion!

Events and circumstances also have the habit of upending even the best laid plans, as the 1997 Asian economic contagion did to the Seventh MP. I thought that experience would have disabused Malaysian leaders of their obsession with Five Year Plans.

Disconnect From Reality

Like its predecessors, this Tenth MP has a glaring disconnect from reality. Only days earlier a minister in Najib's own department warned of impending bankruptcy should we stay the present fiscal course, specifically with respect to subsidies. The Tenth MP only perfunctorily addresses the issue with the promise to rationalize "energy pricing gradually to match market price." Only a promise, no concrete actions!

A few months earlier, the National Economic Action Council (a unit of the Prime Minister's office) unveiled its brave New Economic Model (NEM), one cognizant of market realities and the need to be competitive instead of hiding behind protective barriers and special set-aside programs. Or so it claimed.

Alas only the talk was brave, the courage was fleeting. NEM was an exercise in futility. The Najib Razak who earlier boldly challenged Malaysia to transform itself was easily *gertak* (threatened) by the likes of Ibrahim Ali, the populous critic of NEM.

If Najib could easily be made to capitulate by a two-bit politician from the *ulu* of Kelantan, I wonder how he would fare with tough foreign leaders. No wonder the contested Limbang oilfield ended up being given to Brunei, a real tough adversary! What next?

The major concerns of Malaysians are rampant corruption, escalating crime, and an ill-disciplined police force. Yet, hardly a word on those! Not that it would have made any difference. The Ninth MP's remedy for corruption was to rename the anti-corruption agency and set up the National Integrity Institute. Meanwhile corruption remains unabated.

The few good ideas in the Tenth MP, if competently executed (a huge caveat!), would be positive developments. The explicit commitment away from physical to non-physical infrastructure, specifically human capital development, is one. I also applaud the expansion of preschools, lowering to five years the age for entering primary school (only a consideration at this stage), and enhancing the qualifications of primary school teachers.

Old habits die hard; in Malaysia, they never do. Najib could not wean himself from his dependency on GLCs despite their abysmal performances. This Plan, like its predecessors, spawns its own set of GLCs. Nor could Najib unhook himself from the "30 Percent Bumiputra Equity Participation" obsession, despite the irrelevance of that figure and objective.

In his effort to recruit foreign talent, Najib predictably set up the Talent Corporation, another GLC to be run by UMNO operatives, of course. Another rent-seeking exercise! He never thought of giving universities, the real talent corporations, the funds directly so they could do their own recruiting. Najib cannot find a GLC he does not like.

Najib used the metaphor of a soccer team to illustrate his point on teamwork. Had he followed through on that metaphor, he would realize that a team is only as good as its members and leaders. One inept player could cost the team the game. The pathetic dearth of talent in Najib's team was matched only by his own deficits.

The only thing worse than a central "command and control" economy is one where the leaders are also clueless, lack conviction, and are devoid of courage. Najib Razak is all that.

Tackling Subsidies And Their Myriad Manifestations

May 30, 2010
Idris Jala, Minister in the Prime Minister's Department and PEMANDU CEO, has yet to convince his cabinet colleagues, including the Prime Minister, of the need to reduce subsidies specifically and government spending generally. I suggest doing that first before taking his Subsidy Rationalization "Lab" road show to the rest of the country.

Responding to a question, Prime Minister Najib indicated that he would "leave it to the people to decide on whether they [the subsidies] should be maintained or abolished." In doing so he abrogated his leadership on a critical economic issue. He is following instead of leading public opinion; a wet-finger-in-the-air type of leader.

While I did not share Idris Jala's dire prediction of Malaysia becoming bankrupt in nine years—nations, unlike corporations and individuals, could not do that—nonetheless the grim picture he painted was not far from the likely reality. His likening Malaysia's future to today's Greece may or not be valid but there were enough useful lessons to be learned from the current Greek tragedy.

Greece is not bankrupt, nor will it ever be; the Greeks are suffering because of economic mismanagement by their leaders. Subsidy for the poor or for essential goods was only a minor part of the mess. The Greeks were borrowing beyond their capacity to pay; they borrowed just to keep their bloated government afloat.

The other pertinent lesson is that even when faced with a catastrophe, people who have long enjoyed subsidies and special privileges would not readily give those up. This is true of the Greeks (the ugly mass demonstrations and strikes there today attest to that) as well as others. Americans long used to generous subsidies for their home mortgages and health insurances would severely punish their leaders at election time should they dare even touch either issue. And America has a deficit much worse (twice as bad, as a percentage of GDP) than Malaysia.

As a reminder, the current global economic turmoil was triggered by the American expansion of its housing subsidy through "sub-prime mortgages." Again, this was facilitated primarily through two government-sponsored (and thus subsidized) corporations, Freddie Mac and Fannie Mae. It was done with the best of intentions, to make housing affordable to the poor.

Those factors notwithstanding, in the many deliberations on the current economic crisis, I have yet to hear an American leader or economist suggest doing away with or even trimming the housing subsidy. And America does not lack for wise leaders or smart economists!

If Idris Jala or anyone thinks that Malaysians would readily give up their subsidies, he is blind to the universal precept of human behavior.

Likewise with special privileges, which after all are subsidies manifested differently. Do not expect Bumiputras to give that up easily either.

Picking An Easy Target

Idris Jala showed the frightening and unsustainable trend of rising debt and increasing deficits. There are only two ways out: increase revenue through economic growth, and reduce spending, or more accurately, curtail expenditures that do not contribute to economic growth. As any businessman knows, you spend money to generate money.

Idris Jala should have focused on those two central themes. Instead he strayed onto ending subsidies, specifically on petroleum and essential food items. He ended up being portrayed as someone targeting the poor, and not without good reasons. That distracted him. It is easy and tempting to prey on the poor; though large in numbers they lack economic and political clout.

Of the record RM74B spent on subsidies in 2009, about 57 percent were on social services; 33, fuel and energy; 7, infrastructures; and 3, foods. As for the beneficiaries, only 2 percent were farmers, fishermen, and the poor.

Those subsidies on social services and infrastructures could be viewed more as investments as they could potentially enhance the nation's human and physical capitals, and thus the nation's productive capacity. Even here Malaysia could increase the efficiency by plugging the leakages.

Ending subsidies for foods would address only a tiny part of the problem (3 percent). Besides, the per capita consumption of such staples among the poor is comparable to or only minimally less than the rich, but the poor spends proportionately more of their income.

Idris purported to show that Malaysians enjoy the cheapest price in the region, with cooking oil costing only RM3.30 as compared to RM8.70 in Singapore. In making that comparison, Idris used the exchange rate instead of the purchasing power parity (PPP) or the Economist's Big Mac Index. Had either been used, the price differential would be less impressive. I do not know whether Idris is disingenuous, trying to mislead, or being intellectually dishonest in using the sterile exchange rate.

Idris proposed mitigating measures to help the poor. That would inevitably require massive administrative machinery. For the amount involved, it would be preferable as well as politically wise to leave things where they are, except for sugar. I would remove its subsidy not for economic but public health reasons. With rampant obesity and diabetes, any initiative that would lower sugar consumption would be good. Likewise, I would hike taxes on alcohol, tobacco, and gambling, but not high enough to stimulate a black market.

Petroleum is different; its per-capita consumption among the rich is considerably higher than among the poor. Its subsidy disproportionately benefits the rich. Idris proposes cash rebates to motorcycle and small car owners. Another bureaucracy!

I am for ending petroleum subsidy, phased in to minimize dislocations since it is such a crucial fuel literally and figuratively in a modern economy. Instead of cash rebates I would eliminate taxes on buses, taxis, and other conveyances to transport passengers. That would effectively halve the price of a Proton to be used as a taxi, making it easier for owner-operators.

Subsidize season tickets for bus and rail to ease the burden on commuters, as Canada is doing. Vancouver has a per capita income many times that of Malaysia, yet its car-ownership figure is considerably lower. As a side benefit to that, the air in that city is not polluted, and its streets a pleasure to stroll. Singapore uses differential toll rates and efficient mass transit to discourage driving.

Ending subsidy on petroleum would save not only money but also the environment. Focusing only on petroleum and sparing food subsidies (except sugar) would also make the exercise an easier sell. Besides, petroleum subsidy is massive; food subsidies are small change in comparison and evoke considerable emotional response. It is not worth expending political capital and risking public wrath for the promised minuscule returns.

Hidden Subsidies

Idris should not stop at the obvious and massive petroleum subsidy. He should pursue other equally expensive and rapidly growing but hidden ones. They are pernicious precisely because they are not overt; the public is thus not apprised or aware of the costs. There would be no figures to put on fancy graphs and pie charts for your Power Point presentation.

One is the preferential awarding of contracts to Bumiputras. However noble the objective may have been, unless we know what the added costs would be, we cannot begin a cost-benefit analysis or assess the program's efficacy. Few would quibble with the extra 5 or 10 percent to have a contract awarded to a Bumiputra in the name of social equity and correcting past inequities, but many would grumble if that figure were to balloon much beyond that or be in the multibillions.

It is customary that contracts below a certain amount be awarded exclusively to Bumiputras. Even if the added costs were only 10 percent each (a very conservative estimate!), in the aggregate they would impose a considerable burden on the government. I suggest that Idris's "lab" do a study on this.

Then there are the overt as well as hidden subsidies to the myriad GLCs. Many are perennial "corporate welfare bums," forever hooked on government bailouts. The Malaysian corporate scene is littered with the carcasses of the likes of Bank Bumiputra. I challenge Idris to analyze that!

Such studies would require much thought and wise analysis; they cannot be done by posing simplistic questions via SMS.

The only difference between the recipients of cooking oil subsidy versus those preferred Bumiputra contractors and "corporate welfare bums" like Bank Bumiputra is that the first group is weak while the latter, powerful.

If Idris Jala had been diligent and fearless in analyzing the twin problems of ballooning deficits and increasing spending, he would begin with the obvious and massive petroleum subsidy, flush out the hidden subsidies represented by non-competitive bids of government contracts, and then get rid of those money-losing GLCs. That would make a significant dent on the national deficit and spending. That would also invigorate the economy, thus enhancing revenue.

He does not need a road show for that; all he has to do is convince his colleagues in the cabinet, beginning with the Prime Minister.

NEM And NEP – Only One Letter Different

March 27/2010

With threatening clouds overhead, there are no prizes for predicting the flood, only for designing or building the ark. The recently released New

Economic Model (NEM) Report draws attention (not that Malaysians need it!) to the darkening skies, and then goes on advising citizens to build their arks.

That is as far as the report goes. There are no hints on whether the clouds would bring a tropical drenching or just a midday sprinkle. There are also no suggestions on the type of vessel Malaysians should build. A barge, yacht, or sampan would all keep us afloat, but beyond that they serve vastly different purposes, not to mention their enormously varying costs. If the forecast calls for only a light sprinkle, then a simple umbrella would do; no need to expend scant resources on an unneeded ark.

Malaysians were told that following "public input," another report would be released by June, in time for its recommendations to be incorporated into the Tenth Malaysia Plan and the 2011 Budget. This second report, citizens were further assured, would contain specific policy prescriptions—the ark design as it were.

This report was silent on how this "public input" would come about. Before deluding ourselves that we could participate in robust public debates, let me intrude a cautionary note. Acknowledging that there would be opposition, the report urged the government to take "prompt action when resistance is encountered."

Be assured that those UMNO-Putras and others glutton on the NEP-spawned patronage system would be spared this "prompt action." They as well as the PERKASA boys could continue with their shrill voices opposing NEM. For Pakatan folks and others, be forewarned!

Major Conceptual Flaws

On a general level, this report suffered from three glaring conceptual flaws. One, it failed to recognize that the bane of past policies was their implementations. Two, it ignored the major role culture plays in the successful execution of any economic initiative. And three, there was no attempt at learning from the successes and failures of past policies.

This last deficiency was surprising as well as disturbing. If NEM were to supplant NEP, then we should know the strengths and weaknesses of that earlier policy. Or if it was basically sound, then what or who perverted it, and where the failures were in its implementation.

No one would argue with the twin objectives of NEP, that of eradicating poverty and eliminating the identification of race with economic functions. Those are laudable goals; more so the second for a racially diverse society like Malaysia's. The report pays tribute to NEP for reducing poverty and minimizing inter-communal inequities.

That is where the report ends. In an earlier chapter, the report duly lists the numerous problems facing Malaysia today: widening inequities especially among Bumiputras, talented citizens leaving (brain drain), the rise of a rent-seeking class, entrenched corruption, and the failure of institutions.

What happened in between? Unless that is analyzed, there is little assurance that the laudable goals of NEM would not be similarly derailed. The failure or unwillingness to acknowledge and learn from the mistakes of the NEP would doom us to repeat them.

There should have been some critical analysis of the NEP, at least an elaboration of the positive elements and highlighting the negatives.

The one chapter that should be in the report would be one titled, "How did we get in the mess we are in today?" I reckon that would be filled with narratives on the failures of local institutions and those entrusted to run them. It was this that doomed NEP.

On the role of culture, it is surprising that a committee made up of mostly Malaysians and those familiar with Malaysia would come up with a report that is totally oblivious of this reality. This cultural dimension is crucial not only in economics but also in management and healthcare. Of all people, Malaysians who are daily immersed in a diverse cultural environment, should be aware of this.

An initiative that would be embraced by urbanite Chinese in Penang would fall flat among Iban rural dwellers of interior Sarawak. The solo entrepreneur model would find fertile ground in Penang, but not in Kenawit. There, the social system would be more supportive of cooperative-like ventures.

Challenges for the urban poor regardless of race are radically different from those in rural areas; race only compounds those differences. The failure to recognize this doomed many an imaginative plan. When that happens, those policymakers would resort to blaming and stereotyping the poor victims. Malaysians have heard that many times.

The colonials brought modern schools to Malaysia with the best of intentions. Non-Malays responded to that gesture and benefited immensely. Malays did not and suffered the consequences in terms of our economic and social development.

It would be wrong as well as cruel to conclude that Malays did not value modern education, as many (and not just the colonials and non-Malays) were wont to. For when those schools were named Tuanku Muhammad School instead of Convent of the Holy Infant Jesus, Malay parents readily enrolled their children. The content was still essentially the same, but the packaging was different; it was sensitive to the customers' culture and taste.

American consumers readily respond to their leaders' exhortations to increase their spending to pull the country out of recession. For the Japanese on the other hand, the more their leaders urge them to spend, the more they save and hoard. Same economic circumstances and the same economic rationale, but the responses and results are diametrically different. Culture explains that.

"Most of economics," Landsburg put it in his *The Armchair Economist*, "can be summarized in four words: 'People respond to incentives.' The rest is commentary."

Alas what are viewed as incentives in one culture could be definite disincentives in another. That is the central challenge. Policymakers ignore this at their own peril.

The British attempted to encourage Malays to save by increasing the interest rates on Postal Savings Accounts. Instead of increasing their deposits, Malays withdrew theirs! Malays viewed the increase as an inducement to a life of sin. Those sneaky white devils!

Economist Ungku Aziz created Tabung Haji and labeled the investment returns as "dividends." Malays swarmed to that institution, making it the largest in the region. Essentially the same content, but different packaging! The Ungku understood economics well and fully comprehended its central axiom: People respond to incentives. He went beyond; he knew what those incentives were for Malays.

A corollary to this is that the incentives you offer would influence your responders and their responses. Offer honey, you get bees; rotten meat, maggots. When the committee decries the economic rent-seekers emerging under the NEP, it should carry the analysis further to find out the incentives offered. Rest assured that if NEM were to offer rotten meat as NEP did, NEM would too get its share of maggots.

On the crucial issue of implementation, the report only tangentially addressed the strengthening of institutions when that should have been the major focus. Malaysian institutions are blighted with bloat, incompetence, and corruption; they just cannot deliver.

Consider the current initiatives to improve the civil service. First there was PEMUDAH, self-described as "a high-powered taskforce to address bureaucracy in business-government dealings." It was chaired by no less than the Chief Secretary. Then there was the appointment of Koh Tsu Koon as the Minister in Charge of "Performance Management." He had hardly warmed his seat when yet another minister, Idris Jala, was made in charge of–you guess it–KPI (Key Performance Index)!

Who was in charge here? Meanwhile the civil service continued its bloat and ineffectiveness, as exemplified by Najib's own cabinet. And if you were to get your driver's license, you would still need the services of runners and touts, as well as some *duit kopi* (coffee money–bribe).

Corruption would not be dented–much less ended–merely with the report blandly declaring "zero tolerance" for it. Make the Anti-Corruption Commission independent, answerable only to Parliament or the King, and appoint a seasoned professional to head it. If you could not find a native, recruit from the FBI or Scotland Yard. That one move would more effectively curb corruption and improve local institutions than all the KPIs, National Integrity Institutes, and NEM's and others' declarations of "zero tolerance." It would also be much cheaper.

Accurate Portrait, But No Revelation
The report was refreshingly different from the usual government publications in that it was readable and the content well organized. The chapter headings too were clear and simple; they accurately reflected the contents, with such titles as "Where We Are?" Where Do We Want To Be?" and "How Do We Get There?" An index would have been useful, but the well laid-out and sufficiently detailed "Table of Contents" made up for that deficiency.

This report is remarkably free of gross grammatical gaffes and awkward syntax. The committee staff had done a credible job with the executive summary. The report was available online almost immediately. These features are rare with government publications, and thus merit special commendation.

The full report is available only in English, a glaring omission considering that NEM would supplant NEP. As everyone knows, NEP is dear to most Malays, especially those of PERKASA persuasion. Any tampering of NEP, even if it involved only one letter of the initials, risks raising the hackles of those folks. Having the full report in Malay would have been a splendid start at trying to influence them, quite apart from being a politically smart gesture. Malay after all is the national language.

Those proficient only in Malay would have to be satisfied with the *Ringkasan Eksekutif* (Executive Summary). My hunch is that they would find the going rough, what with such phrases as "Menginovasi hari ini untok hari besok yang cemerlang," (Innovation today for a glorious tomorrow) and, "Inisiatif Pembaharuan Strategik" (Strategic Renewal Initiatives). I would have phrased it differently, *"Cara baru untok menjamin masa depan yang cemerlang"* (A new way to ensure our bright future).

Dark clouds there are—and many—hovering over Malaysia, from the hundreds of thousands of skilled citizens who have migrated, to the anemic growth in productivity. The report rightly points to the lack of political will to overcome these myriad problems. Kudos to the committee for that forthrightness!

The report painted a gloomy picture for Malaysia if it were to stay the course. Few would disagree with that. I wish those luminaries would help citizens sketch and build the appropriate ark, one that would meet the nation's unique needs and challenges, instead of merely warning of the impending flood.

The report did not lack specifics. For example, it aimed for an economic growth of at least 6.5 percent annually. Its target population too was specific, the bottom 40 percent of Malaysians.

One specific suggestion on improving the government machinery is the proposal to "corporatize" and rename the Malaysian Industrial Development Agency (MIDA) to Malaysian Investment Development Agency. The committee pats itself for the brilliance of substituting "Investment" for "Industrial," as then the agency could continue keeping its acronym and logo!

If only they recognize that changing even a single letter in a corporate name would entail changing the entire letterheads, advertising plates, and web pages. The exercise would consume as much effort as if you had changed the entire name. It would have been more productive if the committee had recommended changes to MIDA's mode of operations and strategies. After all, Warren Buffett's Berkshire Hathaway did not need to change its name to diversify beyond its initial textile base.

The Report went out under the signatures of all but one (Dr. Norma Mansor) of NEAC members. Of the ten who signed and thus responsible for the report, three are non-Malaysians while two are Malaysians (or at least born locally) though they had spent their formative careers abroad.

Of the remaining five–the 'natives'–only one, the chairman Amirsham Aziz, had substantive private sector experience, having spent his time in banking. He had a brief political career as a cabinet minister, but that was through the appointive senate route rather than through the electoral one. In short, the chairman and his committee are short on political acumen as reflected in the lack of a Malay version of their report.

Referring to the 'natives,' all have formal training in economics except for one. Dzulkifli Razak, former Vice-chancellor of Universiti Sains Malaysia, was a pharmacist. Two of the 'natives' were former academics but now government bureaucrats. The resumes of the committee members are impressive, with seven having doctorates, all but one in economics.

I have no quarrel with the committee's assessment of Malaysia's current dismal state. I wish that the committee would have been more forceful in pointing out whether the Najib Administration's many recent moves were in the spirit of or contrary to the committee's aspirations. For example, the committee noted the need for devolution of authority to lower levels, yet Najib's recent response to the request for local elections runs counter to that.

The committee decried the failure of local educational institutions. Yet it did not address whether the recent rescinding of the policy of teaching science and mathematics in English would accelerate or reverse this decline.

I hope that in its final report the committee would be more forceful in addressing these contradictions. The committee owes this obligation not only to the Najib Administration but also to all Malaysians. Doing so would help Malaysians design and build a better ark.

Potpourri of Malaysiana

Sultanah Aminah Hospital's Fire Rekindled Old Ugly Memories

October 25, 2016

Like many, I was saddened by the tragic death of six patients from the fire that started at the Intensive Care Unit (ICU) of Hospital Sultanah Aminah (HSA) Johor Baru last Tuesday, October 25, 2016. My condolences to their families and loved ones. Those patients came to be treated and instead ended up being killed.

Having worked at that facility in the late 1970s I have endless fond memories of the place and the many wonderful people I had worked with, as well as the countless grateful patients I was privileged to treat. As a surgeon, that ICU was familiar turf to me.

There was something else hauntingly familiar to me on seeing those frightening videotapes of the huge fireballs and the bellowing black smoke. My family and I had just been through a massive forest fire in the Santa Cruz Mountains in California that forced our temporary evacuation. In addition, the familiar bright red bricks of the hospital building, unchanged over the years but for the telltale stains from tropical black molds, opened the floodgates to my old memory banks.

While I have many pleasant memories of that place, I also remember the more than a few not-so-wonderful ones, as with the all-too-frequent VVIPs' visits. That sediment of my memory was stirred by videos of visits to the hospital by the many VVIPs only hours after the fire. The embers were still smoldering when the sultan and his chief minister, as well as the Deputy Prime Minister and his equally huge federal entourage flooded the hospital.

I do not question their good intentions and could appreciate the boost in morale among those visited—patients, nurses, doctors, firefighters, and others. Well-meaning though those visits may be, they also interrupted and interfered with the immediate and pressing business at hand, that of ensuring the welfare and safety of patients as well as the public. Those colorful videotapes and glossy pictures of appreciative hosts and the genuine concerns expressed by those important guests did not reveal the entire picture.

What you did not see were the crowds of patients kept waiting for their treatment or whose transfer to safety was delayed because their doctors, nurses, and other personnel were occupied with entertaining those big shots. Nor would one appreciate the consequences of scarce resources being diverted from patient care and services towards hosting those luminaries.

There were also a few occasions of VVIP visits during my brief tenure at HSA. Two I recall for specific reasons and both happened at a time of acute crisis at the hospital, though not as critical as this fire.

The first was by the Ministry of Health's then new Director-General who had just taken over from the retiring Dr. Majid Ismail, a former Queens scholar and an accomplished orthopedic surgeon.

This new DG had a point or two to prove, one being that he was a worthy successor to his distinguished predecessor. This new official was determined to not only show the flag but also demonstrate that he was not the typical senior civil servant afflicted with the sultan syndrome—departmental heads who behave like detached sultans but clueless as what to do except issue endless edicts.

On the appointed day, this gentleman arrived. Late of course, in fact very late. By the time we finished the obligatory long line of introductions, it was decided that since it was close to lunch time, we would retreat to the nearby country club. The rest of the day was thus a washout.

It was a Thursday. Later I discovered that it was a favorite day for federal officials to visit Johor. With Fridays and Saturdays being the weekend there, those officials had an early start for their shopping spree across the causeway.

The second episode occurred when the sultan and his consort were involved in a car accident. Both were hospitalized in the royal suite, which coincidentally was just above the ICU. Within hours (and for weeks afterwards) the hospital was inundated with VVIPs from all over the country.

Late on that first night at the height of the crisis, a colleague was called to the hospital to help on a complex obstetrical case. He had not heard of the accident and on seeing so many strangers loitering around and one in his private office, asked him to vacate. It was unfortunate that the gentleman happened to be one of Malaysia's many sultans.

Within 24 hours that good doctor was banished out of state. I heard of the incident the very next morning when there was confusion in the operating suites as the doctor's surgical cases were left in limbo.

Had there been a tipping point to my prolonged and wrenching decision to emigrate, the summary banishment of my colleague was it. I saw the basic indecency and unfairness of it all, to the doctor and patients.

No, that specialist was not a *pendatang* or contract consultant from abroad (not that it mattered); he was in fact one of the sons of the soil.

Fires erase memories. The fire at HSA ironically rekindled my old ugly ones.

A Taste Of Malaysiana In Central Valley, California

October 21, 2012

Hundreds of Malaysians who have visited or studied in California over the years know of or have met "Kim" Ahmad Sabian (Pak Mat) and his wife Rose Mohamad. They know the couple through Rose's signature Malay cooking. They have catered to former Prime Minister Mahathir who on a visit to Silicon Valley during one Ramadan many years ago felt the sudden craving for Malay food for his *suhor* (predawn) dinner. They have also hosted countless touring diplomats and ministers who discovered that being away beyond a few days from their favorite *sambal belacan* and *nasi lemak* was too much to endure.

On the Saturday before Ramadan this year, Pak Mat and Rose were once again gracious hosts, this time for their California friends, families, and neighbors. There were also guests from far away Malaysia—Rose's sisters and brother, and their families. The occasion was the wedding of their daughter Rosanna to her high school sweetheart, Kosal. My wife Karen and I have known Rosanna since she was a little girl, so the occasion was extra special for us.

It was a traditional Malay wedding in all aspects, from the food and decorations to the *akad nikah* (exchange of vows) and *bersanding* ceremony, embellished with elements of Americana. You would be hard pressed to savor a similar experience even in Malaysia.

Rosanna, being American born and raised, is very much the girl next door: poised, confident, elegant, and working her way through college. The occasion was a creative and exquisite blending of traditional Malay wedding, to highlight Rosanna's heritage, with elements of Americana to reflect the couple's upbringing. It is this artful fusion of the two that elevated the ceremony to new heights and made it that much more memorable.

Akad Nikah

The day began in the morning with an intimate *akad nikah* ceremony in the living room of the family's Stockton home. The room was made to resemble a *serambi* (verandah) of a traditional Malay house, with a lush carpet substituting for *tikar nipah* (palm mat). In deference to comfort and modernity, there were two chairs for the bride and groom, flanked by another chair on each side for the official witnesses. On the floor were trays bearing gifts the couple had for each other.

Figure 1: Couple and Bride's Parents and Brother Hisham

All around were family members and close friends standing at the back or sitting *bersela* on the carpet. The ceremony began with the family's Imam Yusoof invoking a *dua* to bless the gathering. Then he explained in

English the meaning of marriage in Islam, a divinely sanctioned contract between a man and a woman. It would be entered upon freely and willingly by both parties. As such, he emphasized, the relationship of wife and husband is complementary and respectful.

Figure 2: Bride and Groom

The Imam drew liberally from the *seerahs* (practices of the Prophet Muhammad s.a.w.) to illustrate his point. He recalled how the Last Prophet of Allah, even though he was an acknowledged leader adored by millions, yet at home he was the humble husband readily sharing in the household chores. No household task was beneath this great man. The Imam was clearly addressing not only the young couple but also the many who were already married or contemplating marriage.

Then the Imam asked Rosanna whether she had freely consented to be the bride of Kosal. When she replied in her clear voice in the affirmative, the Imam noted this, and directed the two witnesses, one of whom was me, to also acknowledge this fact. Likewise, the Imam posed a similar question to Kosal.

With that, the Imam solemnized the marriage and recited some *duas* both in English and Arabic, invoking Allah's blessings upon the young couple. I did not know what it was, perhaps it was the *dua* being recited in English so we could understand the prayers and what the Imam was saying, but there was not a single dry eye in the room. The Imam touched everyone with his *dua*.

That was after all the true meaning and purpose of *duas* and prayers, to touch us emotionally and not merely the meaningless incantations of foreign phrases that no one could comprehend.

Then followed the giving of dowry from the groom and the exchange of rings and gifts; those too, were simple. After the ceremony, my wife told Rosanna that after factoring in for inflation, devaluation, and conversion rate, her dowry was approximately the same amount what she (my wife) received from me (RM49) at our wedding over 42 years earlier! Rosanna's greenbacks were creatively folded origami-style into a bird, an American eagle no less!

Rosanna and her family were mindful that the dowry was but a token and symbol of the love and commitment the young couple had of each other. It was not, as it has now degenerated into, a culturally sanctioned extortion of the groom's family by the bride's.

The *bersanding* (reception) ceremony that evening was truly a Malay event, specifically a Minang tradition, reflecting Rose's Rembau origin. Although held in a hall rather than at the family home, the event was far from being one of those sterile modern catered ones. Rose and her family had done all the decorations *and* cooking. The *pengantin* (wedding) dais was duly decorated with *bunga mawar* floral arrangements. The only thing missing was a live *kompang* troupe. The digital taped audios more than made up for that deficit.

The family's male members were the *orang pangkar*, the hosts, serving the guests, including the head table, which was served by the bride's younger brother, Hisham, just as it was in my village of yore.

The Bride and Groom

In traditional Malay wedding, the bride and groom are indulged upon as *raja sehari*, royal couple for the day. Just as we pay tribute to the king and queen, so too the assembled guests to the bride and groom on the dais. That is the essence of the *bersanding* ceremony.

It began with the parents of the bride and groom, followed by other family members and then friends and guests. It was also a chance for them to bless and express their best wishes to the young couple.

What otherwise would have been a strange ceremony in an equally strange land went off smoothly. Yes, a few of the guests took a while getting into the swing of things especially with the *berinai* and rice sprinkling rituals, but with Rose's sister Norlela doing a splendid job as the Mistress of Ceremony, everyone quickly and smoothly became Malay that evening. At the end, the bride and groom went around each table meeting all the guests and to have photo opportunities with them.

While the ambience was traditional Malay, this was after all a wedding in California. The couple's first dance, to the tune of *Right Here Waiting* after the *bersanding*, was as Americana as you can get.

The warmth and intimacy of the celebration was such that the guests lingered long after the event. That after all is what events like weddings are for, apart from celebrating the joining of a man and woman as husband and wife, to renew the bonds of family and friendship.

Late in the evening when the last guests had departed, there was the groom and bride minus their earlier elaborate wedding attire, rolling up their sleeves and helping with the clean-up. Rose and Pak Mat's new son-in-law Kosal had quickly adapted into his new Malay family, now becoming the *orang pangkar*. That more than anything brought back fond memories of the traditional weddings in my old kampong in Negri Sembilan.

Economic Development Reverses Brain Drain

June 15, 2011

A recent World Bank Report concludes that Malaysia risks jeopardizing its economic development if it does not ameliorate its "brain drain" problem. The Bank singles out the country's affirmative action program as a major contributor to the problem.

Brain drain, as the Bank rightly acknowledges, is a universal problem. For the Bank to conclude as it did, it must present comparative international data showing that Malaysia's problem is worse off than those without similar affirmative action programs. Alas, this is precisely the glaring deficiency to the report, its lack of comparative data.

The Report nonetheless contains a wealth of valuable data. However, as the information sage Edward Tufte observed, nature's laws are causal; they reveal themselves by comparison and difference. This absence of comparisons makes the report's conclusion not credible.

The Bank has it backwards. Brain drain does not impact economic development rather the other way around. Have a robust economy and then watch talent—and not just native ones—flocking black. We saw this with Japan of the 1960s, South Korea in the 1980s, and Ireland in the

1990s. Ireland is a particularly pertinent example. Today with its economy sputtering, Ireland is again suffering a brain drain.

There is no indication that Malaysia's problem is worse off than that of China, India, or Singapore. On the contrary those countries may suffer even worse, and they do not have any domestic affirmative action program, except for the perfunctory one for India's "untouchables."

In California there are more émigrés from Singapore than from Malaysia, on a per capita basis of their home population. Nearly all my college mates in Canada in the 1960s who were from Singapore are now émigrés. Considering the republic's much smaller population, we can infer that it has a bigger brain drain problem. Heck, even its former head of state emigrated! Yet that does not impact its economic development.

China suffered through massive "brain drain" for the past few decades; it still does. Yet it continues registering spectacular economic growth. Only now with greater opportunities, the consequence of that growth, China is seeing an improvement to if not reversal of her brain drain problem.

Despite that, China now has a new problem. According to China Merchant Bank's report, those Chinese with assets over 100 million yuan, a stunning 27 percent have already emigrated while another 47 are considering it. In Malaysia, at least according to the World Bank Report, only the smart Chinese are emigrating; the rich ones stay put. I let readers conclude who really are the smart ones!

Snared by the Race Trap

The Report's other major disappointment is its less-than-rigorous teasing out the race factor in its analyses. Its authors, like many commentators both native and foreign, get unnecessarily entangled with the nation's sensitive race issue. No surprise that the report succeeded only in unleashing suppressed chauvinism and resurrecting ugly stereotypes.

Consider its findings that the majority of emigrants are Chinese and those with tertiary qualifications from or recognized by foreign (specifically Western) institutions. Only those not attuned to the Malaysian scene would miss the redundancy to that statement.

To tease out the delicate race factor, you must present data that show Malays with similar qualifications as the emigrating non-Malays do not emigrate, at least not in comparable proportions. The Bank does not have that data.

Anecdotal evidence may indicate otherwise. When I visit American campuses, the one frequent question posed to me by Malay students is: How do I get to stay back? Most Malays are on scholarships and tightly bound to their contracts. Emigration for them is not an option for at least ten years; that alone would skew the figures, race-wise.

The West is a magnet for the talented. Outstanding athletes and artists excepted, talent to the West means those conversant in English and have qualifications issued by its institutions. In Malaysia that means non-Malays. They may hate Malaysia's affirmative action program but that is not enough for them to emigrate to Australia or America; they must have the needed qualifications recognized there.

Now if Malaysian Chinese were to emigrate to China and Indians to India, then that would indicate something rotten in Malaysia. I do not see that happening, at least not yet. This salient fact indicates that the "pull" of the West far exceeds the "push" out of Malaysia. In China and India, the "push" factor is overwhelming, reflecting their general economic status and not because of any domestic social policies *a la* affirmative action. There, the prime consideration is to get out; regardless whether you are among the rich, talented, or the unskilled, hence the all too frequent tragedies of their poor citizens caught in abandoned rusty trawlers on the beaches of Europe and America.

The Bank noted that Malaysia's brain drain is worse only within the last decade, a period that coincides with Malaysia's less-than-robust economic performance. Malaysia's Affirmative Action policies have been a fixture for over half a century. If that were to be the reason for emigration, as claimed by the Bank, then we would expect the rate to be constant all those years.

There are many good reasons to jettison the current corrupt and ineffective affirmative action program but hoping that it would solve Malaysia's brain drain problem is not one of them.

The Report's many nuggets of useful information escape comments both by its writers as well as by the mob of commentators. The latter is no surprise as any issue that parallels (or seems to) the racial divide inevitably invites such Pavlovian race-tinged responses. That the Report's writers who are experts would fall into the same trap was a surprise.

Consider the Report's findings that fewer than 10 percent of its respondents (Malaysians who emigrated) spoke the national language. If you were born and raised in Malaysia, you would have to be literally an idiot or a hermit not to know the national language as it is widely spoken. Both idiots and hermits have their place, but they are not regarded with esteem in any workplace.

Their poor fluency in Malay reflects their lack of commitment to Malaysia. To them Malaysia is only a staging ground, to prepare themselves for subsequent migration to greener pastures. There is nothing wrong with that; it is only human. The error is in imputing evil motives on those they leave behind and who have kindly provided them their launching pad. They should be grateful, not spiteful to Malaysia. The quota lines (yes, America has quotas too!) for green cards for those from China and India are closer to infinity; not so for those Malaysian-born.

Focus on Retaining Talent

It is futile to tailor your policies in the hope of attracting people who have long ago decided to emigrate. Instead, the emphasis should be on two areas. One, treat your present personnel so well that they would not even *consider* leaving. Two, attract talent worldwide without regards to whether they are Malaysians, former Malaysians, or complete foreigners. The market for talent is global; there is no place for nostalgia, insularity, or misguided notions of nationalism.

Contrary to popular perception, pay is not the only consideration, but a decent one would help smooth out the many other frustrations, including those of affirmative action. Once you treat your current talent well, word would spread out and you would be inundated with enquiries.

Quit tinkering with the tax code or hiring expensive foreign consultants to produce yet another thick report that would soon be forgotten. Disband the costly Talent Corporation; it is just another bureaucracy whose budget for foreign travel rivals that of the Foreign Ministry. Divert those funds to compensate the talented you currently have at home.

You do not have to match exactly the global pay rates to attract talent. A modest increase in the current pay scale in the range of 30 to 50 percent would go a long way in encouraging Malaysians to stay put. We all know the variables of purchasing power and the cost of as well as standard of living even within a country. A US$100K pay in San Francisco, and you would be lucky to afford a one-bedroom condo. In Wyoming, you could live in a mansion. For that same pay, in Malaysia you too could live in a mansion, with maids, drivers and gardeners to boot. Salaries in Singapore may be considerably higher but try finding a house with a yard for your children to play. Yes, you can afford a fancy sports car—so you could drive around the island in less than an afternoon.

Attract talent from wherever and practice meritocracy on a global scale. All things being equal, I would choose talent already in Malaysia. You cannot beat local knowledge and perspective. My next choice would be a complete foreigner. I prefer that individual over a Malaysian émigré, especially one who cannot speak Malaysia's national language.

The rationale is simple. The one trait I value most in an employee is curiosity, for with it comes the eagerness to learn. The complete foreigner has demonstrated his curiosity and adventuresome spirit by wanting to work in a foreign country. He considers that a challenge; his learning curve would be steep. He would also be enthused about his new assignment. A Malaysian who cannot speak our national language clearly shows his lack of interest in his surroundings. He is not even curious enough to learn a language that is widely spoken. An uncurious worker is rarely an asset.

A returning émigré would also carry with him his old baggage; he may find it difficult or unwilling to re-adjust. When faced with a problem his only response would be, "Back in old England .... " If he were to be reprimanded by a superior who is other than his own kind, he would more likely dredge up his old prejudices.

Malaysia should not have any hang-ups about recruiting talented foreigners. Nonetheless her priority should be on retaining the talents she already has and on producing more. Not too long ago, Malaysia commissioned the same World Bank to review our universities on improving their performance. Few could recall that report now.

Prime Minister Najib had a penchant for employing legends of foreign consultants. Unlike his predecessor Abdullah, Najib at least read those reports. However, if you do not have a handle on a problem to begin with, calling in the various experts would only confuse you. Consider this World Bank report. Just a month after its release, the Bank published another study, "Eight Questions About Brain Drain," prepared by yet another set of its experts. This second report essentially questions the findings of the earlier one. Dismiss these expensive consultants and divert the money to reward the talents you already have.

The executive talent of a leader is inversely related to his penchant for calling in consultants. The more inept a leader is, the more likely he or she is to call in various experts. Najib reaffirms my conviction. If he is not already befuddled, this latest World Bank Report would do it for him.

Healthcare As A Bottomless Pit

January 17, 2010

[Invited editorial, *Malaysian Journal of Medical Science*, 17(1):1-2, Jan-Mar 2010.]

As a young surgeon at the General Hospital Kuala Lumpur in the 1970s, I remember pleading with Tan Sri Majid Ismail, then Director-General of the Ministry of Health, for funding of my research project.

A distinguished clinician turned policymaker, Majid was professionally interested in my proposal. Nonetheless he politely declined funding it, but not before offering me a comforting explanation. Between funding me and building a Klinik Desa (rural clinic) in Ulu Kelantan, the choice was clear, he gently told me. Besides, he assured me, I would have minimal difficulty securing funding elsewhere while those poor Kelantanese had no choice.

Tan Sri Majid said something else that reverberates in me today. "Healthcare is a bottomless pit," he advised me, "but the resources to meet those literally endless worthy needs are limited, so society must set its priorities and draw the line somewhere."

The job of government is to ensure a minimal acceptable level of care for all, he added, and beyond that it is for individuals to set their own limits with their own resources.

Malaysia does this with its dual public and private healthcare systems. Tan Sri Majid was adamant in maintaining this clear separation lest there be confusion in the respective missions and objectives.

America today is in the midst of a wrenching debate on healthcare reform, specifically its massive price tag and the provision for a "public option," a government-run insurance company.[1] Similar debates occur elsewhere, Malaysia included. These deliberations would be elevated greatly if we were to heed Tan Sri Majid's observation on resources being necessarily limited and the necessity to set priorities.

It is understandable for America, the richest country, to have difficulty acknowledging the first. As for the second, the setting of priorities is too often confused with rationing, a highly emotive issue.

This need for setting priorities is never more urgent today. In the past, the best that physicians could do was to bring patients back to their pre-morbid state. Today the goals go far beyond, from enhancing lives (cosmetic surgery) to eliminating genetic diseases through bio-genetic engineering, and aggressive preventive measures.

Consider the wonders of modern drugs. In the past they were for curative purposes in a limited setting, as with antibiotics for infections. Today the biggest expenses are for drugs in maintaining chronic conditions (anti-inflammatory medications), enhancing lifestyles (Viagra and oral contraceptives), and reducing risk of diseases (the statins).[2]

In public health, in the past interventions were limited to specific communicable diseases as with childhood immunizations. Today we have the various screening tests for cancers.

Regular exercise, good diet, and smoking cessation too are also health enhancing and good preventive measures. Issues would arise if we were to insist that health insurers pay for our lean cuisine and health club membership. Where to draw the line, in the public health as well as clinical setting, is the greatest challenge.

Often forgotten is that there is minimal correlation between outcomes and expenditures in healthcare. America spends twice as much as Britain (relative to the economy), yet it would be hard to argue that Americans are as healthy as the Brits, let alone twice that.[3]

While the bulk of the healthcare dollar is expended on hospitals, pharmaceuticals, and physicians, nonetheless the costs are primarily physician driven.[4] Many are thus misled into believing that focusing on physicians specifically is the key to improving citizens' health and or controlling costs.

In truth, much of our present good health is due more to civil engineering marvels as central sewer and water treatment plants as well as modern refrigeration. Malaria, still a scourge in the Third World, was eliminated in California's Sacramento Delta through the building of levees and consequent drainage of the swamps, not advances in parasitology.

This observation is worth emphasizing. With rapid urbanization, the inadequacy of these basic infrastructures has turned many Third World cities into public health time bombs.[5] Stroll through an exclusive neighborhood of Kuala Lumpur and you would see garbage strewn all over, stagnant drains spewing unbearable stench, and septic tanks leaking their waste. Esthetics aside, those are significant health hazards.

These infrastructures are prerequisites for our good health, yet they are not considered as healthcare expenses. Malaysia spent hundreds of millions on the aborted new bridge to replace the existing causeway in Johor Baru, yet that city does not have a water treatment plant. The returns on investment for a new water treatment facility would be much more in terms of health and thus productivity of citizens.

In between necessary infrastructure spending and for providing basic medical care, there is the legitimate need for publicly funded medical research even, if not especially, for a developing country like Malaysia.

I did research in transplant immunology before returning to Malaysia but felt minimal inclination to continue it even though the country then had an active kidney transplant program under the capable leadership of Drs. Hussein Awang and Bakar Sulaiman. For one, I did not think that we could compete intellectually and resource-wise with programs in the West. For another, I was more attracted to the neglected but more relevant area of immunology of parasitic infections. You can be assured that there is minimal interest in the West to undertake such research, hence the need for countries like Malaysia to undertake them. They are also best done locally as we have the most at stake.

I am grateful to the wisdom that Tan Sri Majid had imparted on me. All of us involved in healthcare, from the policymakers to administrators and practitioners to researchers ought to participate in the exercise of acknowledging our resource limitations and setting up priorities.

References:
1) American Health Care Reform Debate. www.healthreform.gov
2) Drug costs: Economic Burden of Illness in Canada, 1993. Health Resources Centre, Canadian Public Health Association, 1565 Carling

Avenue, Suite 400, Ottawa, Ontario K1Z8R1; Tel: (613) 725-3769; Fax: (613) 725-9826.

http://www.phac-aspc.gc.ca/publicat/ebic-femc93/pubinfo-eng.php

3) Peterson, Chris L and Rachel Burton: "U.S. Health Care Spending: Comparison with other OECD Countries." Congressional Research Service (CRS) Report to Congress, Sept 17, 2007. http://assets.opencrs.com/rpts/RL34175_20070917.pdf

4) Centers for Medicare and Medicaid Services, Office of the Actuary, National Health Statistics Group, 2007 National Health Care Expenditures Data, March 2009.

5) Patel, Ronak B and Thomas F. Burke: Urbanization—An Emerging Humanitarian Disaster. Perspective: Global Health. *New England Journal of Medicine*, 361:741-743, August 20, 2009.

The Perfect Murder That Wasn't

August 23, 2009

The revelations from the coroner's inquest into the death of opposition political activist Teoh Beng Hock following an "interview" with the Malaysian Anti-Corruption Commission (MACC) Officers eerily reminded me of a similar tragic death of the CIA scientist Frank Olson in 1953. Olson was found dead sprawled on the street outside a New York high-rise hotel where he had spent the night with his colleagues.

The official report classified it as suicide. Two decades later, as a result of disclosures from the Rockefeller Commission, President Ford apologized to the deceased's family, accompanied by a sizeable monetary settlement, over the 'tragic accident' of Mr. Olson.

Still not satisfied, the family secured a court-ordered reexamination and Olson's body was exhumed in 1994. Despite being over four decades later, through expert independent forensic examination the gruesome truth was finally revealed. His death was neither an accident nor a suicide; it was plain cold-blooded, premeditated homicide. His colleagues murdered him. They did it by knocking him unconscious and then threw his body out.

The lead investigator, James Starrs, recounted the details in his book, *A Voice for the Dead: A Forensic Investigator's Pursuit of the Truth in the Grave.* More significantly, prior to Starrs' investigation, the Olson case was celebrated in the annals of the CIA, as well as the Israeli Mossad, as the example of how to execute (pardon the morbid double entendre) the "perfect murder" so as to be seen as either an accident or suicide.

I do not imply that this was the case with Teoh's death. I doubt whether MACC's officials have heard of the Olson case or read Starrs' book. However, we have seen many 'accidental' deaths involving Third World opposition leaders. Locally, Anwar Ibrahim's notorious bludgeoned face was initially dismissed as "self-inflicted!"

As Starrs stated, forensic science can be superior to a confession and even eyewitness accounts. It is the most empirical and objective of all judicial methods in finding out the truth.

That notwithstanding, if Teoh were murdered, the murderer (or murderers) would not likely leave obvious clues around unless he (or she) was unbelievably stupid, or very brazen and thus wish to make a point. Meaning, there would not likely be any dramatic revelations or Perry Mason moment during the inquest. That however would not necessarily discourage the Perry Mason pretenders and wannabes from among the many participating lawyers in the subsequent inquest.

The path to the truth in this case, as with Olson's, would be long and arduous, with many twists and turns as well as false passages. We may never know what really transpired. Nonetheless that did not discourage many amateur 'forensic scientists,' especially in the local blogosphere. Their exuberantly confident analyses suggest that they might have been reading too many medically related articles in *Reader's Digest* and viewing too many CSI series.

As with the Olson case, the pivotal clues (at least initially) would not necessarily come from the autopsy table but from careful interviews of the involved personnel, examining their phone records, and accounting for their activities on that fateful day.

Wise Move to Videotape the Proceedings
The Attorney-General has been much criticized lately, and deservedly so. In this instance I compliment him for videotaping of the inquest and then posting the tapes unedited on the web. That singular move did more to

demonstrate the government's commitment to transparency than all the ministerial speeches and assertions.

I would have gone further and put all the exhibits including the victim's photographs (subject to the next-of-kin's consent) on the web.

I was impressed with the professionalism of the coroner, Azmil Mustapha Abas, and lead counsel Tan Hock Chuan. I was less so with the other lawyers representing the various interested parties. Azmil's calm demeanor reassured the various witnesses, a key to getting the most out of them. Tan skillfully led the expert witnesses such as forensic pathologist Khairul Azman Ibrahim to describe the clinical findings in understandable layman's terms, and to consider each of the three possible causes of death–accident, suicide or homicide–despite the pathologist being under the weather. I hope he was screened for H1N1 before his court appearance as he was coughing a lot during his testimony!

There was a brief digression in court on the National Language Act. It served no purpose except that I wished our language nationalists were present to witness how inadequate our national language still is even in a relatively non-technical court setting. Imagine litigations involving complex finance!

I brought up this language issue for another reason. It is obvious that even highly educated Malaysians (like lawyers) are unable to string simple sentences in either complete English or Malay. Thus, counsel for Teoh's family, "Can you *beri tahu kami maana Perunding Kanan* ...." (Can you tell us the meaning of Senior Consultant?)

There was nothing technical there, just simple ideas, yet they could not coherently articulate them using a single language, confirming that 'rojak Malay' and 'pidgin English' are Malaysia's two official languages.

It was apparent that the counsel for Teoh's family confused an inquest with a criminal trial. In the former you want your witnesses to agree (or at least not disagree) with your interpretations of the evidence. With the latter you want to chip away at the credibility of your adversary's witnesses. Badgering and belittling an expert witness may make you look smart to the gallery but would not advance your cause.

Teoh's counsel's suggestion that the government provides pathologists with tape measures so they could hang themselves precariously outside windows to measure the height of buildings was simply laughable. If you want to know the height, get the architect's blueprints or sixth grade geometry texts! Besides, after you have fallen from 13 stories high, what' the difference of a few feet? Precision without meaning! Such precisions are meaningless.

A key to undermining or at least challenging an expert witness's testimony would be through careful questioning of his or her credentials and experiences. Teoh's counsel tried this, but not very effectively. He asked how many such similar forensic cases Dr. Khairul had done. More appropriate would be to ask when his last similar case was, and the effect of his findings on the final verdict.

I am never impressed with credentials and titles, especially the Third World variety. When I was in GHKL, there was a Sikh surgeon with the imposing title of "Director of Casualty Department." He also had the prestigious (I assume) "Senior Consulting Surgeon" appellation. All he did was sit in his office and never saw a patient; he was waiting out his "medical board" (disability retirement).

You may have an imposing title of Professor of Surgery, but if the only 'cutting' you had done recently was the carving of your wife's turkey dinner, that fact could only be established through careful cross-examination.

I was an expert witness once when the opposing attorney tried to undermine my credibility by asking whether I was being paid to testify. I unhesitatingly replied, "Definitely!" and then quickly added, "But not enough to compensate for my being away from the operating room!" His attempt to portray me as a professional armchair 'expert' backfired. He had obviously not learned what skilled trial lawyers intuitively know, that is, never ask your witness a question you do not know the answer ahead of time!

Having once been a government doctor in Malaysia, I have great sympathy and empathy for the government's expert witnesses. I am certain that when Drs. Seah and Khairul left the courtroom, they had a mountain of work waiting for them at their respective labs. They have other pressing priorities than to appear slick and confident in court. And especially with Dr. Kahirul, as he was feeling miserable! Besides, they do not have the luxury of time or resources to prepare for such appearances; nor are they paid extra to do so.

What the seekers of truth and justice for Teoh should have done was not to demand an inquest or a royal commission but the right to a court-approved independent and independently funded forensic investigation, a *qui tam* inquest as it were. Such investigations are not cheap, and the government rightly has other priorities. It would not be fair to ask the government to devote its scant resources to that pursuit. However, there should be enough support from NGOs, friends, and supporters of Teoh as well as those who seek truth and justice to fund such an endeavor.

Short of that, we should not expect a Perdana quality inquest on a Perodua budget.

Enough Of Pledges; Malaysians Need Actions

August 2, 2009

Prime Minister Najib Razak pledged to improve six key areas (crime, corruption, and poverty reductions as well as education, infrastructure, and public transportation. He would have met widespread applause if only he had indicated just a wee bit more on how he would go about achieving those lofty goals. Malaysians are fed up with unrealistic optimistic targets and stirring slogans. What the nation is in dire need of are leaders who could execute things and get Malaysia there.

Najib referred to those objectives as national "Key Results Areas" (KRAs). If not executed with diligence and imagination, Najib's KRAs could very well end up as KeRA (monkey). Kera would then join up with Najib's earlier *glokal* Malay to be the target of endless jokes.

The very manner with which Najib made the announcement did not give Malaysians much confidence. He made it at a huge gathering of civil servants and on a working day. You could imagine that during that entire morning, work at the various government offices would be at a standstill.

The afternoon too would be a washout, what with those officers busy rehashing his earlier speech. With their superiors absent, the subordinates would even be more sluggish than usual. I pity members of the public who had urgent business with the government on that day.

Najib had acquired many of the bad habits of his predecessors. Both Mahathir and Abdullah Badawi used to convene their ministry officials for a monthly lecture *a la* a high school assembly. Just like a headmaster, Abdullah would stand on the podium sermonizing in his soporiferous monotone voice, putting everyone to sleep. That is, if he himself had not dozed off first. Meanwhile work at the various government offices would come to a screeching halt.

Chief Secretary Sidek Hassan had not thought of advising Najib to use other more effective and much cheaper ways to communicate, like newsletters or even taping the message onto a CD and then distributing it. Perhaps Sidek was in awe of Najib, imagining him to be the civil service's Steve Jobs. Apple's Jobs used to gather his employees in a huge hall at the launch of a new product or to make significant announcements.

If only Najib had a fraction of Job's charisma and executive ability, perhaps such large gatherings could have been excused and defended as a means of rallying and inspiring the troops. Having seen the videotapes of the assembly with Najib at the podium, it seemed more a torture session, torture for those civil servants to remain awake!

Najib deluded himself if he thought that simply assigning a minister responsible would solve the problem of execution. None of the six ministers he selected had excelled themselves or impressed citizens with their executive talent. Muhyiddin, for education, was associated more with his flip flopping on the policy of teaching science and mathematics using English. As for Hishammuddin, responsible for crime reduction, his previous tenure in Education did not enthrall parents with his competence.

Then there was Ong Tee Keat, responsible for infrastructure development. This poor soul had yet to explain the rapidly ballooning boondoggle that was the Port Klang Free Zone Development scandal.

I would have been more impressed had Najib, in assigning the areas of responsibility, also indicated the price for nonperformance. Would Hishammuddin be relieved of his cabinet post should he fail to reduce the crime rate? Heads must roll when there is a major lapse. That is the only way to make ministers and civil servants accountable and take their responsibilities seriously. If there were to be no price to pay for failure, there would be little incentive to perform, much less excel.

Take crime reduction; Najib was reinventing the wheel. All he had to do was revisit the recommendations of the Royal Commission on the Police of four years ago. Along the same vein, if during the tenure of the present Police Chief Musa Hassan the crime rates have soared, that is compelling enough reason to fire him, or at least not renew his contract.

My hunch is that Najib would renew Musa's contracts, thus making a mockery of the commitment to crime reduction. Najib would do more for crime reduction by firing the glaringly ineffective and incompetent Musa. Otherwise all those lofty goals would be but *cakap kosong* (empty talk), KRA morphing into KeRA.

Similarly with Najib's battle to curb corruption; he would do well to get rid of the present director of the Anti-Corruption Agency, Ahmad Said Hamdan. His agency's record in the two latest high-profile cases was abysmal. Then there was the tragic death of one of his agency's 'friendly' witnesses.

Renaming the old Anti-Corruption Agency to the Malaysian Anti-Corruption Commission would not combat corruption if you are still stuck with the same personnel, procedures, and mindset.

A Better Approach

A more effective approach would have been for Najib to gather his assigned ministers and the relevant senior officers to a private meeting where he would lay out his goals and inquire from them the steps that they would recommend in reaching those goals.

Those meetings would be working sessions, dispensing with time-wasting unnecessary protocols. Everyone would literally roll up their sleeves. That would not be the time for you to be in your three-piece suit and have tea. There would be much heavy lifting to be done, with ideas critically examined, resources allocated, and markers put in place.

Such meetings would not only be cheap, but they would also not disrupt the normal workings of the various departments, especially if they were to be held outside of regular office hours. Those meetings would be the time to monitor progress, get feedback, and modify strategies.

Najib's meetings thus far have been heavy on press coverage and laudatory comments in the mainstream media. Too much premature accolades; there would be plenty of time for that later once those objectives were achieved. Meanwhile Malaysians should be critical lest these leaders get carried away with their premature and unmerited applauses.

Like his predecessor Abdullah Badawi, Najib was satisfied with making highly publicized public pronouncements instead of attending to the necessary nitty-gritty of governance. It is attention to such practical and mundane details on which the success or failure of a policy would depend.

Najib should act more as chief executive and less a sultan. He should not be satisfied merely with issuing endless *titah* (edicts). Malaysia already has plenty of sultans; there is little need to add to the roster.

Needing To Show Off

February 5, 2009

The per-capita income of Malaysia's Klang Valley is a mere fraction that of America's Silicon Valley, but one would not know that from visiting the respective shopping malls.

At any one time there would be more (in absolute as well as relative numbers) Mercedes Benzes and other late model luxury cars in the parking lot of the Mega Mall in Klang Valley than at Stanford Shopping Center. Judging from the crowd, the purveyors of luxury goods at Mega Mall do a roaring business compared to their counterparts at Stanford.

I saw more gold Rolexes on brown wrists than on white ones. I must admit that gold is enhanced against a brown background!

Despite the residuum of the dotcom bust, as well as the current [2008] economic crisis, Silicon Valley still has one of the highest per capita incomes in America, and America has one of the highest per capita income in the world. Yet for the most part Americans lack the compulsion to show off their wealth.

That is not unique to Americans. The Norwegians too have a high per-capita income, and their sovereign fund is the largest in the world. Norway is also the Saudi Arabia of the North Sea. Unlike in Riyadh, the most popular cars on the streets of Oslo are those fuel-stingy hybrid models instead of gas-guzzling Cadillacs, the favorites with the Arabs.

To be fair to Malaysians, General Motors sells more luxury models in China than elsewhere. Gucci and Louis Vuitton brands are top sellers there, and Beijing has more gated communities than any other major capitals. Members of the Chinese Politburo and top generals have special license plates to go with their luxury sedans. That enables them to park their cars anywhere and ignore traffic and presumably other rules with impunity.

In Malaysia, UMNO Supreme Council members too are doing the same. I suppose this was what Dr. Mahathir meant when he urged Malays to emulate the Chinese!

Conspicuous Consumption

In his 1889 book, *The Theory of the Leisure Class*, the American economist and social critic Thorstein Veblen coined the phrase "conspicuous consumption" to describe the propensity of the rich towards opulent displays of their wealth.

It was not a surprise that the excesses of the "robber barons" of the Gilded Age would offend the sensibilities of a frugal, Mid-Western Lutheran of Norwegian descent. It was after all a time of undreamed wealth creation, what with the confluence of the Industrial Revolution and the opening of the American heartland, together with the availability of cheap immigrant labor.

Such ostentations were needed so members of the "gentlemanly" or leisure class could differentiate themselves from the working class. As Veblen noted, "the need for such differentiations is seen in all societies and at all times," save perhaps for the ancient hunter-gatherers.

The native Indians of the American Northwest had their potlatch ceremonies where they gathered to exchange lavish gifts which they would later throw away. The lavishness and associated waste offended the sensibilities of those earlier missionaries such that they lobbied their government to ban such practices. How noble of those missionaries to save those natives from their "destructive" culture!

Across the Pacific, it was only recently that the Chinese gave up the practice of tightly wrapping the feet of their infant daughters to increase their desirability as future brides. After all, only the rich could afford to have daughters with dainty feet; huge feet belong to peasant women so they could work the rice fields better. Thus, dainty feet are anatomic manifestations of conspicuous consumption, the need to show off that you are not of the working class.

In the rest of Asia, Malaysia included, huge weddings and exorbitant dowries are but variants of this potlatch mentality.

Malaysian Philanthropy In Its Infancy

Styles, whether sartorial or social, do change. What were once luxuries and the exclusive preserve of the wealthy—cars, washing machines, and hot water on demand—are now the basics even for those on public assistance. Today young professionals just starting out can afford Porsches, albeit through generous bank loans.

Ostentatious lifestyles and visible luxuries are no longer indicators of class, or class differences. In Malaysia if you were to drive a late model higher-end Mercedes you could be mistaken for a taxi driver!

You could "advance" by acquiring a private jet, but then you would have to invest time and effort in acquiring your pilot's license, as John Travolta did. Besides, the "showing off" value of and opportunities from a Gulfstream are limited; nobody would notice you except for the brief time when you are taxiing at the local airport. The Bill Gates and Warren Buffets have access to private jets but through their corporations. Meaning, their cost is partly born by taxpayers as it would be tax deductible.

Among the rich in America and much of the developed world today there is a definite reversal of Veblen's old "conspicuous consumption." The new chic is "inconspicuous consumption."

Warren Buffet personifies this. He lives in the same modest suburban home in Omaha that he has had for the past forty years even though he could afford a Gates-like lakeside mansion. Instead Buffet, like Gates, diverted his vast fortunes to philanthropy, emulating the generosities of the "robber barons" of yore.

Conspicuous consumption is still rampant in America, but only among the rich of visible minority groups, specifically Blacks, Asians, and Hispanics. Before we resort to racial and cultural caricaturing to explain such phenomenon, consider this. Such conspicuous consumptions is still prevalent among Whites, but only those from traditionally poor areas like the South. For the same income level, rich Whites from Mississippi spend more on visible luxuries than those from Massachusetts. Meaning, rich Southern Whites behave like rich minorities.

What governs social behaviors has more to do with your social reference groups than with your race or culture. Rich southern Whites, like rich Blacks, Hispanics, and Asians feel the need to show off their wealth so as to differentiate or prove that they have "escaped" from their poorer peers.

When your peers are the likes of Gates and Buffet, individuals unimpressed with visible luxuries, you would then spend your wealth to pursue your passion, not to impress others. You are thus more likely to endow a professorship at your alma mater, fund your doctor's medical research, buy original paintings, or grow premium varietals for your boutique winery.

Likewise, the invitation list for your daughter's wedding would be short, to include only the couple's best friends and closest family members. The celebration too would be on a scale the very opposite of what those rupee millionaires of Mumbai would put on for their daughters. I viewed the video of a society wedding in Mumbai; it made the one at Windsor Castle hosted for Charles and Diana looked stingy.

Malaysia is still Third World. Its many millionaires including the sultans are only a generation away from the privations of the kampung and city slums. It is not surprising that rich Malaysians would behave more like rich American Blacks or Southern Whites. By displaying their luxury trinkets, these rich Malaysians hope to bury their plebian past. More importantly, they still feel the need to differentiate themselves from the poor masses. The most recent and obscene example was the late Zakaria Mat Deros building his opulent mansion amidst the urban squalor of Klang's Malay village.

With continued development, and with average Malaysians becoming more affluent, we could expect this conspicuous consumption to wither. At least I hope so. Such profligate displays of wealth offend religious as well as social sensibilities.

Malaysia is already seeing glimpses of this trend. Halim Saad, the poster boy of the New Economic Policy, may have been grounded somewhat from his earlier highflying days of pre-1997 economic crisis, nonetheless he has endowed through his Saad Foundation a superb residential school in Malacca that is already besting venerable Malay College.

Tun Daim Zainuddin, another prince of the NEP and a former Finance Minister, endowed the Pok Rafeah Chair in International Studies at Universiti Kebangsaan in honor of his mother. Another former cabinet minister, Zaid Ibrahim, was recently named one of Asia's 48 "Heroes of

Philanthropy," together with Syed Mokhtar Albukhary, Leonard Jugah, and Hishamudin Ubaidulla.

It is heartening that Malaysia has such philanthropists. As for ostentations, I also look forward to the day when the parking lots of Malaysian shopping malls would be filled with fuel-efficient cars, and when cars would be viewed purely as a means of transportation, with citizens opting for mass transits. That would reduce congestion and pollution.

Engage Engineers, Not Doctors To Control Dengue

February 1, 2009

Florida in the summer has the same hot humid climate as Malaysia. Its topography too is like Malaysia, with plenty of swamps and other stagnant bodies of water. Unlike Malaysians, Floridians are not regularly threatened with outbreaks of dengue.

The secret is not that Florida has more and better doctors than Malaysia (although that is true) rather that Florida engages its civil engineers and not medical doctors to control vector-driven diseases like dengue. That is much more effective as well as cheaper, both in financial costs and human sufferings.

While it is commendable that Dr. Ismail Merican, the Ministry of Health's Director-General, is spearheading public awareness of dengue during this latest outbreak–the most severe–he is not the best person to do that. Neither his professional background nor his regular duties would prepare him for this awesome responsibility. Nor is his ministry the most appropriate agency to undertake this formidable task.

Like Florida, Malaysia should engage her civil engineers in local councils and the Ministry of Works, instead of medical doctors in local hospitals and the Ministry of Health. If those engineers would get out of their air-conditioned offices, they would notice those stagnant drains, silted ponds, and ditches with overgrown weeds. If those officers would brave the stench and examine closer, they would see mosquito larva luxuriating in those stagnant waters.

The solution is not to pour toxic chemicals into the water or fog them into the air. Yes, that would be effective, but those same chemicals would then eventually leach into the water tables to poison everyone, that is, if we have not already inhaled them. Get rid of the stagnant waters and you get rid the larva. No larva, no adult mosquitoes, and no vectors to spread the dengue virus.

There is a major role for the Ministry of Health. The most obvious is to educate the public and health professionals in recognizing and treating the disease early. The other is in collaborative research with international agencies for prevention (as in vaccine development) as well as treatment. Its Public Health Division could develop sophisticated surveillance strategies using the Internet, GPS, cell phones, and traps laced with chemicals to attract pregnant mosquitoes. It should get real-time information so that effective and immediate interventions could be initiated, as the Brazilians are doing.

Learning Favors The Prepared Mind

Many Malaysian doctors, engineers, and civil servants visit Florida. What they remember are Mickey Mouse and the Magic Castle. Few would notice the well-trimmed parks, underground drains, and smooth flowing streams. And the absence of pesky mosquitoes!

Those visitors would not realize that the beautiful marinas with their posh waterfront restaurants they patronized were once mosquito-infested swamps. Through the marvels of modern civil engineering, those once sources of pestilence are now major tourist attractions.

Malaysia spends considerable sums sending her officers abroad so they could learn and in turn help improve things back home. However, as per Pasteur's famous quote, learning favors only the prepared mind. You would need to know what you want to learn; you need to know your deficiencies so you could remedy them. Meaning, there would have to be considerable preparations beforehand at home if you were to maximize the learning potential of your overseas trip. If it is only a vague notion of "wanting to learn something new," then you would only be a tourist.

I once had some senior civil servants visit me at my modest suburban California home. They were impressed with the neighborhood, and yet when I queried them what exactly they found attractive, they could not answer me.

Only after I had pointed them out did they realize that there were no overhead power and phone lines (all underground), no open storm drains (all covered), and no front yard fences or tall walls to blight the open park-like ambience of the neighborhood.

When they saw the clean sidewalks and well-trimmed side-street lawns, they attributed that to American city councils being efficient providers of municipal services. That is true. However, I reminded them that homeowners are responsible for keeping the sidewalks and lawns well cared for. If they do not, they would not only be fined but have to reimburse the city for doing that job for them. And that would be much more expensive.

When living in Johor Baru in the 1970s, I paid my gardener extra to cut the weeds and unclog the drains outside my compound. He initially reminded me that those were the responsibilities of the Town Council. When I gently chided him in not wanting to increase his income, he complied. He could not comprehend why I would do something that should have been done by the "authorities." He could not appreciate the benefits that I would enjoy as in not smelling the stench of clogged drains or risk my children being bitten by snakes and mosquitoes.

I could excuse my poorly educated gardener for his narrow perspective, but my neighbors there included a banker and a corporate executive. They shared my gardener's views!

I once suggested to my father's neighbors in Seremban that if they were to contribute a few thousand ringgit each, their neighborhood could have sidewalks and covered storm drains. That would reduce the mosquito population, as well as the stench and unsightliness of stagnant plugged drains.

They balked at the added expense, rationalizing that they had already paid their *cukai pintu* (municipal assessments). It is the responsibility of the Town Council, they argued like my gardener earlier, in between slapping themselves trying to kill the pestering mosquitoes. Yet the costs of these "common space" improvements would be a fraction of what they spent for their gilded gates and high brick fence walls. Had they gone beyond their narrow concerns, they would have gotten not only functionally wider streets but also safe sidewalks, quite apart from making their neighborhood healthier and more wholesome.

They would also recoup many times more their investments through the increase in their property values.

Septic tanks are major breeding grounds for mosquitoes. They should be banned in urban areas; houses and buildings there should be connected to a central sewer system.

Even the lowly septic tanks could stand some improvements. An engineer from East Malaysia invented a system where light Styrofoam balls were placed in the venting pipes. That would allow gases to escape but not mosquitoes. This should be mandated in all septic tanks.

Then there are elementary civil engineering innovations as having V-bottom storm drains or one with a U-shaped channel in the center to maintain fast flow during low volumes. The usual flat-bottom channels would have puddles of stagnant pools during the dry season.

Personal Actions

Mosquitoes have a range of about half a mile. Even if you were to keep your drains flowing and your yards trimmed, but if your neighbors were slothful, you would still have to endure the nuisance of mosquitoes. A neighborhood approach would be needed.

Those factors notwithstanding, there are still many things that individuals can do to minimize the threat of dengue. Installing screens on doors and windows is one; another would be using insecticide-impregnated or even plain mosquito nets, though that is more effective against malaria rather than dengue, which is spread by daytime mosquitoes.

Covering your body as much as possible is also protective. You do not need to be in a burka if that is not your sartorial style; light-colored long-sleeved shirt or blouse, with a sarong, long skirt or pants would achieve the same result.

Even an umbrella is useful. Not only does it protect you against the blistering sun, the constant movement of the umbrella causes micro turbulence underneath it, enough to discourage mosquitoes.

Malaysian officials need not venture far to learn these things. If they had paid greater attention to their colonial predecessors, local officials would know the importance of cleaning up drains during the dry season so that they would not be clogged when the inevitable rain comes. I learned that during my childhood days watching those coolies employed by the Public Works Department scraping the drains. And this was long before I ever heard of Florida and Disneyworld.

Sycophantic Editors Ruin Public Trust

September 7, 2008

The result of the recent Permatang Pauh by-election was a surprise only to those who depended on the mainstream media and the government's massive propaganda machinery for their source of news and information.

A measure of how far detached from reality those who sit in the editorial suites of Malaysian mainstream papers could be gauged by the pre-election editorial of *The New Straits Times* where its Editor-in-Chief Syed Nadzri boldly predicted that Anwar would be defeated. Syed Nadzri believed his own spin!

In coming to such a wild off-the-mark conclusion, Syed Nadzri was either a lousy observer of the public mood or more concerned with sucking up to his political superiors. In either case he did not deserve to be the custodian of such a valuable and essential institution of modern free society.

Syed Nadzri was both. That he was poor judge of the public mood could be deduced from the ever-declining circulation and influence of his paper. Syed Nadzri was only the latest in a long series of those who, through their lack of professional integrity and journalistic skills, have destroyed this once-valued brand name. As one naughty wag put it, that paper should now be more correctly called, *The New S**t Times.*

It pained me to note (what was obvious to all) that since the paper was acquired by UMNO, nearly all its senior editors and journalists were Malays. I refused to believe that a Just Allah had not bequeathed upon the Malay race our fair share of journalistic and literary talent. I also refused to believe that past luminaries like the now-ailing Samad Ismail was an accidental fluke and not the trademark of Malay culture. He should be an inspiration for the present generation of journalists, a measure of what the Malay community could produce.

Instead we have the likes of Syed Nadzri, individuals more adept at sucking up to their superiors. Syed Nadzri obviously learned little from the fate and experiences of his many predecessors who were similarly afflicted. While such a trait may have facilitated their ascent to the top, once there it is no guarantee of career longevity.

Syed Nadzri should have learned, or somebody should have taught him, that while political winds and personalities may change, your professional duties and ideals do not. Yours was to ensure that the public be well informed, the prerequisite of a healthy, functioning democracy.

The slow but sure decline of *The New Straits Times* was interrupted only briefly when Abdullah Ahmad, a former Ambassador to the UN and a Mahathir appointee, took the helm. He survived but only briefly under Abdullah Badawi. At least Abdullah Ahmad left in a blaze of glory, having had the courage to speak his mind.

As I peruse the paper's roster of past Editors-in-Chief, I am struck at how quickly they, with few exceptions, have descended into oblivion once deprived of their perch at the editor's desk. Kadir Jasin is the rare exception. He has his widely read blog where he gives the occasional pungent comments now that he is freed from the tethers of officialdom. Again remarkable because of the rarity, Abdullah Ahmad is one of the few editors whose writings have been respectable enough to appear in reputable foreign publications.

The New Generation of Pseudo Journalists

My observations apply equally to those who helm Bernama, RTM, and TV Tiga, as well as the other mainstream papers like *The Star*, *Berita Harian*, and *Utusan Melayu*. What we have today is a generation of pseudo or pretend editors and journalists. Ever wonder why the public ignores them? They have betrayed the public's trust.

It is instructive that Ahiruddin Atan, Noraini Samad, and Kadir Jasin now reach more readers through their blogs than when they were with the mainstream papers! It would not be long before they would effectively overcome the blemish in their resume that was the time they spent with the mainstream media.

I would be irresponsible if I were to stop here, pointing out only the problems and not offering solutions.

One thing is clear. The present "leaders" in journalism are very much part of the problem. Having been brought up and flourished under the present system, do not expect them to change or be part of the solution. Getting rid of them would be a necessary first step to solving the problem.

Replace them with competent and established editors from abroad if need be. Tie their compensation to the success of their papers. There are many measures of this (circulation figures, advertising revenues) but an important one would be how often articles and commentaries in their papers are being quoted or picked up by other publications.

In addition, I would have as a regular event an annual week-long continuing education series for their reporters, journalists, and commentators where they would hear from the leading practitioners in their respective fields. I would invite established journalists from abroad in various fields (political reporting, economic analyses, and investigative journalism) to lecture and share their experiences.

Include as part of the program a basic writing course as well as courses on effective interviewing. Even more basic, I would gather all the editors, and guided by a competent teacher of English grammar and stylist, craft a uniform editorial format on such things as how to handle long names and honorifics, as well such as simple things as standardized spelling. Is it Kota Baru or Kota Bharu?

Still on the basics, have someone competent in mathematics to teach these reporters and journalists on the meaning and significance of numbers and data generally. Then we would not have such silly statements as, "The price of food increased 5 percent last month." Is that 5 percent over the previous month or over the same month of the previous year? Percentage is a ratio; you must state the denominator or reference point.

As a concrete commitment to ensuring the future quality of the profession, I would groom at least half a dozen young journalists every year for entry into the leading journalism schools in America. With the promise of future infusions of fresh, bright, and well-trained talents, rest assured the quality of local journalism and media would improve.

Only through such careful preparations and nurturing would future local journalists be able to differentiate between news and propaganda, between ministerial speeches and important policy announcements. Malaysia and Malaysians would then be well served. Journalists owe their readers and the public honest professional reporting, not propaganda to serve the needs of their political masters. This is what separates a free democratic society from an authoritarian state.

Rationalizing The Role Of Government

June 29, 2008

Prime Minister Abdullah and his civil servant accountants delude themselves into believing that the government could "save" RM2 billion annually merely by reducing ministerial allowances. The only effective way to substantially reduce the cost of government is to first rationalize its functions.

As for any savings, Abdullah would achieve more by getting rid of his luxurious Airbus corporate jet. If he were to do so, the jet would become a revenue producer instead of at present, a costly expense item. He would move it from the liability to the asset column.

The British Prime Minister does not have a private jet, despite leading an economy and nation considerably much larger. To think that this Imam of Islam Hadhari, only a generation away from the poverty of the kampung, having such an obscenely extravagant taste at public expense!

In the wisdom of the kampung, Abdullah and his ministers *tak sedar ekor* (lit: dogs not aware of their tails; fig: oblivious of their greed).

Proper Role of Government

The government should focus on doing only those things that are properly within its purview and do away with extraneous activities. That would streamline its machinery, reduce its size, and trim costs. Malaysia would also then have a more efficient government that could serve her citizens more effectively.

The government has no business owning a television station or news agency. Dispense with the Ministry of Information, together with the Ministry trying to produce athletes or encourage sports. About the only champions that Ministry could produce were profligate spenders of public funds, as evidenced by its recent debacle over a training facility in London. That now-abandoned project cost the government hundreds of millions of *ringgit.*

Then there is the Ministry of Entrepreneur Development. The pretensions of those civil servants to think that they have the competence to select or train future entrepreneurs! Get rid of it!

In the same vein, do Tourism Ministry officials really think that they are responsible for tourists visiting Malaysia? The operators of Club Med and Hilton Hotels do a far more credible job. They have to; the success of their businesses depends on those tourists.

As for those civil servants in the Tourism Ministry, all they could think of is their next posting abroad, or when they would undertake another "promotional" trip overseas.

I have taken many vacations in Malaysia and have never found the Tourism Ministry or its many agencies useful. Canvass foreign visitors, or better yet, stay at one of Tourism Malaysia's facilities, and you would reach the same conclusion. Abolishing that Ministry would have no negative impact on the industry. On the contrary, freed from bureaucratic hassles, the industry could grow even faster.

Those impressive statistics the Ministry puts out are uninformative. Millions of the "tourists" coming through Johore Baru or Padang Besar are nothing more than aunts and uncles visiting their relatives across the border.

Eliminating these ministries and combining others would reduce the number of ministers, together with their accompanying secretaries-general, directors-general, and hordes of other top officials. Those savings would be instantaneous as well as cumulative.

Bloated Public Sector

By any measure—relative to the economy, population, or labor force—the public sector in Malaysia is bloated. Being primarily a Malay institution, the impact of the civil service on the psyche, labor dynamics, and cultural values of Malays is disproportionately huge.

Young Malays are conditioned not to look beyond the civil service for employment. Malaysian universities and colleges too are unresponsive to the demands of the private sector as most of their graduates are Malays whose career horizons rarely extend beyond government service. Perversely, the obsession with *Ketuanan Melayu* makes the civil service's hold on Malays even more tenacious.

Civil servants enjoy considerable subsidies, from car loans and home mortgages to below-market rents on government quarters and paid pre-retirement vacation packages. Children of civil servants make up a disproportionate number among those admitted into residential schools (again highly subsidized) and recipients of government scholarships. That makes getting rid of the subsidy mentality among Malays that much more difficult.

To those civil servants, gyrations in interest or foreign exchange rates would not impact them. Insulated from the realities of the marketplace, it is no surprise that the policies they formulate are far detached from reality.

If Malaysia were to reduce her public sector, Malays would be forced to venture into the private marketplace, and thus to prepare themselves accordingly. That could just be the incentives needed for young Malays to pursue relevant subjects in schools and universities. Instead of content in being a *kerani (*clerk*)* at the land office, they would opt for auto mechanics, and in the process contribute more to the economy.

The civil service is but overhead, and an expensive one at that. It does not add to the economy; on the contrary it is a burden. It is people, individually or through their enterprises, that produce the goods and services. Reducing the size of government would also discourage corruption and influence peddling. Plot the size of government (adjusted for population and economy) and incidence of corruption, and the correlation would be startling.

A large public sector inhibits the development of a vibrant private sector. The many government-linked companies (GLCs), far from stimulating new independent contractors and entrepreneurs, actively compete with and stunt their development. These GLCs have not nurtured their share of entrepreneurs. How many employees and executives of GLCs have left to start their own enterprises?

More important is what the government does with its size and power. The Scandinavian countries all have large governments, but they use their power and resources to emancipate their citizens through providing superior education and healthcare. Mothers, for example, enjoy subsidized affordable government-run childcare centers.

In Malaysia, the government uses it size and power to snoop on citizens, making sure that they do not hold hands in public. Significant governmental personnel and resources are diverted to controlling what citizens read and view, all non-productive activities.

There is one good thing about Abdullah's reducing his ministers' holiday allowances. They would now know how much those fancy vacations cost. If Abdullah were to go further and dispense with his

Airbus luxury jet and opt for Malaysia Airlines instead, he would experience firsthand the type of service it provides. Apart from saving the government a bundle of money, it would also help disabuse him of the "sultan syndrome," of being a detached leader. Anything that would bring him closer to the real world would be a good move.

Ensuring The Oil Bounty Would Not Be A Curse

June 28, 2008

With Malaysia forced to end or at least reduce its petroleum subsidy, it is well to learn from the experiences of other oil-producing countries.

There are enough lessons in the world today on how Malaysia should manage her precious God-given oil bounty. Prudently done, as in Alberta, Canada, and Norway, it would bring peace and prosperity. Anything less and it would be a curse; the new wealth would breed corruption and tear the fabric of a society, as seen in today's Iraq and Nigeria.

Malaysia should emulate and build on the Albertan and Norwegian models. Malaysia should, like Canada and Norway, remove all subsidies on petroleum products. That would encourage conservation and reduce pollution. It would also prod Malaysians into the global economic reality instead of being insulated from it.

To have this giant step accepted by citizens, the government should divert the savings into a separate trust fund for use by future generations when the oil would run out, with a small portion devoted for current use as in subsidizing cooking gas for the poor, and users of public transportation.

The Lessons from Norway and Alberta

Norway, with a land mass slightly larger than Malaysia and a population only twice that of Perak, 'sterilizes' its oil revenue by diverting it into a separate trust fund for use by future generations. The wisdom of that initiative is that the new wealth did not disrupt the social and economic fabric of Norwegian society. There was no runaway inflation as in Nigeria, and the Norwegians did not become lazy profligate consumers dependent on their new oil wealth, as with the Arabs.

The Norwegians pay the same world price at the pump for their petroleum, currently at about RM 7 per liter, nearly three times the new Malaysian price. One consequence is that while they have one of the highest per-capita incomes, car ownership among Norwegians is one of the lowest in Europe. To them, a car is simply a means of transportation, not for ostentation. Everybody knows that they are already wealthy; they do not need to flaunt it. Further, the cars on the streets of Oslo are fuel efficient brands like Volkswagen rather than luxurious Mercedes. Stiff taxes for gas-guzzlers also encourage that choice of fuel-efficient cars.

Among the many positive consequences to that policy is that their roads are not congested, and air less polluted.

Today the Norwegian Petroleum Trust is the world's second largest sovereign fund, and fast expanding. It may have already exceeded a trillion (a million million) US dollars. When the oil wells run dry, as they inevitably would, the Norwegians could still enjoy their present lifestyles as the Trust Fund's income could cover the country's budget till perpetuity.

Like everyone else, the Norwegians do not like paying high prices for their petrol, or anything else for that matter. They willingly do so because they see the direct and tangible benefits of such enlightened policies.

The Albertans too pay world price for their energy, with their government diverting the extra bounty into a separate Heritage Fund. Unlike the Norwegians who invest in global stock markets, the Albertans invest in their schools, universities, and hospitals.

Consequently, Alberta is the only place where the rich send their children to public schools! The University of Alberta (my alma mater) is now regarded as one of the finest, thanks to the generous funding from the Heritage Fund.

Malaysian Petroleum Trust Fund

Malaysia can improve on the Norwegian and Albertan models. Commit to remove all subsidies on energy, and do so in a phased and predictable manner, spread over a couple of years or even longer, coupled with a properly thought out plan to protect the poor.

For example, continue subsidizing cooking gas for the poor, and only for them. It should be easy to devise such a poverty-ameliorating program with minimal leakage. Malaysia could model it after America's "food stamps" program.

Likewise, subsidize and thus encourage public transportation. In British Columbia, Canada, season pass holders (rich and poor) for public transit get a rebate from the government. There is a public good in this; for by not using their cars for commuting, the air is less polluted and streets less congested, and thus would require less maintenance.

The money saved from removing the subsidies should be diverted to a special Petroleum Heritage Fund. The corpus (or principal) would be invested locally in a broadly diversified portfolio to include stocks, bonds, real estate, and venture capital. The fund should be a passive investor, concerned only with profit making.

The Norwegians limit their holdings in any company to no more than 5 percent, meaning, they are in it purely for the profit potential and not to seek control or management. It is for this reason that unlike other sovereign funds (Singapore's Temasek as well as China's many funds), the Norwegians are the most sought-after investors.

Like the Alberta Heritage Fund, the income from the Petroleum Fund should be used to improve schools and universities, as well as providing affordable housing and better health care. Just as the corpus must be invested locally, the income too must be spent locally. Thus, no scholarships to send students abroad, instead the money should be spent to improve local universities to benefit the greatest number of students.

Malaysia now has many such trust funds, from Tabung Haji to Employees Provident Fund. All too often they serve nothing more than as sources of cheap funds for the politically well connected. They are also not well managed.

To sell this idea, the Petroleum Fund should be professionally managed and free of political interference. This is a high but achievable order. That means its governing board must have wide representations, including nominees of the opposition political parties and NGOs. Anything less and it would be hard to sell the policy.

Pakatan Rakyat's leader Anwar Ibrahim rightly expressed the public fear and mistrust that the funds saved from reducing or abolishing the subsidy would be used to benefit Abdullah's political cronies and family members. Anwar and Malaysians generally have good reasons for this suspicion.

I am not impressed with Abdullah's proposal to provide tax rebates for car owners. If they can afford to buy a car, then they do not need any subsidy or rebate from the government.

Abdullah should spend the petroleum dollars locally to benefit Malaysians, especially residents of oil-producing states. It is morally indefensible and politically foolish to see residents of the three states where oil is produced (Trengganu, Sabah, and Sarawak) are also among the poorest.

If Abdullah does not handle this petroleum subsidy issue wisely, it could prove to be the final straw to his downfall. On the other hand, if he could learn (a big if) from the Norwegians and the Albertans, he could not only salvage his political future but more importantly, leave a significant legacy.

Note To A Malaysian Obama

November 16, 2008

On Tuesday November 4th, 2008, America became, in the words of comedian Jon Stewart, more of a "show" nation and less of a "tell" one. In electing Barack Obama, America showed the world that it was now closer to being that "more perfect Union," to quote the preamble to her constitution. Nations are like people; it matters not where you have been, more important is where you are headed.

In his victory speech Obama cited 106-year old Ann Dixon Cooper from the South who recalls only too well the time when women and blacks were not allowed to vote. The fate of blacks was worse. In his stirring speech Obama challenged Americans to imagine their nation a century hence; what his young daughters would experience should they be lucky enough to live as long a life as Ms. Cooper. Would they too see comparable progress as that witnessed by her?

Obama's victory captured the world's imagination, especially in Kenya where his father was born, and in Malaysia too, but for a far different reason. I had intimation of this when on meeting a group of Malaysian students in New York the weekend before the elections, I was asked whether Malaysia was ready for her own Barack Obama. Before replying, I countered with a question of my own: Was there a Malaysian Obama? More specifically, is Malaysia capable of producing such a leader?

Labeling Barack Obama

Obama is the product of a white mother and a black father. They were no ordinary parents; both had PhDs, his father's from Harvard. Obama however was brought up for the most part by his maternal grandparents, a solid Middle-America couple from Kansas.

In achievements, Barack followed the trajectory more typical of an ambitious white middle-class family: exclusive "prep" school followed by an Ivy League education. While Obama could throw a mean basketball through the hoop, his climb to the top was through academics, not athletics or music. Stated differently, Obama's path to success hews closer to a Kennedy than a Kareem Abdul Jabbar. Obama adopted the faith of his mother and grandparents, not of his Muslim father or stepfather, which is a minority faith albeit a fast-growing one in America.

In his speeches, from the imageries and metaphors he used down to his accent and delivery, Obama is more Jack Kennedy than Jesse Jackson, more Cambridge Massachusetts than Southside Chicago. Obama's favorite expression was, "My fellow Americans!" not, "Yo! Brother!" He favored conservative dark suits and a well-trimmed look, not brash-colored Afro suits and daring hairdo.

Culturally at least, Obama is more white than black. During the early part of his political campaign, he had to fight hard the widely held perception in the black community that he "ain't black enough."

Yet to the white dominant American society, Obama is black, not white. The reason is obvious; he carries the physical features of a black, including or especially his skin color. During the intense campaign there were concerted efforts to paint him as being "not one of us." This would have happened even if he were a conservative with a waspish name like Alan Lee Keyes, another Black presidential candidate, and not a foreign one like Barack Hussein Obama.

Obama had to constantly deny that he was a Muslim. It is doubtful that he would have secured his party's nomination, let alone the election, had he been a Muslim. This does not mean that America is anti-Muslim, rather that it is not quite yet ready to accept someone from a minority faith to be in the White House. A generation ago America had difficulty digesting the fact that a Catholic would be president. This recent election season also saw (during the Republican primaries) misgivings about Mitt Romney's Mormon faith.

In America, the path to "a more perfect Union," while steady, is slow.

Contrast that to Malaysia. There are many children of Malay-Caucasian as well as Malay-Chinese and Malay-Indian marriages exhibiting very "un-Malay" features. Yet Malay culture has been very welcoming of them, unhesitatingly embracing them as Malays. This is not a recent phenomenon. I had many childhood friends and classmates who had distinctly Chinese or Indian appearances because of adoption or mixed marriages, yet they were all considered and treated as Malays.

Why the children of mixed marriages between a member of the majority and a minority are not regarded as the majority in America as with Obama, but they are in Malaysia, is an observation worth pondering. I am certain this is related to an underlying obsession with "racial purity."

As a Malay I am heartened that my culture is very welcoming of those who are adopted, products of mixed marriages, or do not look like us, whatever that presumed "Malay appearance" might be. We are thankfully, not consumed with maintaining our "purity."

Malaysia already has her Barack Obama in the person of Mahathir Mohamad. We do not recognize him as such because unlike in America where her Obama is considered a member of the minority, Malaysia's majority Malays warmly and quickly embrace their Obama as one of their own. Nor is Mahathir alone; earlier leaders like Datuk Onn and Tunku Abdul Rahman were also of mixed ancestry.

By biological heritage Obama has equal claim to being black or white. Yet because of his unalterable physical characteristics, Obama is labeled black. Even if Obama were to resort to the miracles of plastic surgery, skin-whitening cream, and hair coloring and straightening *a la* Michael Jackson, which Obama does not, he would still be labeled black.

For contrast, examine the group portrait of UMNO Supreme Council members. If they were to dispense with their songkok and *Baju Melayu* and instead put on modern attire, some of them could easily be mistaken as delegates from MCA or MIC, that is, until they open their big mouths and chant their chauvinistic slogan of *Ketuanan Melayu*!

Malaysian Obama Wannabe

Malaysians do not recognize their Obamas because our Obamas have adopted and are comfortable with the cultural values of the majority; they consider themselves and are being treated as a member of that majority.

Malaysia's Obamas are comfortable with and have successfully adopted the dominant culture. They are fluent in Malay, not the language of their forefathers, just like Obama cannot speak a word of Swahili, or whatever language his late father used in Kenya.

The heroes Obama invokes are Jefferson and Lincoln, not some Mau Mau chief or Zulu King. Likewise, a Malaysian Obama wannabe must invoke local heroes, not Churchill, Nehru, or Mao. Just as Obama has a fondness for conservative business suits and not colorful Kenyan robes, his Malaysian wannabe must not only be comfortable in songkok and batik but must also look good in them. You would not endear yourself to the majority (which is the first step to earning their votes) if you balk at wearing the songkok when in the palace to pay homage to the King or Sultan, or entering their place of worship wearing a short skirt and dispensing with a headscarf.

Malaysia is not only ready for her Barack Obama, she has already produced quite a few. Dispense with the racial label and ask the more substantive question of whether Malaysia could produce a future leader the caliber and transforming character of Barack Obama, then the answer would be more complex and problematic.

Obama captured the imagination of Americans with his brilliance, eloquence, and charisma. He appealed to their finer instincts; he brought Americans together, transcending class, region, and most of all, race.

Despite all that it is well to be reminded that Obama would not have secured his party's nomination if the Democratic Party had adopted the procedures of the Republican Party, with its winner-takes-all rules in the states' primaries. Had the Democrats done that, Hilary Clinton would have been their nominee, not Obama.

For another, Obama owed his meteoric rise in the Democratic Party to many senior party leaders. His fellow senator and former presidential candidate, John Kerry, spotlighted Obama by giving him a slot to address the Democratic National Convention in 2004 that catapulted Obama to the national scene. Obama followed that with his stirring all-American success story in his bestselling autobiographies, *Dreams of My Father* and *The Audacity of Hope.*

I am certain that a just Allah has also blessed Malaysia with her share of individuals with the leadership talent and charisma of Obama. Whether they would be nurtured by our institutions would be the biggest challenge. Malaysian schools and universities would more than likely stunt their development or poison them with chauvinistic ideas.

Even if such individuals were lucky enough to escape the local system by attending international schools in Malaysia and then proceed to the great universities abroad, there is little reason to expect that they would be welcomed back home. More than likely such scarce talents would have been seduced by the more lucrative and challenging opportunities abroad. Even if they were to return home, they would have been tempted by the more rewarding careers in the private sector.

This problem is not unique to Malaysia but plagues the developing world. It also afflicts economically "First World" but culturally and politically "Third World" countries like Singapore.

Even if a brilliant young Malaysian Obama could fend off those temptations and opt for a career in politics, his path would not be fast or clear. For one, he would have difficulty being accepted by the local party branch as those insecure village leaders would be wary of new challengers. Even if he were to be accepted, there would not be a Kerry-like senior figure to grease the path. Malaysian leaders promote only their kith and kind, not some unknown talent no matter how promising.

The political structure and culture in Malaysia do not lend themselves to such rapid renewals of leadership. The Malaysian pattern is akin to the landing slots at a major airport, with the third or fourth tier leaders all dutifully lining up taking their turns. If perchance one proves later to be a dud, it matters not; his or her turn is coming up anyway.

There are indeed many a Malaysian Obama out there, but nobody cares or would bother to find or nurture them. That unfortunately is a loss for the nation.

Rustam Sani: Patriot And Intellectual (1944-2008)

April 24, 2008

I was saddened to hear of the sudden death of Rustam Sani. In Rustam Malaysia had a true patriot, one whose love for the country was pure. His came from the head as well as the heart. It was patriotism unadulterated by the pursuit of material wealth, public adulation, or political power. A genuine intellectual, he was not one to fit his ideas to the prevailing fashion of the day.

He recognized early the heavy duty and responsibility of being a patriot. His was not one consumed with endless exhortations. As the son of a renowned nationalist, Rustam must have been immersed in the patriotic fervor and fiery speeches of his late father, Ahmad Boestaman. Rustam knew at a young age that the new independent Malaysia would need leaders who not only loved the country but also be well equipped with the necessary skills and intellect to lead it.

He focused on his schoolwork fully aware that he was among the fortunate few to have the privilege of attending school. From his local *sekolah attap* (village school) in Behrang Ulu and later the Methodist School Tanjong Malim, he went on to the University of Malaya via Victoria Institution. From there on to graduate work at Kent and Reading in Britain, and later, Yale.

He was both a scholar as well as practitioner of politics. His intellectual accomplishments were never diminished by his political involvement. He had penned more academic papers and popular commentaries as well as books than many fulltime academics. It was only yesterday that I read his latest (and alas his last) posting on his blog. Rustam was in his usual sharp element; that posting was a trenchant commentary on Mahathir's interview on BBC's *Hard Talk*. Rustam was to have launched his latest books, *Failed Nation? Concerns of a Malaysian Nationalist,* and *Social Roots of the Malay Left,* later this month. Imagine two books at the same time!

As an academic, Rustam molded thousands of young minds. That may be his greatest though not easily visible legacy. Rustam may not have been successful in electoral politics, nonetheless his contributions to the nation dwarfs those of "successful" political leaders.

Rustam is survived by his wife Rohani, son Azrani, and daughter Ariani, as well as daughter-in-law Ku Salha and granddaughter Arissa. My condolences and prayers to them in this moment of sadness. May Allah shower His blessings and Mercy on this great Malaysian patriot and intellect.

Book Reviews

A Wonderful Depiction Of Mother-Daughter Bonding

Book Review: Rosana Sullivan's *Mommy Sayang*, Pixar Animation Studios Artist Showcase Series, Disney Press, New York & Los Angeles, April 2019.

ISBN: 978-1-368-01590-5 / LCCN: 2018033419; Hardcover; 48 pages; $11.72; Age level 4-7 (Preschool and Kindergarten)

May 9, 2019

Storytelling fills our basic need for intergenerational bonding. This is especially so for a mother and child. Storytelling has been practiced since time immemorial. That notwithstanding, few of us, mothers included, are born raconteurs; hence the endurance of fairy tales and booming sales of children's books.

In 2014 Walt Disney Animation Studio and Pixar Animation Studios teamed up with Disney Worldwide Publishing to launch a series of children's books by their artists and storytellers.

The Pixar Animation Studios Artist Showcase series was Disney's way to recognize and provide an avenue to showcase the talents of its artists. Otherwise the only public recognition they received would be the ever-too-brief mention in the lines of credit rolling fast up the screen at the end of a movie or tape.

Most children's books, being produced in the West, are heavy on themes and scenes familiar only to their Western urban readers. Even when those books venture to the countryside as with the Peter Rabbit series, the farm scenes would be heavily sanitized.

Rosana Sullivan's *Mommy Sayang* (Mommy Dear!) is a refreshing exception. Hers is autobiographical, set in a Malay kampung. Her story arc is simple and readily comprehensible but nonetheless profound: a child's secure, comfortable world suddenly turned topsy-turvy with her dear mother becoming unwell. This sudden reversal of fortune is a universal theme, as is a mother's love for her child, and vice versa.

Mommy Sayang follows the infinite curiosities of a child, Aleeya, and her mother's ever patient and attentive responses to her endless inquisitive "Whys." This maternal-love theme is reinforced throughout the book.

After the panoramic kampung scene on the first page, complete with the adjacent rice field, cars parked on the front yards, houses on stilts with the women casually conversing on the steps, the obligatory mosque, and yes, even a water buffalo with a little boy holding the tether, is the sketch of two mother hens with their broods happily pecking on the spacious grounds. On the next page a mother cat nursing her kittens. Mother hens and cat look contended, like all happy mothers.

Then there are the scenes of her mother cooking, serving dinner, and praying. There is the touching picture of her mother's storytelling and kissing her at bedtime that launched Aleeya into her dreams of extravagant flowers in vivid, vibrant colors. The illustrations reveal much about Malay culture, right down to the food eaten. There was the ubiquitous durian on the table served next to a Caucasian-looking guest, and without him grimacing!

Aleeya's world was suddenly turned upside down when her mother became unwell. The whole household routine hitherto predictable and routine was disrupted. Unable to comprehend the sudden change, Aleeya acted out as her aunts and others tried to console her.

She found solace in those beautiful flowers in her yard as well as in her dreams. She picked one colorful hibiscus in full bloom and gave it to her mother, a simple heartfelt expression of a child's love for her mother. As with all Disney stories, with that simple gesture her mother felt better— the healing power of nature's beauty and a child's love. And Aleeya's world was restored!

Rosana, American-born and of Malaysian descent, now resides in Oakland, California. Among the many films she has worked on are "The Good Dinosaur," "Coco," and "Incredibles 2." She recently released her first short animation, "Kitbull," written and directed by her, to critical reviews.

Mommy Sayang is her first children's book, suitable for 3-7 years old. It is delightfully written and even more beautifully illustrated. As you would expect from an outfit like Disney, the technical quality of this hardcover was flawless. This book would make a perfect Mother's Day gift for a young mother. I am getting a few for my many grandnieces who are now mothers or soon-to-be. The book would also be an excellent and enjoyable way to introduce your child to a different culture—that of rural Malaysia.

The focal points of the illustrations are clear and well depicted. We could see the serene reflections on the subject's face, as with the cat and her kittens. The background is uncluttered and conveys the essence of an unadorned Malay kitchen and simple kampung life.

This book is a universe beyond, in content and presentation, to the *A Man, A Pan* English reading text I had in primary school back during the colonial days in the early 1950s. If the Ministry of Education is looking for supplemental reading books in its effort to increase the English fluency of rural pupils, this is the one I strongly recommend.

The only anachronism in the illustrations for me growing up in a kampung in the 1950s would be the gas stove and electric fans. We had neither in those days.

In Arabic, Aleeyah means exalted or sublime. Despite Malaysia's obsession with matters Arabic, modern Malays tend to dispense with the "h" ending, as with "Maria" and "Marina" instead of "Mariah" and "Marinah." The Western influence is still strong and pervasive.

With Rosana's gift for drawing and storytelling, Aleeya will soon be a well-known children's character, adorable to kids and adults. Elsa, meet your competition!

Pamper Those At Home, The Ones Abroad Would Soon Return

Review of Ruslan Khalid's *Quest for Architectural Excellence. A Malaysian Experience.* Marshall Cavendish, Singapore, 2013. 308 pp. US$35.00; RM44.90.

August 5, 2014

During World War II, British aviation experts were consumed with analyzing and fixing returning warplanes that had been fired upon, until it was pointed out that those damages were not critical as the planes could still fly and return home safely. It was counterintuitive but logical; if you want to study the damages that were critical, examine the downed planes.

Last year, the Talent Corporation spent RM65 million on Malaysian professionals abroad to entice them to return. It may be counterintuitive but the money would have been better spent on those now at home so they would not even *consider* leaving. If they are happy, the good word would soon spread, enticing those abroad to return.

My old village wisdom counseled us against the trap of *kera di hutan di susukan, anak di rumah mati kelaparan* (breastfeeding the monkey in the jungle while letting your child at home starve to death).

An emigrating family, like Tolstoy's unhappy family in *Anna Karenina*, is unique unto its own. Instead of studying "big data" on the brain drain, it would be more fruitful to analyze individual cases, not those who emigrate but the ones who return or have stayed.

One such professional was the late architect Ruslan Khalid. He died in November 2, 2012, only days after final-proofing his autobiography, *Quest For Architectural Excellence. The Malaysian Experience.*

Product of London's AA School of Architecture

Ruslan graduated from London's prestigious Architectural Association (AA) School of Architecture and had a successful practice in London before returning home late in 1979. Among his clients in London was the Sultan of Pahang.

His final dozen years or so in Malaysia took only about a third of his 308-page book. Those running the Talent Corporation would learn more from reading those pages than they would from gallivanting around the world enticing Malaysians to return. It would also be a lot cheaper, and the book is an enjoyable read to boot, quite apart from being informative. Ruslan wrote well, with elegance and passion. He had also immersed himself into the upper crust of British artistic society, and readers get a glimpse of that as a bonus.

Ruslan dedicated his book to "all late starters." Presumably, he considered himself one. On the contrary as is evident from the book, he was intelligent, insightful, and very resourceful right from the very beginning. Those qualities of his were not recognized early or at all by his native country, nor were they readily assessed by paper-and-pencil tests.

He obtained *only* (his description) Grade II in his School Certificate Examination in 1952 and a scholarship to a third-rate British architectural school. He recognized that stark reality on his very first day on campus. For an institution to train designers of buildings and structures, the edifice of his school was anything but inspiring. It was like entering a hospital or medical school where the foyer was dirty and ambience unhygienic. Only if you were desperate would you trust it or have any confidence in it.

It reflected the foresight of his colonial interviewers that they awarded him a scholarship despite his Grade II; *they* saw his potential. After all he entered English school only two years earlier, having previously attended only Malay and religious schools. It also reflected the wisdom of his teachers then that he had to take English classes at his Islamic school. Where are those educators today?

On his voyage to England he bunked with three top-scorer students. By the time they reached Bombay, he had already befriended a certain lady from the First-Class Deck while the other three were content jabbering among themselves. As luck would have it, she was the wife of a famous architect, besides being one herself.

With uninspiring lecturers in a third-rate institution, Ruslan flunked his second year. Undeterred and confident of his talent, he pursued his craft through the old apprentice system. His portfolio, together with his contacts with many well-known architects, helped pave his way into AA School as an advanced student on a *British* scholarship.

All these are interesting preamble but the topic at hand is on enticing successful Malaysians to return, and to inquire what made them leave in the first place. This native son's travails at home upon his return late in his life shed much light.

Disappointments At Home

Despite having been a practicing architect for over a decade in London, his application for registration in Malaysia was summarily denied. He did not have the prerequisite two years of local public service. Not wishing to be desk-bound in some ministry, he opted for teaching at Universiti Teknoloji Malaysia. After all he had been a senior lecturer in London.

The ending was predictable, and it came soon. He left after the minimum two years to pursue private practice, which led him to be editor of his professional association's journal. He soon discovered that his profession at home was but the handmaiden for developers. The journal he edited was more advertising channel for the industry than advancing the art and science of local architecture. His observation is still valid today and could be extended to many local "professional" journals.

A few years later UPM opened its architectural faculty. Eager to train future architects in his mold, Ruslan became its founding dean. Again, the quick and predictable ending! Despite being on the Sultan of Pahang's polo team and Prime Minister Mahathir's riding companion, quite apart from having a half-brother in the cabinet, Ruslan was, as he wrote, "relieved of his duties." Mahathir offered his services to have him reinstated, but bitten twice, Ruslan politely declined.

The one incident during his deanship was symptomatic of the country's malaise and obsession with praises from foreigners. He had fought hard to improve the academic facilities when, unbeknown to Ruslan, the Vice-Chancellor had hired a British consultant. As it turned out Ruslan knew him. No surprise that the report was full of praise and confidence of the faculty's future under Ruslan's leadership. The VC used that as an excuse to deny Ruslan's request, deeming that the faculty was already fine as it was!

Again, I can relate to that. As a surgeon in Johor Baru in 1978, I fought hard to upgrade the hospital to be worthy of a teaching institution. Then came a British delegation sponsored by the Ministry of Health. At the exit conference the British spokesman could hardly restrain himself in praising our facility, egged on by the beaming smiles of local officials.

When he finished, I spoke up. I told him that much as I appreciated his generous remarks, he had effectively undercut our efforts. The Ministry would now not approve our request seeing that our facility was already doing well. Then to drive home my point, I told everyone that I had never been to a British teaching hospital, but if they were impressed with our facility, then I did not think highly of their standards.

At the end of the meeting one of the surveyors sought me out to apologize. I told him it mattered not as the damage had already been done and that he surely would be invited again for the next survey, unless of course he was willing to submit an amended report.

These ugly realities would never be uncovered in glitzy official reports or expensive international consultants' surveys; hence the need for personal accounts as with Ruslan Khalid's *In Quest for Architectural Excellence*.

Ruslan Khalid is now gone, may Allah bless his soul and put him among the righteous. Allah had been generous to him, not only in giving him those precious talents but also in letting Ruslan see the blue proofs of his manuscript just before he died. Ruslan had instructed that upon his death, his extensive portfolios be bequeathed to be used to further Malaysian architecture. Invaluable though those portfolios may be, in my mind none could match this legacy—a native son's thoughtful and insightful autobiography. Young Malaysians would be inspired by his story. As for Malaysia, the nation would be the poorer if she does not heed his wisdom.

Growing Up With A Nation That Isn't

Review of Ahmad Kamil Jaafar's *Growing Up With The Nation.* Marshall Cavendish, Singapore, 2013. 256 pp. RM135

July 1, 2014

The life of a diplomat, as the laity sees it, is one of glittering cocktail parties, spacious residences in leafy exclusive neighborhoods, and being pampered in MAS first-class cabins, all paid for by taxpayers.

As such it was a surprise for me to read this opening line in *Growing Up With The Nation*, the memoir of Ahmad Kamil Jaafar, Malaysia's former top diplomat, "The life of a diplomat and foreign policy maker can be pretty much routine and humdrum during the best of times."

Then as if to underscore this point, midway through the book, in the chapter "China—A Transformational Journey," he writes, "Finding myself with ample free time I tried my hand at learning Chinese … and Chinese brush painting."

This was the mid-1980s when China was undergoing, as per the chapter title, transformational changes under Deng Xiaoping. To be bored or have ample free time at such a period reflected more on the caliber of our diplomats generally rather than on Kamil Jaafar's talent, ability, or diligence.

It was commendable for Kamil to learn Mandarin. It would have been even more impressive had he done it *before* being posted there. There was (and is) no lack of opportunities for learning that language in Malaysia. Granted, the Malaysian Chinese accent may be way off the Beijing variety, nonetheless the basics remain the same.

Kamil Jaafar is privileged to have been given the great opportunity and rare responsibility to guide the young Malaysia. There are many others, but most are content to spend their retirement collecting lucrative GLC directorship fees and hitting golf balls. Malaysians owe Kamil a huge debt of gratitude for having taken time and effort to recollect his experiences so others could benefit.

Maximal Recollection, Minimal Reflection

Kamil's memoir, competently written, spans a career of over three decades. He retired in 1996 as the top civil servant in the Foreign Ministry but continued as Special Envoy. He covered a vast expanse of water. However, as any scuba diver would tell you, the world underneath is even more rich, challenging, and fascinating. Skimming the surface may get you far but at the price of missing this wonderful universe below. Stating it diplomatically, Kamil's memoir has maximal recollection but at the expense of thoughtful reflection.

On the rare occasions when he does pause, Kamil is astute and penetrating, revealing much. Recalling a meeting between Prime Minister Mahathir and Chairman Deng, Kamil noted the large spittoon which Deng used only three times during the entire encounter. Kamil congratulated Mahathir, deeming the meeting a success, at least by that criterion. Deng may be a transformational leader of the biggest country, but in mannerisms he was just another coolie. Diplomatically spun, Deng remained faithful to his plebian origin.

During Abdullah Badawi's tenure as Foreign Minister, Kamil felt like his ministry was under the Prime Minister's Department. That reveals volumes on Abdullah's capability and contribution. Apparently, Abdullah was satisfied if not reveled in being sidelined.

Abdullah was a special guest at this book's launching. He obviously had not read the book, or if he did, missed that subtle but devastating jab. Or I could be over reading that passage.

In a post-publication interview Kamil related how tough he was with his subordinates. I wish he had been equally frank and tough on his political superiors. Did he see any parallel between Abdullah's performances as Foreign Minister and later as Prime Minister? As for the other dozen or so foreign ministers Kamil served under, none merited more than just a few bland lines penned in passing. Most were skipped entirely. Perhaps that said it all.

Of all the prime ministers, only Mahathir did not serve concurrently as foreign minister. Yet Kamil devotes more ink to him than to anyone else. His adoration for Mahathir is unbridled, and evident throughout the book. Yet when Kamil lamented on the poor English of our young diplomats and how that handicaps them professionally, he fails to make the connection. Mahathir was most responsible for this sorry state, first as Minister of Education and later as Prime Minister.

Mahathir appointed Kamil as Secretary-General of the Foreign Ministry. That has much to do with this uncritical appraisal of the man.

As for that promotion, Kamil recalled his colleagues urging him to decline it, in deference to the incumbent who had been at it for only six months. That reveals the destructive culture of the civil service, this *tunggu geleran* (duly and patiently waiting your turn), like incoming planes at a busy airport. That, more than anything else, is responsible for the anti-meritocratic norms of the civil service. There is no such thing as fast tracking. You wait your turn patiently.

Kamil rationalized his acceptance thus: "I dare not go against the Prime Minister's decision." I would have preferred had he asserted that he could do a better job. False modesty is hard to conceal while the genuine form is overrated. Besides, a senior civil servant should never fear of going against his political superior if that is the wise thing to do.

Kamil had a brief and less-than-laudatory paragraph on Prime Minister Hussein Onn, recalling a meeting involving a sensitive issue related to a neighboring country. Kamil and his counterparts in the Home Ministry including its minister, Ghazali Shafie, had concocted a nefarious scheme the nature of which was not revealed. When they finished briefing Hussein, he became visibly angry and reprimanded them.

"What you are doing is a bottomless pit. You cannot do to others what you do not want others to do to you," Kamil quoted Hussein, who ordered an immediate halt. Kamil did not describe his or Ghazali's reaction to this dressing down by Prime Minister Hussein.

Hussein was not known to be a decisive leader, but on that occasion when he most needed to be, he was. That brief anecdote epitomized Hussein's integrity and fair-mindedness. I remind readers that the odious phrase "cronyism, corruption and nepotism" entered the popular

Malaysian lexicon only after Hussein had left office. As an aside, he was *not* cited in the index, perhaps an honest line editing slip.

John Kenneth Galbraith, Kennedy's Ambassador to India, wrote in his *Ambassador's Journal* that Kennedy read his (Galbraith's) dispatches because they were a joy. I assume that most diplomatic communications are not, consumed as they are with being detached and laced with bureaucratese as well as bewildering acronyms. They are also written so as not to offend anyone.

Kamil no longer needs to be deferential to his former superiors. He should be critical of their performances. He should go beyond lamenting the current sorry state of Malaysia and analyze the "who, what, where, when, why and how." Which leaders were most culpable for Malaysia not growing up? If luminaries like Kamil shy away from this crucial responsibility, then by default it would fall on the *tin kosong jaguh kampong* (empty tin-can village champions). And the nation would be the poorer for that.

Proposed Diplomat's Assignment

Kamil recalled how as a young diplomat he was clueless as there was no one to guide him. Now having reached the pinnacle of his career, he put forth very few ideas to guide his young successors, except for them to improve their English. That reveals volumes on the state of the Malaysian foreign service today.

To fill this void, I share with our diplomats, young and old, this advice, the one my late father gave me before I left for Canada back in 1963. Observe the country and its people, he counseled me, be perceptive of and receptive to your new environment. Heed the wisdom of our culture, *Alam terkembang di jadikan guru* (Let the expanding universe be your teacher), echoing Wordsworth's "Let nature be your teacher."

On a specific point, my father asked me to ponder this question: Why was it that Canada was offering those generous scholarships to young Malaysians and not Malaysia to Canadians?

Tailoring that query to Malaysian diplomats-to-be, I would advise them thus. Study one feature of your host country that is worthy of Malaysia's emulation, or conversely, the one to avoid falling into. A Malaysian Third Secretary in Venezuela could learn how that country successfully used music to empower poor children and produce superb youth orchestras as well as many accomplished young conductors. The High Commissioner to Nigeria would warn us of the fate that awaits Malaysia if it does not get a handle on corruption, while that to Pakistan, the dangers if religious extremists were to get the upper hand.

With such an assignment tagged onto their regular duties, Malaysian diplomats, novice and seasoned, would never again complain of their posting "being routine and humdrum," or having "ample free time." Thus occupied, they would also not likely get themselves into mischief or otherwise embarrass the nation.

Ampun Tuanku: Sultans' *Daulat* A Myth

Book Review: *Ampun Tuanku. A Brief Guide to Constitutional Government.* Zaid Ibrahim. ZI Publications, Petaling Jaya, 2012. ISBN 9 789675 266263, 256 pp, RM 35.00.

April 19, 2009 *(First Of Three Parts)*
As a youngster in 1960 I had secured for myself a commanding view high atop a coconut tree to watch the funeral procession of the first King, Tuanku Abdul Rahman. My smug demonstration of my perched position drew the attention of the village elders below. They were none too pleased and immediately ordered me down.

"Sultans have *daulat*," they admonished me, "you cannot be above them." Apparently even dead sultans maintained their *daulat*. I did not dare challenge my elders as to what would happen once the king was buried; then we all would be above him.

This attribution of special or divine powers to rulers is not unique to Malay culture. The ancient Chinese Emperors had their *Tianming*, Mandate from Heaven. Even that was not enough to protect them.

Even though it has deep roots in Malay society, this *daulat* thing is a myth. The Japanese, despite their own "Sun Goddess" tradition, had no difficulty disabusing Malay sultans and their subjects of this myth during the Occupation. The surprise was not how quickly the sultans lost their power and prestige, or how quickly they adapted to their new plebian status, rather how fast the Malay masses accepted this new reality of their rajas being ordinary mortals, *sans daulat.*

Only days before the Japanese landed, any Malay peasant who perchance made eye contact with his sultan, may Allah have mercy on him for the sultan certainly would not. When the Japanese took over, those rajas had to scramble with the other villagers for what few fish there were in the river and what scarce mushrooms they could scrape in the jungle. Nobody was bothered with or took heed of the *daulat* thing. So much for it being deeply entrenched in Malay culture!

To pursue my point, had the Malayan Union succeeded, Malay sultans today would have been all *tanjak* (ceremonial weapon) and *desta* (headgear), nothing else; they would have as much status and power as the Sultan of Sulu. Across in Indonesia, hitherto exalted Malay sultans are now reduced to ordinary citizens. They and their society are none the worse for that.

Today's slightly better educated Malay sultans and crown princes (there are no crown princesses, let it be noted) would like Malays to believe in yet another myth, this time based not on culture but the constitution. They believe that it provides them with that extra "something" beyond their being mere constitutional heads.

This new myth, like all good fiction, has just a tinge of reality to it. The Reid Commission had envisaged the Conference of Rulers to be the Third House of Parliament, after the elected House of Representatives and the appointed Senate. It was to be a greatly reduced or refined House of Lords as it were, to provide much-needed "final thought" to new legislations.

That assumption had considerable merit, at least in theory. As membership is hereditary, those rulers would be spared from having to pander to the masses as those elected Members of Parliament, or please their political patrons as with the senators. As a bonus, this third house would be non-partisan and stable. Only through death could its membership be changed.

An expression of this "Third House of Parliament" function is that all senior governmental including ministerial appointments must be ratified by the Conference of Rulers. Unlike the transparent deliberations of the "advice and consent" function of the United States Senate where senior appointees are subjected to open confirmation hearings, the proceedings of the Conference are secret. We know only those who have been accepted, not those rejected or why.

A rather long preamble to my reviewing Zaid Ibrahim's *Ampun Tuanku. A Brief Guide to Constitutional Government.* Zaid addresses what should be in his view the proper role of sultans in the Malaysian brand of constitutional monarchy, specifically whether they have this "something extra" beyond what is explicitly stated in the constitution. As a lawyer Zaid is uniquely qualified to write on the matter. He is no ordinary lawyer, having once headed the country's largest legal firm and served as the nation's *de facto* Law Minister.

The title notwithstanding, this highly readable book is more persuasive than descriptive; more political science treatise, less legal brief. The expository flow is smooth, logical, and highly convincing. It is refreshingly free of legal jargon or references to court cases and precedents that typically pollute commentaries by lawyers. To Zaid, the constitution does indeed grant Malay sultans that something extra, but not in their capacity as the titular head of the government, rather as their being head of Islam and defender of the faith.

Zaid explores the many wonderful opportunities possible as derivatives of this second function without having to invoke additional "special powers." I will pursue his novel ideas and wonderful suggestions later. At 40 pages, his chapter on this issue ("The Rulers and Islamization") is the longest and deserves careful reading especially by the royal class. He puts forth many innovative ideas that if pursued would benefit not only Malays and Malaysians but also the sultans.

With active and enlightened engagement by the rulers and Agung, Islam would emancipate Malays just as it did the ancient Bedouins, and in the process enhance race relations. That would be a pleasant if somewhat radical departure from the current environment where Islam not only deeply polarizes Malays but also sows much interfaith and interracial distrust.

In all other aspects the sultans and Agung are bound by what is explicitly stated in the constitution. Malaysia is a constitutional monarchy, Zaid stresses, and our sultans and Agung must abide by the wishes of the rakyat as expressed through their elected representatives in the executive branch. If citizens have made their wishes clear through an election that they would prefer a certain party and individuals to lead them or certain legislations enacted, the sultan must abide by that decision regardless of where his personal or political sympathy lies.

There are no penumbras or derivatives of rights and privileges emanating from those hallowed clauses of our constitution. The matter is clear: Sultans are bound by the law. Sultans cannot claim extra power based on *daulat* or divine mandate, as the Sultan as well as the Raja Muda of Perak tried to argue recently. In short, *daulat* is fiction.

This principle is central and must be defended against any incursion or erosion. Zaid was rightly distressed, for example, when the Sultan of Trengganu (who was also the Agung at the time) prevailed in making his choice of Ahmad Said as Chief Minister when the citizens had explicitly elected the state UMNO leader Idris Jusoh. This erosion of the executive power was possible only because of the weak leadership of then Prime Minister Abdullah Badawi. Similar incursion occurred in Perak, this time on a much more blatant and ugly level.

The situation in Perak was particularly instructive. Before becoming sultan, Raja Azlan Shah once served as the country's Chief Justice. As Zaid reminds his readers, in that capacity Raja Azlan clearly articulated that the powers of the Agung are well circumscribed by the constitution. As sultan however, he claimed his "special powers." That was his justification for imposing his solution on the state's political crisis during the post-2008 election crisis to favor the Barisan coalition.

Such palace incursions and the executive branch's acquiescence undermine the very principle of Malaysian democracy. On a more practical level, if that proves to be the new norm, Malaysian Chief and Prime Ministers would then be beholden to their Sultans and Agung, not the rakyat. Ministers (*menteris*) would revert to their role in feudal Malay society, as hired hands of the palace and not as the people's choice as their chief executive of the state.

In a democracy, *daulat* (sovereignty) resides with the people, not the rajas. The Malaysian constitution is clear on that point, as Zaid repeatedly reminds us. Malaysians must constantly defend that principle lest it be eroded.

Ampun Tuanku: Origin Of The *Daulat* Myth

April 26, 2009 (*Second of Three Parts*)
Zaid begins his book by briefly tracing the history of Malay sultans. Unlike the Japanese Imperial family that stretches as far back as 600 BC, or the British to the 11th Century or even earlier, Malay sultans are of recent vintage. The Raja of Perlis was established only in 1834, while that of Johor only slightly older (1819).

In modeling the Malaysian constitutional monarchy along the British one, the Reid Commission assumed that Malay sultans were like English kings. That was the first major blunder. To Zaid, that also underscores the pitfall of trying to adopt wholesale foreign concepts or models, not just in law but also much of everything else.

Those English monarchs have had centuries of working with a democratically elected government. Earlier, a few of them have had to pay dearly for their errors. As a result, today their system works well. Not so with Malay sultans. Up until British rule, Malay sultans were literally Gods; those sultans could take your life. Displease the sultan or prevent him from grabbing whatever you own including your daughter or prized *kerbau* (water buffalo), and you risked being beheaded, banished, or enslaved (*kerah*). Those sultans were not above the law as there were no laws then; *they* were the laws.

Malays like me have a lot to be thankful to those colonials for ending those odious royal traits of Malay culture. No, that is not an expression of my being mentally colonized, rather one of heartfelt gratitude.

Malaysia has a disproportionate number of monarchs, 9 out of the nearly 40 worldwide, as Zaid and others have noted. The error in that frequently cited statistics is the assumption that our sultans are comparable to those other kings and queens; they are not. There is little in common between Malay sultans and the British Queen or Japanese Emperor. Malay sultans have more in common with the tribal warlords of Africa and Papua New Guinea, from their insular worldview to their fanciful costumes. The Papuan tribal chiefs have their elaborate colorful headgear, as well as their prominent penile sheaths which they proudly display; Malay sultans have their equally ostentatious *desta* (headgear) and *tanjak* (ceremonial dagger).

Like those tribal chieftains, Malay sultans too are afflicted with their old feudal habits. Modernity has not erased or moderated their medieval mentality. When Malaysia became independent, those odious habits began creeping back. Those sultans are not to be blamed entirely for that.

"The Rulers' unwillingness to remain within their constitutional roles has been further aggravated," Zaid writes, "by a lack of conviction and courage by the institutions that are supposed to protect and preserve [our] … constitution." Stated differently, Malay sultans have many enablers for their errant ways. Citizens have allowed those sultans to regress. *We* tolerated them when they flouted the rules. That only encouraged them.

Members of the Malay royal family are perfectly capable of behaving themselves and keeping within the rules if they were to be told in no uncertain terms that their tantrums would not be tolerated. Consider their behaviors during colonial times and the Japanese Occupation. It was the sultans who *sembah* (genuflected to) the colonial and Japanese officers. Today when these Malay princes and princesses are down in Singapore, they obey even basic traffic rules. They would not dare pull their silly stunts down there; they would be immediately punished.

If America, when those sultans skipped on their Vegas casino gambling debts, the Malaysian ambassador was ever ready to bail them out. The ambassador was being the official enabler.

Just as a child whose earlier tantrums had not been corrected would grow up to be an intolerable brat, likewise when Malay sultans strayed earlier on and there was no one to restrain them, that only encouraged them to go beyond. A few decades later their excesses would trigger the constitutional crises of the 1980s and 1990s that led to the amendments ending respectively the rulers' power to veto legislations and stripping them of their legal immunity in their personal conduct.

Both were possible because of the strong executive leadership of Prime Minister Mahathir. When you have an administration with a less-than-robust electoral mandate and a leader with a banana stem spine, the sultans are emboldened to re-exert themselves; hence the insistence on invoking their *daulat* or special status.

With that, old ugly feudal traits began to re-surface and be resurrected. Consider the sordid spectacle a few years back in Singapore involving the Kelantan Royal family. They tried to kidnap the estranged Indonesian wife of one of the princes. Had that incident happened in Malaysia, rest assured that a "helpful" minister or religious leader would have "counseled" the poor young girl to return to her obnoxious husband.

In Singapore where everyone is equal under the law, that prince would not dare claim his special status. More to the point, no one would grant him that. As a result, that poor Indonesian spouse of the prince was able to escape from her palace prison.

On a much more grotesque scale, there was the case involving a Brunei prince and his British lawyers. As the dispute fell under American jurisdiction, we got to see in open court the peccadilloes of that prince. Not pretty, in fact hideous. You could assume that his counterparts in Malaysia are no different, only that their ugly acts are willfully concealed.

Because of the constitutional amendment of the 1990s, the late Yang di Pertuan Negri Sembilan was successfully sued for his unpaid debts. In the past, his creditors would not have even dared challenge him. To the royal class, peasants should be grateful that their "tributes" were accepted.

While the royal tribunal is an advancement, its learning or even deterrent value is minimal or non-existent as the proceedings are secret. Had they been open, the lavish lifestyles and obscene unpaid bills of our sultans would be exposed. They could not then readily claim their *daulat* under such ugly earthly circumstances.

Zaid advocates that those royal tribunal proceedings be open to the public, as with any court hearing. I agree. Such exposures would also help humanize our sultans, showing to the public that they are susceptible to the usual human foibles and weaknesses. Deadbeats, even royal ones, do not have *daulat*!

Ampun Tuanku: Missed Opportunities For Sultans As Head Of Islam

May 4, 2009 (*Last of Three Parts*)
The constitution explicitly states the secular role of sultans. There are no penumbras or derived powers. In practice however, as Zaid noted with everything pertaining to the law, if you have enough money you could

always hire a smarter lawyer who would argue otherwise. That is what the sultans are now doing as they can afford expensive legal counsel; hence their novel claim of "something extra" based on *daulat.*

Legal theories do not arise out of nowhere. It is the current weak political leadership of Najib (and Abdullah Badawi before him) that emboldens the sultans to reassert themselves and challenge established principles and practices.

That notwithstanding, there is one area in the constitution that is indisputable and unchallengeable: The sultan as head of Islam. This is where he could rightly claim his special status as his authority there is absolute. Creatively managed, that provision could prove to be a splendid opportunity for them to serve not only Malays but also non-Muslim Malaysians.

"Where Islam is concerned," Zaid writes, "the Malay Rulers have a golden opportunity to make their mark." That they do not is the greatest missed opportunity, for them as well as for Malaysians and Malaysia.

This special role in Islam for the sultan has a strong foundation. The concept of a supreme head of the ummah goes back to the days of the Rightly Guided Caliphs and Prophet Muhammad, s.a.w. Not surprisingly, modern Muslim leaders including our sultans have conveniently latched on to that deep symbolism.

Historically and for very practical reasons, the British were only too happy to relegate matters of Islam to the sultans. That was also politically shrewd as it placated both the natives and their sultans. It helped as Islam then was peripheral if not irrelevant to the politics and economics of the country. So that was an easy concession on the part of the colonials. Further, with Malays consumed with their sultans and religion, that eased the British to exploit the economic riches of the land with the help of immigrants who were unencumbered with either.

Today the situation is different. Malays are still obsessed with their religion and to some extent (although decidedly less so) so too their sultans. Islam today is central to everything that is Malaysian, especially politics and economics. The increasingly shrill contestation of Islam between UMNO and PAS attests to this. Islamic financial institutions are now major players in the economy, and zakat collections are in the billions.

At one level the Malay obsession with religion and the afterlife distracts us from making our rightful contribution to the country, especially in matters economic. On another, this presents lucrative opportunities for the sultans to intrude into Islamic financial matters and economic spheres, their being head and defender of the faith.

With his legal background, Zaid rightly focuses on the increasingly assertive role of syariah in the administration of justice. In the past, syariah was concerned primarily with family law, as with divorce and inheritance. Now it encroaches into areas hitherto the purview of secular (both civil as well as criminal) courts. Syariah is now on par with, and in many instances, superior to secular courts, in effect above the constitution. *Fatwas* (decrees issued by religious functionaries) now have the power of law, thus usurping the legislature.

If those were not problematic enough, with syariah usurping the criminal courts, Malaysians today face the reality that the punishment they get would depend not on the crime they have committed rather their faith. A Muslim caught committing adultery could face "stoning to death" under syariah while non-Muslims would not even be prosecuted, or if prosecuted would be slapped with a small fine for indecent exposure perhaps. Even in matters pertaining to family law, they can get messier especially where one party to the dispute is a non-Muslim. The victims are not just the living. Recent cases of "corpse snatching" are but one ugly manifestation.

This judicial abdication by the secular courts, in Zaid's view, occurred because their judges are mostly Malays who want to appear "pious and upright Muslims … to fit into the 'correct' image of a good Muslim."

Islam emancipated the ancient Bedouins and made them give up their odious practices such as female infanticide and "an eye for an eye" sense of justice. Perversely today, the more Malays and Malaysia become "Islamized," the more backward, corrupt, polarized, and dysfunctional Malays and Malaysia have become. The irony!

"Islam–the great purifier and liberating force in the world–has been reduced to a cult in Malaysia," writes Zaid. Not any ordinary cult but a rogue one, with corrupt, toxic and in some cases deviant leaders.

As acknowledged leaders of Islam, sultans have a major role to correct these glaring pathologies. That they have abdicated this crucial role is a major factor in Malays becoming deeply polarized and increasingly marginalized economically. That is a tragedy not only for Malays but also Malaysia. Ultimately this too would negatively impact the sultans.

The sultans have shirked their responsibilities because they are ill equipped to play this important role as head of the faith. They have limited knowledge of Islam and worse, they lack the curiosity to learn. As they are Islamically-challenged in all spheres, they become captives to the utterances of the ulama class (at least those state-sponsored ones), an arrangement reminiscent to what the Saudi royals have today.

The personal behaviors of these sultans also preclude them from playing exemplary roles in Islam. They frequent casinos and night clubs, not mosques and suraus. The apparent notable exception is the current Sultan of Kelantan. His visible piety softened what otherwise would have been a severe negative public perception of filial betrayal and palace coup after he took power from his incapacitated father. His modest and pious lifestyle also embarrassed the other royals. There is a picture going viral of him removing his shoes before entering a mosque during Ramadan. This was juxtaposed to that of the Johore crown prince being fitted with his polo riding boots by one of his subjects. The contrast could not have been more revealing as well as jarring; two strikingly different portraits of the head of Islam.

At another level, Malay sultans do not pay any income or other taxes. It can be argued that this is the norm for monarchies elsewhere, those being the privileges of being head of state. In Islam however, nobody is exempted from its precepts. One of the five cardinal obligations of a Muslim is to give *zakat* (tithe) in the amount of 2.5 percent of the value of your assets. This applies to leaders and followers, imams and ordinary believers, and sultans as well as subjects.

As head and defender of the faith a sultan must be an exemplary Muslim. I challenge Malay sultans to declare how much *zakat* they have contributed. On the contrary, they are *consumers* and *beneficiaries* of zakat.

In the final analysis the fate of Malay sultans lies less with what is written in the constitution or their accepted role as head of Islam, rather how they perform both in their official roles as well as personal capacities. As for the former, we have the Sultans' of Perak and Trengganu performances following the last elections to go by; for the latter, the thuggish behaviors of the Johor princes and the debt-skipping late Yang

Di Pertuan of Negri Sembilan. With such examples, Malaysia cannot be optimistic on the future of her sultans.

The sultans may be the constitutional heads of state but to most non-Malays they are irrelevant; they are after all *Malay* rajas. Those non-Malays who found the sultans useful do so because they provide reliable conduits to lucrative government contracts. The sultans are the rich Chinese social and economic lubricants. That relationship is less symbiotic, more parasitical. I leave it to readers to determine which party is the parasite. Then there are those non-Malays who flaunt their fancy royal titles and who are genuinely proud of their status as Malay *hulubalangs* (knights).

Few Malays, especially the young, urban, and educated, have favorable views of their sultans. Those in the kampung still display at least outwardly their loyalty and fealty, but that is more an expression of cultural courtesy rather than genuine respect.

I visited my kampung in Negri Sembilan near the royal town of Sri Menanti during the reign of its former ruler and was surprised by the outward displays of loyalty by the villagers despite and especially considering the blatant "un-Islamic" and "un-Malay" behaviors of the princes. One would conclude that this tolerance and acceptance by the villagers turned them into enablers for those royals' excesses.

When that Yang Di Pertuan died, the *Undangs* bypassed his eldest son in their choice of a successor. He had been his father's choice as he had installed him much earlier as the crown prince. The relief and joy of the villagers to the *Undangs'* choice was palpable. Only then could one discern the citizens' subtle loathing of the members of the previous royal family.

On a grander scale, one would be hard put to deny the "love" the Iranians had for their late Shah, judging from their behaviors during the 2,500-year Persepolis "anniversary" celebration in 1971. Who could have predicted that barely eight years later the Shah of Shahs would be hounded out of his country!

The Shah of Iran, Egypt's Farouk, and the King of Afghanistan all enjoyed the effusive adulations and loyalty of their subjects. Today they are all gone. Recalling their names would evoke only loathing among their former subjects.

Malay sultans would do well to ponder that. As they reflect, they would do well to read Zaid Ibrahim's *Ampun Tuanku*. Better yet, invite him to address their next Conference of Rulers. That would be the best way for them to avoid the fate they had endured during the Japanese Occupation. Beyond that, they could become truly modern monarchs who could be the source of pride and inspiration for Malaysians.

If they were to continue with their present feudal profligate ways, it would only be a matter of time before they would meet the fate of their brethren in the greater Nusantara Malay world. The Sultans of Sulu and Jogjakarta are ready reminders.

Saya Pun Melayu! Me Too!

Book Review: Zaid Ibrahim's *Saya Pun Melayu* (I Am Also Malay). Foreword by Tengku Razaleigh Hamzah. ZI Publications Sdn Bhd, Petaling Jaya, 2009. 312 pages. RM 35.00

April 19, 2009

The Annual UMNO General Assembly is also the season for the release of new books on local politics written in Malay. It must be a profitable venue and time, for the number of new titles keeps growing every year.

Foreigners would mistake that to reflect a healthy intellectual discourse, or at least a vigorous political debate. The reality is far different. With such titillating titles as "50 Dalil Mengapa XYZ Tidak Layak …" (Fifty Reasons Why XYZ Is Unfit For …) and the promiscuous use of "half-past six English," this 'genre' poisons the political atmosphere, quite apart from degrading the national language.

As for content, these books are nothing more than *warong kopi* (coffee shop) gossips transcribed. Observers and political scientists hoping to gain an insight on Malaysian politics would do well to avoid these books. And they have. These books will never be cited in reputable publications or quoted by respected commentators.

Enter Zaid Ibrahim's *Saya Pun Melayu* (I Am Also Malay). It too was released to coincide with the recent UMNO General Assembly. There the similarity ended. This gem of a diamond sparkles with insights and wisdom. Like a diamond, this book has innumerable multifaceted sharp edges that cut through rock-headed politicians. I would be insulting Zaid if I were to compare his thoughtful and well-written book to the thrash that littered the hallways of Dewan Merdeka, where the recent UMNO General Assembly took place.

Greater Impact Than *The Malay Dilemma*

A more appropriate comparison would be Mahathir's *The Malay Dilemma*, written some 40 years ago, at a time when UMNO and Malays were going through a critical crisis. Zaid's book will have an even greater impact than that earlier slim volume.

Like Mahathir's, the first run of this book quickly sold out, but unlike Mahathir's, this book has not been banned. This is not due to any greater enlightenment on the part of the authorities today, rather a tribute to Zaid's skillful and subtle approach. Whereas Mahathir is frontal and polemical, meant more to shock if not insult readers, Zaid, ever the accomplished corporate lawyer, takes a softer and polite approach. In contrast to Mahathir's anger and indignant rhetoric, Zaid is more sorrowful and disappointment over UMNO's current malaise. Zaid persuades readers with his rational arguments; Mahathir barrages them with his accusations. Mahathir caters to one's baser emotions and sense of victimization, while Zaid caters to the intellect and pristine values of Malay culture.

Malay culture is partial to Zaid's *halus* (soft) ways, of subtleties and obliqueness. It is that what makes him so devastatingly effective, as when he upbraided his former cabinet colleagues who are lawyers. Rais Yatim, Syed Hamid Albar, Hishammuddin Hussein, and Azalina Othman, among others are chastised for failing to live up to their professional ethics and obligations as shown by their disrespect for due process of law and basic human rights. In Malay, Zaid's polite criticisms are very damning. It would be difficult to maintain this tone with this style had the book been written in English. Potential translators should ponder that.

The book is in three parts. The first is the author's reflection on and prescription for Malaysia's current predicaments. Zaid tackles such "hot" issues as *Ketuanan Melayu* (Malay hegemony), the rule of law, and the role of the monarchy in a democracy. It also includes accounts of his very brief tenure as Abdullah Badawi's Law Minister.

The second is a brief memoir of sorts where he traced his humble origin in a village deep in Ulu Kelantan to become a highly successful corporate attorney who created the nation's largest law firm. It also includes his tenure in UMNO politics, and his current philanthropic works where he has been recognized by *Forbes* magazine as Asia's Inaugural Heroes of Philanthropy. The last part contains short profiles of Malaysians he admires (which includes former Chief Justice Salleh Abbas), his hopes on the future of Malays, and the current state of Malay, specifically UMNO, politics.

UMNO No Longer Represents Malays

One could be excused in assuming that those rent-seeking, keris-brandishing, and race-taunting types that infest UMNO today represent the best if not the essence of the Malay race. Or that the angry menacing Mat Rempits, the jungle version of Hell's Angels so eagerly being embraced by UMNO Youth, are the future of the nation and of Malays.

Zaid's ideas and approaches are the antithesis of UMNO's. In deliberately choosing the simple title, Zaid is emphasizing that his is also a legitimate if not the prevailing viewpoint. To me, Zaid represents more of the essence of Malayness while those corrupt, pseudo-modernized UMNO types just happen to be Malays. They are the ones who soil Malay culture and give it a bad odor.

Zaid writes teasingly that he has already set a record of sorts by being the shortest serving cabinet minister. Here is another observation also worthy of the record books. He is the only minister whose reputation is enhanced on leaving office! Not to belittle Zaid's own fine personal qualities and considerable achievements, that says a lot on the caliber of people leading Malaysia today.

Zaid takes to task UMNO leaders for presuming to speak on behalf of all Malays. It is clear now that they do not. In the chapter *"Masa Depan Melayu"* (The Future of Malays) in Part III, Zaid suggests that Malays must be outward looking, willing to learn from others, and not be obsessed with empty slogans. The road to *Ketuanan Melayu*, he writes, is not by shouting your lungs out at every gathering, rather through diligence, hard work, and most of all, superior education.

Zaid relates his experience as a university student leader on a three-month trip to America visiting the top campuses (*"Memburu Cita Cita"* – Pursuing You Dreams; Chapter 8 Part II). This was in the 1970s, the height of the anti-Vietnam protests. He was struck that even though America was at war, its government was still tolerant of dissent.

I have met many Malaysians who have lived for many years in America and yet miss this important aspect of American exceptionalism. Their America is the shopping malls, porno shops, and blighted downtowns.

Decades later as Abdullah's Law Minister, he was appalled when the government he was a part of detained dissenters like Raja Petra and Teresa Kok under the ISA. Not surprisingly, Zaid's departure from the cabinet soon followed.

Zaid's ideas and observations resonate with me, as well as many Malaysians. Here is the voice of a successful Malay professional and a member of the political elite. That he now quits UMNO is a loss for it but a gain for Malaysia. Another blessing is that he is now free to pursue his philanthropic works as well as his involvement in NGOs. And being an effective critic of the government!

The most valuable part of the book is his brief memoir (Part II). Zaid clearly subscribes early to the values he writes about. His divorced father took him away from the village to live with him in Kota Baru where he could attend an English school (Sultan Ismail College). When he reached secondary level, he felt the urge to leave, to see the greater world beyond.

He chose English College in Johor Baru, at the very opposite end of the peninsula. The school however accepts new students only if their families were transferred there. He wrote to the principal stating that indeed he had a "family" (his distant cousin) transferred to the Army base there. His father willingly signed the letter for him and supported his decision.

Unlike in Kota Baru where his classmates were almost all Malays, down there he had an environment more reflective of Malaysia. From there to Sekolah Tun Razak in Ipoh for his Form Six, where he excelled in debates, and then to UiTM for his law studies.

Except for about seven months in London at one of the Inns to qualify for the English Bar, and the earlier trip to America, Zaid spent his formative years in Malaysia. It is remarkable that he could have such an open and receptive attitude. We have many who spent years at the best British universities only to return quickly to their old kampung mentality upon coming home.

Zaid has what the Stanford psychologist Carol Dweck refers to as a "growth mindset," in contrast to a "fixed mindset." Those with the growth mindset believe that their fate is dependent on how adaptive they are in seizing opportunities, and on their ability to grow and gain from their experiences. They do not believe that their fate is dependent on what nature has bestowed upon them, the benevolence of some remote emperor, or what had been written in the book of life. The "fixed mindset" view their talent and ability as fixed, and that their lot in life is ultimately tied to their innate nature, especially their intelligence and 'giftedness.'

Zaid is always learning from others and improving on what they had done. He writes of his early experience articling in a prestigious law firm where he was offered a position. That was an early career coup, a young lawyer's dream. What soured it for him were the whisperings among his colleagues that he was offered the position simply because the firm wanted to increase its Malay representation. After much soul searching, Zaid declined the offer. He did not wish to be perceived as the token Malay. That must have shocked the firm's senior partners. Another "dumb" Malay refusing to seize opportunities!

Zaid too must have questioned himself a thousand times in the years following that tough decision, especially when he had difficulty trying to borrow from MARA (a measly RM25,000.00) to start his own law firm. In the end he created ZICO, a law firm that easily bested the one where he articled. Not only is it the largest, it is also one of the few that could handle the complex needs of multinational corporations, and the first to venture abroad.

That is the potential or where a growth mindset could lead one.

Going back to MARA, an institution I am a never a fan of, Zaid relates an incident visiting his alma mater soon after being appointed Law Minister. He wanted to spend a few minutes to give the students a "pep talk." On the appointed day, he was surprised by the overflowing crowd. Then as is typical, the Vice Chancellor, one Ibrahim Abu Shah (a "Dato' Seri Prof. Dr." no less!) hogged all the allotted time, pouring embarrassingly effusive praises on Zaid. He was left with a scant few minutes for Q&A!

A few months later, after Zaid resigned as a minister and gave his talk at the Asean Law Forum where he challenged the wisdom of *Ketuanan Melayu*, that same Ibrahim called Zaid a traitor to the Malay race! As Zaid says, our intellectuals are also now speaking like politicians. Zaid may not realize this; they do so because they are essentially politicians who happen to wear academic robes. Scholars and intellectuals, they are not.

I wish many Malaysians would read this book. Our policy makers would benefit more from reading this volume instead of the World Bank's dense treatises on rural poverty. The tribulations of his childhood that Zaid so well described are still very much the reality today for a vast number of young Malays. Zaid was fortunate in that his father saw the value of a good education. Many parents are trapped between needing their children to work to lessen the family's burden or going to school. If our government were to adopt programs like Mexico's *Progressa* where parents are being paid for keeping their children in school, then we would help those parents make the right decision that would benefit them (children and parents) and the nation in the long term.

If UMNO leaders were to read this volume they might just be disabused of their delusion of *Ketuanan Melayu* and their ethnocentric mindset. On the other hand, they might not like it when they realize their own stupidities. For young Malays, Zaid is an inspiration of what is within their grasp if only they could see through the fraud of *Ketuanan Melayu* that is being perpetrated upon them. For non-Malays, this book might just erase some of their negative stereotypes of Malays they may harbor.

I thoroughly enjoyed this book not only because of the remarkable personal story but also for the style of writing. Malay writers writing in Malay (and often also in English) tend to use non-declarative sentences. Instead of saying, "I like vanilla ice cream!" they would write, "On matters of ice cream taste, I like vanilla!" The latter takes twice as many words, and you, the reader has to shift gears. Very irritating! It slows you down.

This book is a valuable contribution to the political discourse, and it comes at a time when it is badly needed. Rest assured that this book will be talked about for years.

Calling For A New Breed Of Politicians

Review of Saifuddin Abdullah's *Politik Baru: Mematangkan Demokrasi Malaysia.* English version: *New Politics: Towards A Mature Malaysian*

Democracy. Institut Terjemahan Negara Malaysia, Kuala Lumpur, 2008. 88 Pages, RM 30.00 (Sabah & Sarawak: RM35).

March 4, 2009

It is *de rigeur* for ambitious politicians to pen their memoirs or put in print their political thoughts. Barack Obama did both, first with his autobiographical *Dreams From My Father: A Story of Race and Inheritance*, and then his *The Audacity of Hope: Thoughts on Reclaiming the American Dream*. That strategy worked!

I am not privy to Deputy Minister for Entrepreneur and Cooperative Development Saifuddin Abdullah's political aspirations, but he has written *Politik Baru: Mematangkan Demokrasi Malaysia*, and its English translation, *New Politics: Towards A Mature Malaysian Democracy*. Both versions are included in this one cover.

Saifuddin has written three other books. Impressive! He is way ahead of another leader both in literary as well as political milestones. At a comparable stage in his life, Dr. Mahathir had yet to write a book or hold any ministerial appointment.

What Malaysia has in Saifuddin is a new breed of politician, committed as well as reflective.

Straightforward Thesis

In *Politik Baru*, Saifuddin puts forth the thesis that Malaysian politics desperately needs players who are wise, knowledgeable, and with integrity to launch the nation into her next trajectory of development. Amen!

To achieve that, government leaders specifically and the political process generally must engage leaders in the private sector and civil society with a view of enticing them into politics to augment the talent pool.

Saifuddin may be young but in framing the issues thus, he demonstrated early his superior political skills and acumen. The politically tone deaf like me would have stated the problem differently and more frontally. That is, current politicians are a bunch of opportunists who are also corrupt and incompetent. No surprise then that the government they lead acts in highhanded fashion, ignoring the needs of the private sector as well as trampling on the sensitivities of civil society.

Had Saifuddin presented the issues as I did, it would be unlikely for a government-linked corporation to publish his book, much less have Deputy Prime Minister Najib Razak launch it.

Saifuddin demonstrates the *halus* (subtle) ways of Malay culture. Sometimes that can prove to be much more effective; the operative word there being "sometimes." Mahathir catapulted his political career by writing his brutally direct if not frankly insulting *The Malay Dilemma*.

In his book Saifuddin frequently uses catchy if not poetic phrases, as in, "*Politik ilmu dan bukannya politik ampu; politik hikmah dan bukannya politik fitnah; serta politik bakti dan bukannya politik undi.*" ("Knowledge politics instead of ingratiate politics; wisdom politics instead of defamatory politics; and service politics instead of vote politics.") Another, "*UMNO perlu diisi dengan ahli politik yang 'berjuang' dan bukannya yang 'berwang.'*" (UMNO must be filled with politicians who 'struggle' and not politicians who seek wealth.")

The English version is not as cute; it lacks the alliterative assertions or rhyming ring of the original Malay, but more on the translation later.

Participatory Democracy in Perspective
It is not surprising that Saifuddin calls for the greater participation of civil society as he was once active in the Youth movement. True to his word, soon after being elected to Parliament for the first time in 2008, he set up a community liaison committee that would have included the PAS state assemblyman in his constituency. However, subsequent directives from above precluded him from having that state politician. I hope Saifuddin would not be discouraged and that he would still meet regularly in an unofficial basis with that opposition politician, as well as others.

Saifuddin does not explore why Malaysian politics has degenerated or why current politicians do not share their earlier compatriots' deep sense of duty and service to the community. My own theory is that unlike earlier leaders who were inspired by the struggle for merdeka, today's politicians lack such transcendental ideals and aspirations; hence they are easily corrupted by material gains.

Further unlike the past, today's best and brightest have other much more rewarding avenues for their talent. If they have not already succumbed to the seduction of the First World, there is the lucrative private sector or more fulfilling careers with NGOs at home.

Attracting talent is a major challenge. Generous compensation is not the entire answer. America does not pay its leaders on the same scale as the private sector, yet there is no shortage of capable and willing candidates. However, paying them poorly would attract only the corrupt and the less-than-talented, a destructive combination.

Then there is the matter of getting the best candidate, one of UMNO's major systemic weaknesses. I agree with Saifuddin that having potential candidates debate each other is one of the better ways of assessing them. Although he does not specifically say so, UMNO's "no contest" tradition for its top leadership positions is one it can do without.

Saifuddin would prefer political leaders be knowledgeable ("berilmu"). He digresses somewhat with his philosophical deliberations on the meaning of knowledge and ends up declaring his preference for intellectuals and scholars as leaders. Such individuals, in Malaysia as well as elsewhere, rarely prove to be good leaders or executives, quite apart from their being politically inept.

While Malaysians should strive for competent, dedicated, and incorruptible leaders, they should nevertheless be realistic and deal with the cards they have. To prioritize, I would put competence first. The public would readily overlook if not forgive an otherwise competent leader's their other weaknesses. Witness America's continuing admiration for Jack Kennedy despite his unsavory personal morality. Malaysians tolerated the corruption of the Mahathir era because his was a competent administration, and the level of sleaze was at least manageable.

Contrast him to Kelantan's Nik Aziz, a pious and honorable leader, *berintegriti* (with integrity) as Saifuddin put it, but he was totally lacking in management competence. I would not tolerate him leading the nation, despite his admirable piety, honesty, and humility.

The worst would be a leader who is both incompetent as well as corrupt. That was what Malaysia had with Abdullah Badawi. No surprise that he was booted out early.

In engaging the private sector and civil society, Saifuddin advocates a more participatory form of democracy, beyond the rituals of regular elections. While supportive of that, I would not buy too much into it.

India and the Philippines have participatory democracy on a scale a quantum leap higher that what they have in Singapore and South Korea, but no Singaporean or South Korean would trade places with the Indians and Filipinos. The reason is obvious: Singaporean and South Korean leaders are competent despite their being repressive (Singapore) or corrupt (South Korea). Their competence enabled them to grant their citizens their most basic and greatest freedom, the freedom from hunger and privation.

It is for this reason that I am not enamored with Saifuddin's idea of electing town councilors. In theory that would be the essence of grassroots participatory democracy, in practice it would only bring the current political gridlock down to the local level. Witness the ongoing paralysis in Perak and elsewhere where the party in power is different from the one nationally. Now imagine the local, state, and federal governments all under different political parties! To reemphasize, I would put competence ahead of everything else, including ideology. Town dwellers just want their potholes filled and garbage picked up!

To enhance citizens' participation, Saifuddin calls for their empowerment. The World Bank defines that as "the process of enhancing the capacity of individuals or groups to make choices, and to transform those choices into desired actions and outcomes." Saifuddin searched hard to find the right Malay word for this before settling on his *penghakupayaan*.

I have a simpler and more accurate concept that is readily understood by the masses. We would empower them if we were to grant them their personal *merdeka* (independence) to make their own decisions. Repealing the Universities and Colleges Act for example, would grant Malaysian students their personal *merdeka*.

Malaysia must properly prepare her citizens for their *merdeka* lest they corrupt that precious gift as a license for anarchy. Make the relevant information available to them and train them to think critically. A good start would be freedom of the press and a decent education system.

In many ways the issue of press freedom is now mute. The Internet has democratized access to information and no government, not even the most repressive, has a monopoly on information. The deficiencies of the local education system however are not so readily overcome or bypassed. Those remain the biggest obstacles to empowering citizens.

Saifuddin is silent on the Internal Security Act (and other intrusive laws) and affirmative action. These issues are central to all Malaysians and must be faced directly. Leaders with higher aspirations cannot pussyfoot around these defining issues. The ISA and other oppressive laws are the antithesis of empowering citizens.

Saifuddin may have internalized the clear but unspoken boundaries set by his party. If so, my advice would be this: An important aspect of leadership, and a measure of courage, is one's ability to push back those boundaries.

Calling for the private sector and civil society to be "partners in development" would require an appreciation of their proper roles. This is problematic in Malaysia as the government is heavily involved in business and civil society. The views of those in Petronas and Khazanah may not accurately reflect the aspirations of the genuine entrepreneurs. While the UMNO government would readily work with civil society groups that it sponsors or are sympathetic to its cause, there is much less tolerance for the others.

Another wrinkle is that with few notable exceptions, civil society in Malaysia is race based. The government often has to mediate the conflicting demands of GAPENA, the Malay writers' association, and Suqui, the champions of Chinese education.

I am surprised by the omission of credit to the translator of this volume. Translation is an art, and the translator's work must be acknowledged and recognized. Perhaps the translator does not wish to be recognized here, and for good reasons. The translations are too literal. The imagery that would have been appropriate in Malay is totally meaningless in English. Saifuddin's likening politics to a *taman* (garden) that must be carefully tended to, while appropriate in Malay, is not when translated into English. Instead, the better word would be 'landscape.'

The average Malay reader would have considerable difficulty with Saifuddin's original Malay text because of his profuse use of bastardized English words like "integriti," "adversarial," "manipulatif," or even the simple "debat." All those words have their more accurate and comprehensible Malay counterparts. Try "amanah" for integrity.

Another distraction, again endemic with Malay writings, is the lack of consistent style and editorial standards. In the English version he refers to the Malaysian Integrity Institute and then went ahead to use its Malay initials "IIM" that bear no relation to its English name. Malaysian editors and writers must agree on a common stylistic standard so readers would not be distracted or confused.

As a politician, Saifuddin faces the twin challenges of first changing UMNO along the lines suggested in his book, and second of ensuring that he is not changed in the process. Both are formidable undertakings. His writing this volume is an excellent beginning.

Saifuddin cannot do it alone. Even as talented and intelligent a leader as Obama had plenty of help. His party elders recognized his talent and helped pave the way for him.

Senior UMNO leaders likewise need to help nurture and gracefully make way for promising young talent like Saifuddin. Malaysia and UMNO need a new breed of politicians in the mold of Saifuddin Abdullah, someone with fresh ideas who can express them cogently, and then engage citizens intelligently as he has done with his *Politik Baru.*

Thrust Forward Our Best Arguments, Not Our *Kerises*

Review of Suflan Shamsuddin's *Reset: Rethinking The Malaysian Political Paradigm.* ISBN 10:9834352131; ZI Publications, Malaysia, 2008, 214pp

September 9, 2009

From UMNO Youth's Hishamuddin wildly jabbing his *keris* in the air at imagined enemies to the malicious distribution of Pakatan Rakyat's purported "Babi Cabinet" list, political discourses in Malaysia are coarse and degenerating fast. *That* should concern all Malaysians.

Malaysians are also becoming sharply polarized along racial lines. Malaysian leaders blissfully ignore this dangerous trend as they continue egging on their supporters. Prime Minister Abdullah, as head of UMNO, has yet to admonish Hishammuddin for his ugly race-taunting antics, thus implicitly encouraging others to do likewise.

This deepening polarization has many Malaysians worried. One of them is Suflan Shamsuddin. In his book, *Reset: Rethinking The Malaysian Political Paradigm,* Suflan puts forth his analysis of the current national dilemma and advances his own unique solutions.

Suflan blames the nation's race-based political parties. If he had his way, he would "reset" the current system such that only racially inclusive parties that consciously broaden their appeal to all communities could partake in elections. Non-inclusive parties that cater to a narrow racial base could contest only if they were to come under an inclusive coalition.

Suflan's rationale is clear. These parties would then have to broaden their appeal and not, as at present, cater to their most chauvinistic followers. Under his plan, race-exclusive parties like UMNO, MCA, and MIC that come together under an "inclusive coalition" like Barisan Nasional would be allowed to contest elections, but not PAS, unless it were to come under a similar coalition, which it did in the last election [2008] under Pakatan Rakyat.

To Suflan, only the Democratic Action Party (DAP) and Parti Keadilan Rakyat (PKR), the two race inclusive parties, would be allowed to contest under their own banner.

This is the weakness of his argument. While PKR is genuinely multiracial in its ideals and membership, DAP is not. While DAP's constitution may explicitly state that it is non-racial, the reality is far different. Malays are as rare in that party as a meat dish in a vegetarian restaurant. Gerakan still has its inclusive ideals, at least in the beginning; today it is exclusively Chinese and fighting to displace MCA in the Barisan coalition.

You cannot rely on a party's name or professed ideals on whether it is inclusive or not. After all, North Korea calls itself the Democratic People's Republic of Korea. They fool only themselves.

In truth, today's political realities demand that parties broaden their appeal across racial boundaries unless they are satisfied with their perpetual fringe opposition status. Even the insular folks in PAS recognize this, however clumsily. In the last election it fielded its token non-Muslim candidate, and a woman at that! The remarkable success of the opposition parties in the last election when they coalesced under the Pakatan Rakyat banner is another proof of this.

The test on whether a party is racially inclusive or exclusive lies not with its constitution or avowed declarations of its leaders, rather on how it is being perceived by voters. Prohibiting any party ahead of time is not the answer. Let voters decide. They have a good track record having buried such old entities as Parti Negara and the Socialist Front.

PKR's recent spectacular success indicates that Malaysians are now warming up to the idea of non-race-based parties; there is no need for any legislation as per Suflan's suggestion. Nor do I fully agree with his assessment that the political system is to be blamed for our present predicament. I too wish that our politicians would not pander to and stir up the baser racial instincts of their followers.

The greater blame must fall on leaders. It was Prime Minister Abdullah's willful neglect that permitted the nation's racial sore to reopen and spew out its putrid poison.

Earlier leaders like Tunku Abdul Rahman and Tun Razak managed to rein in and in many instances disassociate themselves from the excesses of their more chauvinistic followers. The greatest threat to a plural society like Malaysia is a weak and ineffective leader. Sadly, that is what she has in Abdullah. Note that even Mahathir could overcome his earlier reputation as a Malay ultra-nationalist by being a decisive leader.

As Suflan rightly observes, "[Malaysia] has survived ... distrust, prejudices and antagonism between communities ... by recognizing natural political cleavages along racial lines .... We successfully relied on communal representation ...."

In making his case for race-inclusive parties, Suflan, like others, also implies that Malaysia's greatest threat is interracial conflict. I disagree. The most likely and dangerous threat is not inter-racial rather intra-racial, specifically conflicts among Malays. Malays are dangerously polarized along cultural, religious, and socioeconomic lines. Worse, those fracture lines converge; affluent, liberal, urban, secular Malays versus their poorer, rural, conservative, Arab-oriented brethren.

Further, disputes between Malays and non-Malays are over material matters, like scholarships, access to contracts, and economic opportunities. Those are what Albert Hirschmann calls "divisible conflicts;" they could be resolved through negotiations and compromises. Splits among Malays on the other hand are over core values; they are "indivisible conflicts," not readily solvable and thus more dangerous. The Islamists would insist that hijab is mandatory for Muslim women. Liberal Muslims think otherwise. Settling for half a hijab as with a head scarf would not be an acceptable compromise with either side.

UMNO Youth leaders have regular golf games with their PAP counterparts in Singapore, but they have yet to engage PAS Youth members in any similar gesture. They do not even attend the same mosque!

Re-Examining The Social Contract

The bulk of the book deals with Suflan's analysis of the current malaise and schisms in the political system, and on the path that led the nation to be where it is today. Suflan contributes enormously to the national dialogue. His is a nuanced discussion, the arguments deliberate and rational, with no diatribes, grandstanding, name-calling, or demonizing any party or personality.

Whether discussing *Ketuanan Melayu*, the New Economic Policy, the social contract earlier leaders had struck, or the special place of Islam and Malay rulers in the constitution, Suflan presents the various viewpoints objectively and conveys the passions of their respective proponents. He does not advocate any position, rather for us to understand and appreciate the different perspectives. His is an exercise in educating and informing, from someone well qualified by experience and training to do so.

Trust comes only through better understanding the various communities' concerns, aspirations, and perspectives. As Suflan observes, without trust, not even the most elaborate contract would save a relationship. This caution is particularly relevant to those who think that by merely tinkering with the constitution or passing legislations we would reduce distrusts or build relationships.

We could abolish the NEP overnight through legislation but that would not solve the nation's race relations unless we also address the basic issues that brought forth that policy. By the same token the country could remove the egregious abuses of the NEP through executive actions without waiting for changes in statutes, and thus remove the bulk of the grievances Malaysians have towards that policy. Doing so would not stir the racial hornet's nest.

Suflan is a corporate attorney with a multinational firm based in London. The forte of such lawyers is in bringing various parties together and closing the deal. Their skills are in earning the trust and respect of all sides through frank discussions of potential pitfalls and emphasizing the mutual benefits. This book reflects Suflan's professional style. It attempts to bring Malaysians together by pointing out the dangers of relentlessly pursuing our current narrow and divisive path as compared to the rewards that would accrue should Malaysians change to more inclusive stratgeies.

Contrast that to the styles and personalities of trial lawyers *a la* Karpal Singh who relish courtroom histrionics in order to sway judges and juries.

Theirs is to demolish the credibility of the other side. Malaysian politics would do well with more Suflans and fewer Karpals. Those who advocate forcefully for the narrow racial interests of their followers may win their little battles but would eventually lose the war.

Malaysian politics faces yet another major problem. In the past, politics attracted the bright and talented with aspirations of public service. Today those Malaysians are lured to the lucrative private sector or multinational corporations. Suflan is a ready example. Attracting such talents to politics is a major challenge. Malaysian leaders have yet to recognize this.

As a result, Malaysia has an abundant of "half past six" (third string) leaders. Some are outright flunkies who think that they can buy their way into anything, including their seemingly impressive doctorates. They are also ruthlessly ambitious, a dangerous combination. We will continue having them until we attract talents like Suflan to politics.

With *RESET*, Suflan initiates an important dialogue; he invites all Malaysians to partake in it. We would also do well to emulate his style: cool, rationale, and hearing as well as respecting all sides. That is, instead of thrusting our *kerises* forward, Malaysians should be thrusting their best arguments.

Third World Reality Beneath Malaysia's First World Veneer

Review of Ioannis Gatsiounis' *Beyond the Veneer: Malaysia's Struggle For Dignity and Direction*. Monsoon Books, Singapore. 2008 273 pp; Indexed; 2008. US $15.95

July 10, 2008

Soon after Abdullah Badawi led his Barisan Nasional coalition to a landslide electoral victory in 2004, I wrote a blistering critique of his leadership. He had hoodwinked voters, I wrote, with his slick "feel good" campaign, and that sooner or later Malaysians would see through his emptiness. I had the piece previewed by my good friend and frequent collaborator Din Merican. He suggested that I hold back and instead give Abdullah a chance. I did.

Little did I know that at about the same time (October 2004) an American journalist in Malaysia, Ioannis Gatsiounis, had written for *Asia Times* an essay titled, "Abdullah's Honeymoon is Over in Malaysia." Although more restrained in tone, he nonetheless, as judged by the title, revealed a similar lack of enthusiasm for Abdullah as a leader. His "soft but firm" leadership, Gatsiounis wrote, "has shown … to be more soft than firm."

That kind of perceptiveness is rare for a foreign observer, or a local one for that matter. Today, as judged by the current headlines, Gatsiounis's prescient judgment of Abdullah has become common wisdom.

Such insights and perceptiveness do not come easily or quickly, even for the most astute of observers. Gatsiounis has been reporting from and on Southeast Asia since 2000, beginning first in Jakarta and later in Kuala Lumpur where he now resides. That gives him an intimate knowledge of Malaysia and a nuanced understanding of her racial dynamics and political tensions. He is not easily persuaded by smooth press releases or slick PR gimmicks.

This volume, *Beyond the Veneer: Malaysia's Struggle For Dignity and Direction*, contains his 42 essays written from about 2003 onwards. There are three commentaries on the recent [2008] "most crucial general elections in the country's 50-year history," one written just before the elections, and two, right afterwards.

"The Malaysian government's authoritarian instincts," Gatsiounis wrote in his first post-election essay ("A New Democratic Era in Malaysia") "were finally checked by democracy at Saturday's highly anticipated elections."

Noting the immediate fractiousness among the opposition parties on power sharing, Gatsiounis observed ("The Malaysian Race Card") that the "Chinese and Indians have become more vocal in opposing discriminatory policies, but they have given little indication that if they were granted greater equality they would rise above their own clannish tendencies." As I said, Gatsiounis is a perceptive observer.

No Christaine Amanpour Brand Of Journalism

Today because of budgetary restraints, American media are cutting back on their foreign news operations, relying instead on what I would call the Christiane Amanpour-type of coverage. Fly in your celebrity journalist, interview the top local honchos, pick some cute quotes from the "man on the street," choose some recognizable backdrops (which in Malaysia would be the Petronas Twin Towers), and then file your brief three-minute report that would appear just before the toothpaste commercial in the evening news.

It is not surprising that Americans are so poorly informed on matters beyond their borders. Such ignorance would ultimately percolate up to the leaders and policymakers. The results, as can be seen in Iraq and Afghanistan, can be devastating both to the natives as well as their "saviors."

Thanks to the Internet, I have read many commentaries by Gatsiounis that have appeared in such publications as the *International Herald Tribune*, *Newsweek*, *Washington Times* as well as *Asia Times*. His reporting is the very antithesis of CNN's Amanpour.

His is more along the *Independent*'s (Britain) seasoned Middle East correspondent Robert Fisk. Had Tony Blair listened to Fisk's wisdom, he would probably still be Prime Minister today. More importantly, he would have spared himself, as well as those British soldiers in Iraq as well as common Iraqis much grief.

Malaysia is, as evidenced by the observations in this book as well as explicitly stated in the introduction, "trying to run the rat race of globalization on one good leg." That is the leg Malaysia shows to the cameras, the gleaming Petronas Towers and the ribbon of smooth highways. The other, the bad leg that is severely handicapping the country, is the rampant corruption, deepening rich-poor divide, deteriorating institutions, and the increasingly and dangerous polarization along racial lines. To Gatsiounis, Malaysia has all but ensured that its "diversity is a weakness and not a strength." I could not agree more.

There are no interviews of the powerful in this volume except for one longer than usual essay ("Malaysia's Leader-in-Waiting") based on a 40-minute interview with Deputy Prime Minister Najib Razak, a man very much in the news today, but for all the wrong reasons.

Gatsiounis observed that while Najib Razak "displayed a firm understanding of the kind of world Malaysia is entering and the attributes it would need … to be competitive, … he has also been a staunch defender of UMNO's status quo … which has hindered Malaysia's competitiveness and social harmony."

Najib, like all UMNO leaders including supposedly better educated younger ones like Khairy Jamaluddin, is not so much defenders of UMNO culture rather that he is trapped by it, unable to escape its suffocating clutches. These leaders' collective response to the March 8, 2008 electoral thumping was not to seek changes but more of the same. Meaning, UMNO's implosion is inevitable, and would be soon.

Instead of interviewing the powerful, Gatsiounis relied on his own observations. According to official accounts on the massive public *Bersih* rally calling for clean elections, shopkeepers were fed up with the demonstrators who had disrupted businesses. By Gatsiounis' reckoning ("Opposition Steals a March in Malaysia"), those shopkeepers welcomed the increase in foot traffic. Their businesses were rudely interrupted only when the police came rushing in wildly brandishing their truncheons and firing their water cannons.

With such critical and penetrating reporting, I am surprised that Gatsiounis is not on the radar screen of the Home Ministry. One reason could be that those officials think that he writes primarily for foreigners. Those bureaucrats could not be more wrong. Through the Internet, Gatsiounis commands a sizable local audience, as evidenced by the praises on the book cover by such local luminaries as Ramon Navaratnam, Khoo Kay Peng, and Ibrahim Suffian.

I asked Gatsiounis whether he felt intimidated by the authorities. Much to my surprise as well as relief, he answered no, although obviously he is aware of the realities. He wisely avoids flouting those restraints.

Malaysian journalists and writers regularly blame the myriad of restrictive rules for their timidity. They must exercise self-censorship to survive, they claim. That is more an excuse. As Gatsiounis has shown, one can still be true to one's professional ideals even under such trying circumstances. In truth, Malaysian journalists and pundits grovel to the powerful less for self-preservation, more for ingratiation.

A challenge in publishing a collection of essays is organization, whether to arrange them thematically (as this one) or chronologically. The disadvantage of the latter would be that readers would have to jump from one topic to another. A combination would be better. On the section dealing with Abdullah for example, arranging the essays chronologically would help. After all, a highly critical commentary on his leadership written in 2008, when Abdullah had clearly and fully exposed his incompetence, would not have the same impact as one penned earlier.

A further modification would be to have as a footnote at the bottom of the title page the date when the essay was written, instead of at the end. That would save readers from having to flip to the end of the article to find out when it was written.

With the current headlines filled with sordid details of the sexual escapades (real and imagined) of the politically powerful, and of police reports and sworn affidavits submitted and then retracted by those who wish to ingratiate themselves to the powerful, we are again being reminded of the pitiful lack of solid reporting and penetrating analyses in the Malaysian media. By publishing this volume, Gatsiounis extends his reach among Malaysians, making them (to be hoped) better informed. More to the point, this book reminds Malaysians of what they miss in their daily news and information.

Flat Earthers Versus Good Samaritan

Book Review of Ha-Joon Chang's *Bad Samaritans: The Myth of Free Trade and the Secret History of Capitalism*, Bloomsbury Press, New York, 2008. $21.00 288 pp.

April 6, 2008
It must be frustrating to be a leader of a developing country. Just as you are becoming convinced of the virtues of free trade and globalization, there emerges a countervailing viewpoint suggesting that those are nothing more than attempts by the developed world to maintain their economic hegemony.

To me, the differences between the two viewpoints are more apparent than real. To former Prime Minister Mahathir however, this merely vindicates his conviction all along. And the man can speak with considerable authority.

He had defied the then prevailing economic thinking–the so-called Washington consensus–and successfully steered Malaysia out of the treacherous 1997 Asian economic contagion. In the process he made those brilliant economists at the IMF and US Treasury Department eat more than their share of humble pie. His ways were unique if unorthodox and at variance if not the very opposite to the then accepted wisdom.

The surprise is that Mahathir's remarkable achievement is not more analyzed or appreciated. The 1997 economic crisis and Mahathir's bold contrarian approach to solving it provided one of the rare "experiments of nature" in economics.

It is interesting to note that with America currently [2008] experiencing a severe economic squeeze, the result of its sub-prime mortgage mess and other follies, many of the solutions advocated by the champions of free market in the Bush Administration bear remarkable resemblance to Mahathir's methods. These include the government's prompt and unhesitating "rescue" of a major Wall Street firm (Bear Stearns), the lowering of interest rates (with scant regards to its negative impact on the value of the dollar), and the priming of the economic pump with generous tax rebates.

When Mahathir did similar "rescues" a decade ago amidst the Asian contagion, he was accused of bailing out his cronies. Now nobody would dare suggest that Treasury Secretary Paulson, a former major Wall Street figure, of doing the same thing for his former buddies in the corporate financial world. As for the decline of the dollar, the direct consequence of lower interest rates, it was deemed acceptable to avoid recession and unemployment. Exactly the rationale Mahathir utilized earlier!

Malaysia emerged out of the 1997 economic crisis much faster and with fewer scars than countries like Indonesia that followed the "severe but necessary" prescription of the Washington consensus. Mahathir was right then; I hope that Paulson would also be right today.

Cause Versus Effect

This wind of change is also evident outside the corridors of political power. Consider that a book by the Korean-born Cambridge University economist Ha-Joon Chang, *Bad Samaritans: The Myth of Free Trade and the*

Secret History of Capitalism, is fast making the bestseller list. His provocative point is that the developed countries are preaching the very opposite of what they had practiced, with respect to economic and development policies.

Unlike other economists who rely on complex econometric models and esoteric mathematics (no equations or Greek alphabets in his book!), Chang is into economic history. He studied what countries did, in contrast to what they now preach. He also reminds us that many economic conclusions are based on statistical correlations.

Correlations are just that; they do not mean or even infer causation, nor do they differentiate between cause and effect.

Take the widely accepted notion of the poor: They are poor because they are lazy, so we are told repeatedly. This observation is of course made only by the rich, never by the poor.

Could it be, as Chang challenged us, that they are lazy *because* they are poor? The poor are more likely to be malnourished, unhealthy, and thus lack vigor to undertake any hard work. Even if they are capable of hard work, because of their poverty they could not afford an education and thus their hard work is valued less. It is callous if not cruel to label those poor hardworking rice planters and fisherman in Kelantan as lazy. Try spending an hour in their day under the blazing Malaysian sun!

If we assume that they are poor because they are lazy, then we are dealing with basic human nature, difficult to change. But if they are lazy because they are poor, then we are dealing with external conditions, and thus potentially solvable. It makes more sense and at the same pragmatic to approach the problem from this perspective.

Today we are being told that unfettered free trade and globalization are the recipe for economic development. We are lectured ad nauseam by Western experts and commentators of this truism, most persuasively by Thomas Friedman of *The World Is Flat* fame.

Chang concluded from his reviews of historical data that trade liberalization has been the *outcome* rather than the *cause* of economic development. Many of today's developed nations, America, in particular, was once ardent advocates of protectionism. It was Alexander Hamilton who coined the term "infant industries" and the need to protect them.

Chang refers to his native South Korea which made the remarkable transformation from a backward agrarian society to a modern industrialized one by resorting to unabashed protectionism and aggressive state interventions in the marketplace, all anathema to free market doctrinaires. He remembers as a young man ostracizing those who would dare smoke foreign brands of cigarettes. Precious foreign exchange should be used to support local industries, not foreign ones! Now that the nation is developed, South Koreans have no compulsion buying expensive Gucci handbags.

Had South Korea been diligent in enforcing copyright laws as per WTO dictates, Chang would not have become an economist as practically all his textbooks while in college in South Korea were pirated versions!

South Korea proves that active participation in international trade does not require free trade. In economics as in other human endeavors, dogmas should never come in the way of pragmatism. Extremism in the pursuit of a truism is a vice. A familiar hadith says it better: In everything, moderation.

As Chang wisely noted, "The secret of success is in a judicious mix of protection and open trade, with areas of protection constantly changing as new infant industries are developed and old infant industries become internationally competitive."

Sifting Concept From Content

Globalization makes the world smaller, with physical distance reduced to irrelevance. At the same time other distances—cultural, institutional, and linguistic—become more pronounced. Indonesia is physically, culturally, and linguistically close to Malaysia, while America is far away in all dimensions. Yet trade between Malaysia and America is a universe beyond that of Malaysia and Indonesia. Malaysians are more likely to have heard of or even visited San Francisco than Surabaya.

Trade benefits its participants; we should encourage and facilitate trade. While the benefits may never be equal or perceived to be so, there is no such thing as unfair trade, only that we can always make it fairer. The best way to achieve this is not to discourage trade but to increase it even more. As the participants get more sophisticated and more engaged, they are more likely to make the necessary compromises lest their now valuable relationship be lost. Exploitative trade, like other exploitative relationships whether business or personal, rarely endures.

In the past, jute farmers in Bangladesh were at the mercy of middlemen. Nonetheless both benefited more by trading than by not partaking in it. Through globalization, specifically modern technology like cell phones, jute farmers now have access to real-time market information. This liberates them; they are now no longer dictated by the middlemen. Information makes the playing field more level.

Technology destroyed the monopoly and monopsony of the middlemen far more effectively than any rigid communist mandate. The middlemen can still make their profits but not through the ignorance of their clients but by providing better services, as it should be.

The recent electoral humiliation of Barisan Nasional would not have been possible if not for the Internet, an accoutrement of globalization. Globalization is liberating. We should not ignore globalization or discourage trade in our purist pursuit of unattainable fairness. It would be more fruitful to prepare your citizens for both trade and globalization.

Protection may be necessary, but it is only good if you use that space and opportunity to enhance the competitiveness of your people and infant industries. Otherwise it would be the surest and quickest route to complacency and mediocrity. If you cannot provide indigenous competition, introduce some from outside.

Trade must be actively promoted; it does not happen spontaneously, as revealed by our trade figures with Indonesia. For this reason, I am optimistic on the future of the Taiwan-China conflict because of the increasing trade and other economic ties between the two countries.

Globalization also brings the reality of a diverse world closer to each of us. A plural society like Malaysia is uniquely positioned to prepare its citizens for this new reality than those from culturally and ethnically homogenous societies. The Malaysian diversity is an asset, not a liability in this era of globalization.

I see no conflict in the truth and wisdom expressed by Friedman and Chang as they both offer pertinent lessons for Malaysia.

An American Voice

City's "Statement of Support" The Right Thing To Do

[My guest column in *Morgan Hill Times* February 1, 2017]

At a time when our nation is gripped with fear and hysteria, some of the leaders in our nation's capital are content letting the noxious seeds of hatred and distrust take root in and soil our beautiful landscape. Our founders had anticipated this, hence their wisdom in asserting that the government closest to the people governs best. A derivative of that wisdom would be that leaders closest to the people lead best.

Testament to that insight is the City of Morgan Hill's "Statement of Support and Assurance to the Morgan Hill Community" voted unanimously by council members on December 14, 2016. It reaffirms the commitment to making Morgan Hill "well respected and inclusive." Respect for all our residents is foremost among our values.

Having lived and practiced as a surgeon here for nearly four decades, I, like many others, have taken those values for granted. And rightfully so. We demonstrate every day those values of tolerance and inclusivity, both as individuals as well as a society.

When the young girl Sierra LaMar disappeared, we shared in the grief. Many volunteered in the search and to support her family. They still do, years later. When our high school marching band won national awards and performed in the Macy's Thanksgiving Day Parade, we shared in the reflected glory. We congratulated those talented students and their dedicated teachers.

Our community has an active interfaith organization, well represented with members and leaders of the various faiths, that meets regularly. We build bridges, not erect walls between us.

As individuals and as a community we do not claim to be angels, nor have we been angelic all the time. Nonetheless, when we see the noxious seeds of hatred and bigotry attempting to sprout amidst us, we act fast, as we did with the race-tainted hooliganism at our school.

That crucial message was sent out quick and clear to the young and adults alike. Our community will not tolerate such nonsense even if manifested as a prank.

Neither we nor our nation claim to have it right all the time. A casual reading of our history would disabuse us of that smugness. We dehumanized a subset of humanity in our midst because of their skin color. We disenfranchised half of our citizens based on their sex. More recently, we incarcerated a whole group of people based only on suspicion because of their ethnicity and national origin.

In all those instances, there were elegant and sophisticated contemporary commentaries defending those odious actions. Their sophistry could not hide nor justify the basic inhumanity and ugliness of those deeds.

While we may not have done everything right, there is one ideal we are committed to. That is "to strive for a more perfect union," as stated with such elegant brevity in the Preamble to our Constitution, and to give full inclusive meaning to that other simple phrase, "We, the people."

Those ideals notwithstanding, never underestimate the ability of one individual to wreak havoc. An idiot with a matchstick could burn down a whole town, what more a leader with access to the nuclear code.

Back to the idiot, he could only do mischief if he had access to a matchstick, the town littered with dried tinder, and it did not have a functional fire department. As residents, it is our duty to keep the metaphorical matchsticks out of the reach of potential mischief-makers, maintain a clean environment to ensure it does not have combustible debris, and keep our fire department in top form.

I have great faith in our civic leaders, institutions, and shared values. The city's statement is testament to that faith. I commend Mayor Steve Tate and the Morgan Hill city leaders for reasserting and reassuring us that our core values remain steadfast.

Index

About The Author

Malaysian-born and Canadian-trained, Bakri Musa is a surgeon in private practice in Silicon Valley, California. Although he left Malaysia in 1963, he has kept close track of her social and political developments.

He has given presentations on Malaysian affairs at Stanford University's Shorenstein Asia-Pacific Research Center, The Woodrow Wilson International Center for Scholars, The University of Buffalo, and Rochester Institute of Technology.

Apart from scientific articles in scholarly journals, his commentaries have appeared in mainstream Malaysian papers *The New Straits Times* and *The Sun Daily*. He was a long-time columnist for the on-line portal *Malaysiakini* (Malaysia Now) and a regular contributor to The Malaysian Insider.

Beyond Malaysia, his commentaries have appeared in The New York Times, International Herald Tribune, and The Far Eastern Economic Review. His editorial on Malaysian affirmative action program was aired on National Public Radio's "Marketplace."

The author has written eleven books on Malaysian socio-political affairs and maintains a blog (www.bakrimusa.blogspot.com) that serves as repository of his essays and commentaries. He also has a following on Facebook and other social media outlets.

www.ingramcontent.com/pod-product-compliance
Lightning Source LLC
Chambersburg PA
CBHW051215130726
47988CB00001B/99